World Music Pedagogy, Volume VI

World Music Pedagogy, Volume VI: School-Community Intersections provides students with a resource for delving into the meaning of "world music" across a broad array of community contexts and develops the multiple meanings of community relative to teaching and learning music of global and local cultures. It clarifies the critical need for teachers to work in tandem with community musicians and artists in order to bridge the unnecessary gulf that often separates school music from the music of the world beyond school and to consider the potential for genuine collaborations across this gulf.

The five-layered features of World Music Pedagogy are specifically addressed in various school-community intersections, with attention to the collaboration of teachers with local community artist-musicians and with community musicians-at-a-distance who are available virtually. The authors acknowledge the multiple routes teachers are taking to enable and encourage music learning in community contexts, such as their work in after-school academies, museums and libraries, eldercare centers, places of worship, parks and recreation centers, and other venues in which adults and children gather to learn music, make music, and become convivial through music.

This volume suggests that the world's musical cultures may be found locally, can be tapped virtually, and are important in considerations of music teaching and learning in schools and community contexts. Authors describe working artists and teachers, scenarios, vignettes, and teaching and learning experiences that happen in communities and that embrace the role of community musicians in schools, all of which will be presented with supporting theoretical frameworks.

Listening Episode music examples can be accessed on the eResource site from the Routledge catalog page.

Patricia Shehan Campbell is Donald E. Peterson Professor at the University of Washington. She is editor of the Routledge World Music Pedagogy Series, and board member for Smithsonian Folkways Recordings and the Association for Cultural Equity.

Chee-Hoo Lum is Associate Professor, Visual and Performing Arts Academic Group, at the National Institute of Education at the Nanyang Technological University, Singapore. He is the coordinator of the UNESCO UNITWIN: Arts Education Research for Cultural Diversity and Sustainable Development.

Routledge World Music Pedagogy Series

Series Editor: Patricia Shehan Campbell, University of Washington

The **Routledge World Music Pedagogy Series** encompasses principal cross-disciplinary issues in music, education, and culture in seven volumes, detailing theoretical and practical aspects of World Music Pedagogy in ways that contribute to the diversification of repertoire and instructional approaches. With the growth of cultural diversity in schools and communities and the rise of an enveloping global network, there is both confusion and a clamoring by teachers for music that speaks to the multiple heritages of their students, as well as to the spectrum of expressive practices in the world that constitute the human need to sing, play, dance, and engage in the rhythms and inflections of poetry, drama, and ritual.

Volume I: Early Childhood Education
Sarah H. Watts

Volume II: Elementary Music Education
J. Christopher Roberts and Amy C. Beegle

Volume III: Secondary School Innovations
Karen Howard and Jamey Kelley

Volume IV: Instrumental Music Education
Mark Montemayor, William J. Coppola, and Christopher Mena

Volume V: Choral Music Education
Sarah J. Bartolome

Volume VI: School-Community Intersections
Patricia Shehan Campbell and Chee-Hoo Lum

Volume VII: World Music in Higher Education
William J. Coppola and David G. Hebert

World Music Pedagogy

School-Community Intersections

Volume VI

Patricia Shehan Campbell
University of Washington

Chee-Hoo Lum
National Institute of Education, Singapore

Routledge
Taylor & Francis Group

NEW YORK AND LONDON

First published 2019
by Routledge
52 Vanderbilt Avenue, New York, NY 10017

and by Routledge
2 Park Square, Milton Park, Abingdon, Oxon, OX14 4RN

Routledge is an imprint of the Taylor & Francis Group, an informa business

© 2019 Taylor & Francis

Library of Congress Cataloging-in-Publication Data
The Library of Congress has cataloged the combined volume edition as follows:
Names: Roberts, J. Christopher, author. | Beegle, Amy C., author.
Title: World music pedagogy.
Description: New York; London: Routledge, 2018– | Includes bibliographical
   references and index.
Identifiers: LCCN 2017050640 (print) | LCCN 2017054487 (ebook) |
   ISBN 9781315167589 () | ISBN 9781138052727 |
   ISBN 9781138052727q(v.2: hardback) | ISBN 9781138052796q(v.2: pbk.)
Subjects: LCSH: Music—Instruction and study.
Classification: LCC MT1 (ebook) | LCC MT1. W92 2018 (print) |
   DDC 780.71—dc23
LC record available at https://lccn.loc.gov/2017050640

ISBN: 978-1-138-06847-6 (hbk)
ISBN: 978-1-138-06848-3 (pbk)
ISBN: 978-1-315-15792-4 (ebk)

Typeset in Times New Roman
by Apex CoVantage, LLC

Visit the eResource: www.routledge.com/9781138068483

Contents

Chapter 3   **Participatory Musicking**   **47**

Chapter 4   **Performing World Music**   **77**

Series Foreword

Turning and turning in the widening gyre
The falcon cannot hear the falconer;
Things fall apart; the centre cannot hold;
Mere anarchy is loosed upon the world.

(from "The Second Coming", W. B. Yeats)

There is a foreboding tone to the stanza above, which at first may seem out of sync with a book on the pedagogy of world music. After all, music education is an intact phenomenon, arguably innocent and pure, that envelops teachers and their students in the acts of singing, playing, and dancing, and this field is decidedly not about falcons. Instead, music education conjures up long-standing images of spirited high school bands, choirs, and orchestras; of young adolescents at work in guitar and keyboard classes; of fourth grade xylophone and recorder players; of first grade rhythm bands; and of toddlers accompanied by parents playing small drums and shakers. At a time of demographic diversity, with a wide spectrum of students of various shapes, sizes, and hues laid wide open, music education can press further, as the field has the potential to hold court in a child's holistic development as a core avenue for the discovery of human cultural heritage and the celebration of multiple identities based upon race, ethnicity, gender, religion, and socioeconomic circumstance.

Yet there is a correspondence of the stanza, and the disquiet that Yeats communicates, with this book and with the book series, the Routledge World Music Pedagogy Series. I refer the reader to the start of the third line and also to the title of a novel by Nigerian author Chinua Achebe. A landmark in the world's great literature, *Things Fall Apart* has been very much in mind through the conception of this project, its design and development by a team of authors, and its thematic weave in these tempestuous times. Achebe's writing of cultural misunderstanding, of the arrogance and insensitivity of Western colonizers in village Africa, and of competing cultural systems is relevant.

We raise questions relative to music teaching and learning: Do things fall apart, or prove ineffective, when they do not reflect demographic change, do not respond to cultural variation, and do not reasonably reform to meet the needs of a new era? Can music education remain relevant and useful through the full-scale continuation of conventional practices, or is there something prophetic in the statement that things fall apart, particularly in music education, if there are insufficient efforts to revise and adapt to societal evolution? There is hard-core documentation of sparkling success stories in generations of efforts to musically educate children. Yet there is also evidence of frayed, flailing, and failing programs that are the result of restrictive music selections and exclusive pedagogical decisions that leave out students, remain unlinked to local communities and ignore a panorama of global expressions. There is the sinking feeling that music education programs exclusively rooted in Western art styles are insensitive and unethical for 21st-century schools and students and that choices of featured music are statements on people we choose to include and exclude from our world.

Consider many school programs for their long-standing means of musically educating students within a Western framework, featuring Western school-based music, following Western literate traditions of notation, including Western teacher-directed modes of learning, and being Western fixed rather than flexible and spontaneously inventive musicking potentials. All good for particular times and places and yet arguably unethical in the exclusion of music and music-makers in the world. Certainly, all practices deserve regular review, upgrades, even overhauls. Today's broad mix of students from everywhere in the world press on diversifying the curriculum, and the discoveries of "new" music-culture potentials are noteworthy and necessary in making for a more inclusive music education.

The Nigerian author selected the Irish poet's phrase as meaningful to his seminal work, much as we might reflect upon its meaning to muster a response to the societal disruption and contestation across the land and in the world. The practice of musically educating children, youth, and adults may not at first appear to be the full solution to the challenges of local schools and societies nor essential to meeting mandates in cultural and multicultural understanding. But music is as powerful as it is pan-human; musicking is musical involvement in what is humanly necessary; and the musical education of children and youth benefit their thoughts, feelings, and behaviors. When things fall apart or seem to be on the brink of breaking up, of serving fewer students and to a lesser degree than they might be served, we look to ways in which the music of many cultures and communities can serve to grow the musicianship of our students as well as their understanding of heritage and humanity, of people and places. Thus, from cynicism springs hope and from darkness comes light, as this book and book series rise up as a reasoned response to making music relevant and useful in the lives of learners in schools and communities.

THE SERIES

Each of the seven volumes in the **World Music Pedagogy Series** provides a sweep of teaching/learning encounters that lead to the development of skills, understandings, and values that are inherent within a diversity of the world's musical cultures. Written for professionally active teachers, in various contexts, as well as students in under-graduate and certification programs on their way to becoming teachers, these volumes encompass the application of the World Music Pedagogy (WMP) process from infancy and toddlerhood through adolescence, in higher education, and into the community.

The books are unified by conceptualizations and format and, of course, by the Series' aim of providing theoretical frameworks for and practical pedagogical experiences in teaching the world's musical cultures. Individual WMP volumes are organized by music education context (or class type) and age/grade level.

For every volume in the World Music Pedagogy Series, there are common elements that are intended to communicate with coherence the means by which learners can become more broadly musical and culturally sensitive to people close by and across the world. All volumes include seven chapters that proceed from an introduction of the particular music education context (and type) to the play out of the five dimensions to the reflective closing of how World Music Pedagogy contributes to meeting various musical and cultural goals, including those of social justice through music as well as issues of diversity, equity, and inclusion.

There are scatterings of music notations across each volume, mostly meant to assist the teacher who is preparing the orally based lessons rather than to suggest their use with students. Many of the chapters launch from vignettes—real-life scenarios of teachers and students at work in the WMP process—while chapters frequently close on interviews with practicing music educators and teaching musicians who are devoting their efforts to effecting meaningful experiences for students in the world's musical cultures. Authors of several of the volumes provide commentaries on published works for school music ensembles, noting what is available of notated scores of selected world music works, whether transcribed or arranged, and how they can be useful alongside the adventures in learning by listening.

LISTENING EPISODES FOR THE SERIES

Of central significance are the Listening Episodes for recordings that are featured in teaching-learning episodes. These episodes are lesson-like sequences that run from 3 minutes to 30 minutes, depending upon the interest and inclination of the teacher, which pay tribute to occasions for brief or extended listening experiences that may be repeated over a number of class sessions. The Listening Episodes are noted in the episode descriptions as well as at each chapter's end, and users can connect directly to the recordings (audio as well as video recordings) through the Routledge eResource site for each of the Series' volumes, linked to the catalog page of each volume through www.routledge.com/Routledge-World-Music-Pedagogy-Series/book-series/WMP.

All volumes recommend approximately 20 Listening Episodes, and Chapters 2–6 in each volume provide illustrations of the ways in which these listening selections can develop into experiences in the five WMP dimensions. From the larger set of recommended listening tracks, three selections continue to appear across the chapters as keystone selections that are intended to show the complete pathways of how these three recordings can be featured through the five dimensions. These learning pathways are noted in full in Appendix I so that the user can see in one fell swoop the flow of teaching-learning from Attentive Listening to Engaged Listening, Enactive Listening, Creating World Music, and Integrating World Music. Appendix II provides recommended resources for further reading, listening, viewing, and development of the ways of World Music Pedagogy.

***

As a collective of authors, and joined by many of our colleagues in the professional work of music teachers and teaching musicians, we reject the hateful ideologies that blatantly surface in society. We are vigilant of the destructive choices that can be made in the business of schooling young people and that may result from racism, bigotry, and prejudice. Hate has no place in society or its schools, and we assert that music is a route to peace, love, and understanding. We reject social exclusion, anti-Semitism, white supremacy, and homophobia (and other insensitive, unfeeling, or unbalanced perspectives). We oppose the ignorance or intentional avoidance of the potentials for diversity, equity, and inclusion in curricular practice. We support civility and "the culture of kindness" and hold a deep and abiding respect of people across the broad spectrum of our society. We are seeking to develop curricular threads that allow school music to be a place where all are welcome, celebrated, and safe; where every student is heard; and where cultural sensitivity can lead to love.

ACKNOWLEDGEMENTS

This collective of authors is grateful to those who have paved the way to teaching music with diversity, equity, and inclusion in mind. I am personally indebted to the work of my graduate school mentors—William M. Anderson, Terry Lee Kuhn, and Terry M. Miller, and to Halim El-Dabh and Virginia H. Mead—all of whom committed themselves to the study of music as a worldwide phenomenon and paved the way for me and many others to perform, study, and teach music with multicultural, intercultural, and global aims very much in mind. I am eternally grateful to Barbara Reeder Lundquist for her *joie de vivre* in the act of teaching music and in life itself. This work bears the mark of treasured University of Washington colleagues, then and now, who have helped to lessen the distance between the fields of ethnomusicology and music education, especially Steven J. Morrison, Shannon Dudley, and Christina Sunardi. Many thanks to the fine authors of the books in this Series: Sarah J. Bartolome, Amy Beegle, William J. Coppola, David G. Hebert, Karen Howard, Jamey Kelley, Chee-Hoo Lum, Chris Mena, Mark Montemayor, J. Christopher Roberts, and Sarah J. Watts. They are "the collective" who shaped the course of the Series and who toiled to fit the principles of World Music Pedagogy into their various specialized realms of music education. We are grateful to Constance Ditzel, music editor at Routledge, who caught the idea of the Series and enthusiastically encouraged us to write these volumes, and to her colleague, Peter Sheehy, who carried it through to its conclusion.

As in any of these exciting though arduous writing projects, I reserve my unending gratitude for my husband, Charlie, who leaves me "speechless in Seattle" in his support of my efforts. Once again, he gave me the time it takes to imagine a project—to write, read, edit, and write some more. It could not have been done without the time and space that he spared me, busying himself with theories behind "the adsorption of deuterated molecular benzene" while I helped to shape, with the author-team, these ideas on World Music Pedagogy.

Patricia Shehan Campbell
December 2017

Acknowledgments

To all those who have taught us, and who have inspired us to make music, to teach and facilitate it, and to seek out more of the world's expressive musical cultures, we offer our sincere gratitude. We owe this volume to those who have helped to shape our ideas on meaningful school-community intersections in the name of knowing local and global musical cultures, including children and youth in our Seattle and Singapore schools, and community musicians and culture-bearers whose ideas spill out of the pages of this work. As we navigate between schools and communities, configuring meaningful interactions and intersections, we acknowledge the efforts of so many who are committed to the cause of musical-cultural diversity, equity, and inclusion. We are duly grateful to the exemplary efforts of colleagues at work in musical communities we know, including Lee Higgins, Shannon Dudley, Bo Wah Leung, Barbara Lundquist, Huib Schippers, Amanda Soto, and Jennifer Walden. Thanks to our colleague-authors, too, who have dedicated long hours to the making of the Routledge World Music Pedagogy Series. We take inspiration from these people named, from our families, and from the many unnamed here who nonetheless have offered us at one time or another their musical-artistic-pedagogical energy and ideas that brought us to the making of this work.

Patricia Shehan Campbell, Seattle
Chee-Hoo Lum, Singapore
March 2019

Episodes

Listening Episode music examples can be accessed on the eResource site from the Routledge catalog page.

1
Teaching and Learning in Context

Recipe for success: A devoted music teacher, her students, her interest in music as a global phenomenon, her belief in the necessity of school-community intersections. The success she and her students know pertains to their study of music for how it is learned and taught, as it is humanly expressed, and as it is culturally reflective of human diversity. The school-community intersections she advances are both local and global and include the music and musicians of such practices as Korean samul-nori; *Appalachian-style* bluegrass; *Japanese* koto; *Argentinian* tango; *Shona* mbira; *Mexican* son jarocho; *Lakota Sioux* powwow; *Chinese* jiang nan si zhu *(silkstring ensemble);* Jamaican *reggaetón;* Javanese *gamelan;* and South Indian trio of violinist, singer, and player of the double-headed drum known as* mridangam. *Some of these musicians are down the block and around the corner from the school, others are within the metropolitan area in which the suburban school is located, and several hail from further afield, visiting the area or coming across the Internet. As a devoted teacher to her K–12 students of various ages and experiences, she facilitates their understanding of music as a presence in all communities, "near and far" from their experience; on all manner of instruments; in various vocal styles; with the integration of dance, drama, poetry, the visual arts, and various curricular subjects. She carries the concept of community close to the heart; over nine years of successful teaching, she has shown her students and co-workers not only that their neighborhood is rich with diverse musical practices but also that a sense of community is created when her students gather to sing, dance, play, create, and even listen together. She has configured a socially inclusive program that leads students to a full reckoning of the diversity of musical expressions that can be listened to (live and on recordings) and learned, and that can form the basis for developing community consciousness and cultural understanding. Like a prism of many-splendored colors, she has embraced "community" in all of its shades of meaning, and the musical education of her students is full evidence of the success of her commitment to the cause.*

Music Happens in Every Living Community

Across the planet, in small villages, and in teeming city neighborhoods, people make music *because they must*, as it is a human penchant for young and old to want to sing, to sound on musical instruments as extensions of themselves, and to listen to music. They respond to music in ways that span from the external need to move and to dance all the way to the intimate meaning-making of music that transpires within themselves. They make music in community, that is, through the interaction of voices and instruments (and dancing bodies) together in a gathered group. Every community, in every culture, knows the music that defines them, contributes to their identity, and carries with it shared meanings. Music and community are linked, too, in that communities are created, re-created, and perpetuated through a network of music-makers, music listeners, and music supporters.

This volume gives accent to music and community, with attention to the diverse musical practices that are performed in communities—by culture-bearing community musicians—and that can be taught and learned in schools. It acknowledges World Music Pedagogy as a multifaceted avenue for knowing diverse musical expressions and that the concept of teaching and learning a diversity of musical expressions is relevant and useable in contexts within schools and communities. It accepts that artists in the community are powerful players in efforts to lead children and youth to an understanding and valuing of music of every sort. It maintains that teachers and artists together, be they music educators or teaching musicians who working within the contexts of schools and communities, can benefit greatly from occasions to work collaboratively to make music and design experiences that nurture the musical capacity and cultural awareness of students. With World Music Pedagogy as a pedagogical sequence, this volume suggests that there is bridging to do between people who make the music and the contexts in which music is made and that beneficiaries of school-community collaborations are manifold in that they serve students, their teachers, the musicians who live and work in the community, families, and the wide span of various other residents who live in the local neighborhoods that surround the schools.

As one of seven volumes devoted to cultural diversity in music education, this volume is intended for all musicians-who-teach. In fact, it is aimed at those who teach in educational institutions that encompass public and private schools (as well as conservatories, colleges, and universities) as well as those who call themselves teaching artists, teaching musicians, and community musicians. It reaches also to performing musicians; to composers and improvisers; and to various others with portfolio careers who give recitals, perform in chamber (and larger) ensembles, and engage in musical collaborations with other musicians. Because we view music education broadly, we recognize that music and music learning occur in a grand variety of contexts. We embrace the community at large as alive with music and musicians and with rich potential for making music, teaching and learning music, and connecting musicians to teachers and students. Thus, we see a need for this volume to address music education in its breadth of possibilities and to reach beyond the narrowly channeled, conventional interpretations of those who teach. Indeed, we challenge convention by enveloping within the teaching-learning process all those who pledge their time and effort in schools and communities to effect the acquisition by people both young and old of musical knowledge, skills, and values.

Interfaces of Music With Community

A successful partnership of school music educators with community musicians, audiences, and "arts agents" in support of school-community connections rests in an understanding of the interfaces of music with community (and schools). A critical launch-point to the discussion is in selecting out the various meanings of familiar terms, "music" and "community", since they are so variously used and so frequently favored in everyday conversation and clarifying their particular meanings to the enterprise we are undertaking here. Certainly critical, too, is an awareness of the diversity that exists both culturally and musically in communities (and across school populations) and a recognition of diversity as it relates to music, community, and conviviality. By conceptualizing these terms, the frame will thus be set for a consideration of pedagogical avenues that facilitate learning pathways for students to experience intricate and increasingly evolved encounters with music and culture.

Music

Music is in the ear of the beholder. It exists as an art form, as a force of socialization, and as an expression of cultural identity. It consists of sounds and silences, of elemental features such as pitch (and melody), duration (and rhythm), timbre, texture, and various expressive features such as dynamics and articulation. Not always do musicians care to include all features in their performance, such as the case of rhythmic percussion music produced by a group of Haitian musicians playing same-size hollowed-out bamboo stamping tubes *(gangos)*, where pitch pales in comparison to the rhythmic complexities of the music. On the other hand, performances may go beyond the musical sound in order to encompass also dance, drama, the visual arts, poetry, and more—at times together in a kind of all-encompassing pageantry whose multisensory experiences are nonetheless referred to merely as "music". In many sub-Saharan African cultures, *ngoma* is the term applied to music as sound-plus, that is, sound that is typically blended with any number of artistic practices.

One person's music may be another person's noise, and there is no guarantee that any two people—particularly from different places in the world—will define music, or identify with music, in precisely the same way. To be sure, carefully designed learning encounters do well to make sense out of what might seem initially to a student like sonic chaos so that the logical structures of music rise to the surface through repeated listening. Likewise, student understandings of unfamiliar music do also develop through a realization of people's uses and values of it and its historical and contemporary roles in cultural life. There is a wide spread of musical possibilities and preferences, of course, which makes the selection of music for casual use or formal learning a challenge in itself. The question arises: "Do I listen, perform, teach, and compose in the style of Beethoven or Beyoncé, Haydn or hardcore punk, Copland or *conjunto*, Mozart or *maqam*? Or all of these and more?"

Music that has been historically prescribed for use in various educational settings frequently excludes the music of many musicians living in local communities, and many more musical expressions found elsewhere in the world may not be found in classrooms. School music teachers have canonized what music is taught and not taught to children and youth, and it's possible that they have learned what's appropriate through their university training as well as from finely experienced master teachers in schools who, intentionally or not, continue to perpetuate the music of their own training without reaching out to the wider world of musical possibilities. Inroads have been made, of course, with exemplar musicians and teachers leading the way in opening ears to a broad musical range. Still, it is astonishing that in this time of demographic diversity and tremendous technological access, music is still in the ear of the beholder whose musical taste may be confined to a narrow band of the rich assortment that is so easily available.

Community

Derived from the Latin *communitas*, the concept of community speaks to people who gather together as a group acting collectively—working, playing, and otherwise conducting themselves with a strong sense of shared purpose. They are bonded by their shared beliefs, and they develop a sense of solidarity that derives from group-thought and collective experience and action. Community is a concept that is receiving considerable play in sociology, anthropology, psychology, the arts, and music in particular (Higgins, 2012). Its academic home is in the social sciences, and yet the term "community" is also so frequently used as to be colloquial and certainly conversational. It is a term favored on local government websites and in circulars, and it appears regularly in school district manuals and curriculum guides. Community signifies camaraderie, a fellowship, and even friendship, of belonging and mutuality (Ansdell, 2004), and it denotes an association of people through one or more cultural facets. There are communities of people who identify by race, ethnicity, gender, class, religion, age, and lifestyle, as there are also regional, national, and virtual communities that connect electronically. There are international communities (e.g., surgeons, school superintendents, and symphonic orchestra conductors in Berlin, Brussels, Boston, and Buenos Aires) as there are also intergenerational communities (e.g., civic groups or religious congregations consisting of families of children, parents, and grandparents). Community signifies people in collaboration, as it also refers to a cooperative spirit among people.

Music and community are wedded in ways that include the conglomerate of musicians living and working in a given location, the individual subcultures of musicians in a location (from choristers to jazzers, rock guitarists, brass-band players, and classical pianists), and the potential of a local population of music fans and supporters, and music aspirants, amateurs, and learners of every age and experience level becoming participants in music-making encounters through their interactions with musicians. Another relevant meaning of community is the sense of oneness that derives from people gathering together for a purpose, including the purpose of making music together or otherwise enjoying music as responsive listeners. Community denotes coalition, too, as in the coalition that develops when people are drawn together for music functions, and the bonding power of music is notable for its capacity to create a sense of community—and a coalition.

Of course, to act collectively and develop solidarity requires a substantial effort from each individual member of a community. Aided by active communication and action, a communion of individuals can emerge who share strong intellectual, social, emotional, and spiritual connections. The development of a sense of community brings with it an invitation to members "to reflect upon the ecology of sociocultural life" (Stige, 2004, p. 91), whether it be within the small social unit of a family; in neighborhoods; in work, worship, and leisure groups; in special-interest networks;

or across a full cityscape of multiple mini-communities. Community denotes a commitment by individual members to the mutual support of one another and a conscious aim by members to interact and intersect with one another. Community members experience togetherness when they strive for an intimate understanding of the context in which they live and when they share a willingness to critically and creatively communicate, negotiate, and collaborate for the good of the group. Community is closely linked to the formation of traditions that result from questioning and affirming identity through collective action. A community can thus be a litmus test for equity, diversity, and inclusion as living and fluid entities within a society that embodies concepts of the local and global in all their manifestations.

The musical and artistic life of a community reflects the community's sociocultural composite and its identities, traditions, and values. Lee Higgins (2012) observes that the music of a community is any and every "music (that is) made by any community at any time" (p. 3.) The music of a community arises in various contexts and through various circumstances. Consider these: A church choir that rehearses on Wednesdays and performs every Sunday morning; a weekly *fandango* gathering at El Centro de la Raza where people sing, play *requintos* and *vilhuelas*, and dance in hard heels on a raised wooden platform; adults and their children, and a few senior citizens, who enjoy participation in Saturday afternoon drum circles at their local community center; a small group of professional string players who meet two Saturdays a month on their own time in order to expand their horizons by creating new and experimental music; a community band of brass and wind players ranging in age from high school seniors to "mature" adults who come together to play for fun (and seasonal community concerts); an internet or online band, where members collaborate musically across varied geographic boundaries without meeting face to face but who can nonetheless share their musical outcomes on social platforms with their local or other virtual communities. Music of a community ranges widely and can be inclusive of a diverse range of people with various musical interests who forge their individual identities into a collective whole.

Community Music

One merging of music and community is the phenomenon of Community Music, an influential movement in group music participation that arose from UK-based local sociomusical activity as early as the 1960s and which has spread internationally into communities and schools across the globe (Higgins & Bartleet, 2018). The crux of the movement is to provide music-making opportunities for all who desire to join in, and the process of group music has asserted the importance of expression by group members from the ground up (rather than top-down by teachers and conductors) of which music to make and how to make it. In Community Music practice, some of the music may be known to group members, familiar and "fixed", and other music may arise from group improvisation activity in which all members work together to make something musically interesting to them. Importantly, Community Music asserts all members should have an equal opportunity to shape the music of the collective, and the task of the professionally trained community musician is to assist in realizing the group's interests and ideas. This informal music-making process is maintained in some settings, while it has also been modified as the principles of group improvisation have gradually made their way from informal to formal educational settings. Community

Music ideals, then, are evident not only in community centers where songwriting, "African drumming", and samba groups are organized but also in school-based music education settings where a more democratic practice of student ideas and interests are shaping the musical experience. In its exemplary form, Community Music involves communal music-making activity, including the exposure and active participation and performance of music to bind people together. The interjections and interventions of a community music facilitator is meant to guide but not lead music-making experiences; this facilitator suggests but does not teach and honors the musical ideas of all present in forging a collective musical expression. The emphasis in Community Music is on "active participation, sensitivity to context, equality of opportunity, and a commitment to diversity" (Higgins, 2012, p. 174).

The concept of community music is, in fact, a metaphor for music education in its finest manifestation, where music teachers succeed in providing students of music with the opportunity to make something beautiful together through group engagement in a process that helps them to gain hold of their collective musical self (which leads to group gratification of the process in which they engage as well as the musical product that they accomplish). In the context of school music classes, community can be viewed from four perspectives: In place (boundedness, rootedness, interconnectedness, feelingfulness, and a sense of empowerment), in time (sense of dynamism, means of regulation, basis for tradition, and awareness of finitude), as process (of becoming, sense of reflective action, dialogue, and pilgrimage [of travel and the spiritual]), and as an end (uniting diverse people in pursuit

Figure 1.1 The classroom as a musical community in the hands of culture-bearing Brazilian musician Eduardo Mendonça

Photo by Susie Fitzhugh

of an objective, having an idealistic vision, codification, practicality, and anticipatory) (Jorgensen, 1995). An examination of music in community in many of the world's cultures allows for an understanding of music in its past and present contexts, valuing differences and similarities, feeling connected to others, accepting and loving musical traditions close to heart, and feeling the empowerment to change and embrace new musical perspectives. Music in local and global communities quite naturally features active musical participation by community members who enjoy making music for which they have a personal buy-in (i.e., music that is already familiar and readily available to them in their lives) or music that draws their curiosity and intrigue (i.e., music that features unfamiliar or unusual instruments or vocal styles). For many community members, there may be little interest in fussing over a plethora of musical styles that may have no direct links to them. Yet at the same time, community members may choose to explore together the worldwide spectrum of music, to take a musical journey beyond themselves, to know something more of the world in and through music (which may even flavor and influence their performance of the music they know well).

Music, Diversity, and Conviviality

We are living, learning, teaching, and having a need for expressing ourselves in a world of tremendous human diversity. The cultures that comprise our cities and towns, our neighborhoods, and even our extended families are increasingly varied by race and ethnicity, gender, class, religion, and other facets. While people are united by the circumstances of their geographic location and the sociopolitical infrastructures that govern their shared civil society, they also proudly celebrate their unique identities. There are mandates for recognizing cultural diversity in civic organizations and for taking responsibility to remove barriers and eliminate naiveté as to the importance of diverse voices within our circles of influence in schools and so many societal circumstances. In music, there are manifesto-like statements that pledge an allegiance to diversifying musical studies—directed at the tertiary level but intended for students who will eventually teach music in schools (Sarath, Myers, & Campbell, 2017). Diversity is a daily reality, and those in the practice of music education have access to a spectrum of wondrous music-cultural expressions to listen to, learn, perform, and even innovate and improvise upon.

For more than a generation, digital natives who grew up in a techno world (and older generations of "digital immigrants" as well) (Prensky, 2001) have come into finger-tip touch with the wide world of music. The ease and accessibility of technology has allowed people to become diverse in their listening experience, to travel from the throat singers of Mongolia to the Griot singers of West Africa in a fleeting moment as they toggle from one YouTube video to another in the comfort of their homes. Sound-worlds have expanded exponentially and are no longer bounded by time, space, or distance. Accessibility to a wide range of musical expressions through technology is not just a passive visual-aural experience, either. One can actively learn the techniques and skills of unfamiliar music easily from the bountiful online tutorials and video clips available, and musical competence is possible from home without ever having had physical in-person contact with a teacher. Many skilled musicians have also established online possibilities for study through Skype and FaceTime, where they can teach students remotely across continents. Technology also offers online music communities the means for making music together across borders, even without ever physically having met one another.

Twenty-first century educators of all subjects and disciplines are faced with a range of challenges and possibilities, as rapid shifts in the geo-political landscape and wide-ranging uncertainties in the economic, social, and cultural terrain impact the future and its implications for today's young people. Among the most important skills critical to equipping students for the unpredictable demands ahead is the ensuing capacity to dialogue with, understand, negotiate, and respect cultural differences across a range of boundaries. There is a dire need for educators to engage students in the processes that can enable them to reflect, interact, collaborate, and thus deal with varied kinds of experiences in order to gain the creative capacities and socio-emotional insights and skills needed for a purposeful future (Robinson, 2001). As students are supported in opportunities for self-discovery, so, too, is it critical that they develop understandings of others, of people outside their own familial territory, of individuals and groups of people of a variety of cultures who live locally and across the world.

Arts education at large, including education in music, dance, drama, and the visual arts, has proven to be a suitable site for employing critical pedagogies that can encourage students to attend closely to one another; to shape artistic expressions together; and to engage in imaginative, experimental, and improvisatory processes that allow for new and innovative approaches to rethinking culture and identity. The branding that occurred generations ago of the arts as "aesthetic education" referred not only to producing and reproducing great works of high art (be they masterworks of Monteverdi, Mozart, or Mozabiquean Chopi-styled xylophone ensembles) but also working toward the expansion of student agency through their own refined sensibility and critical literacy. Attainment of these goals under the arch of aesthetic education was meant to enlarge the capacity of students to grow in sociocultural cohesion and cognitive development. Such aims are current today. To affect change in students so as to lead to their deeper cohesiveness and self-confidence among young people is a noble goal, and music and all the arts are effective in provoking critical thinking and reflection on experience, history, memory, and knowledge. This dialogue with ideas allows for a range of voices that reflect multiple perspectives to emerge in an imaginative and stimulating environment. Within open and contextually grounded frameworks that look closely at the dynamics of cultural difference and multiplicity, all education in the arts can consciously expand the capacity for dealing with conflicts and tensions that curtail social cohesion. In this manner, the arts become a form of critical literacy that advances the students' ability to read, interpret, and respond to issues of local and global diversity and inclusion in their individual environments.

In focusing on musical activities in the community, teachers and their students can draw upon local and global content that is near to them; familiar and relevant to everyday lives; and also distant, intriguing, even "exotic" to the point of stretching their ears and minds in expansive ways. Exercises in knowing the unfamiliar music can result in developing in students an awareness of critical qualities such as respect of others, responsibility, and civic consciousness. By juxtaposing different cultural elements, adapting, and translating diverse vocabularies of artistic expression, and examining world music encounters within local communities, teachers can challenge the normative assumptions by students regarding culture and identity that are typically reductive in order to move toward better equity (Grant & Sleeter, 2011, pp. 55–92).

Equity in this instance refers to students acknowledging and understanding the fluidity of culture and identity, not judging (or stereotyping) the music of a culture based on face-value generalizations but being fair and impartial through the critical examination and understanding of multiple musical contexts and narratives. Bearing in mind that the 21st century is laden with anxieties of dividedness, fears of alienation, and tensions of estrangement, the placement of musical diversity front and center in a curricular plan can help to situate and contextually ground learning experiences and to consciously connect experiences in music with universal values of integrity and justice.

The theoretical notion of "conviviality" as suggested by the eminent cultural studies scholar, Paul Gilroy (2005), is relevant here. In an educational context, conviviality emphasizes the normalizing of multicultural interactions and processes as a part of ordinary social life, with an aim to moving students critically forward in affecting their sociocultural and emotional development. By examining these processes of cultural innovation and interpretation in music education and across all realms of arts education, teachers can provide opportunities and guidance to their students in expanding their capacity to engage as conscious and proactive participants of a diverse global society. Gilroy argues that this form of creative thinking can generate multiperspectival narratives that imitate the complexities and "everydayness" of heterocultural metropolitan lives, thus reducing "exaggerated dimensions of [racial] difference to a liberating ordinariness" (Gilroy, 2005, p. 119). Music teachers need to constantly gear their students toward understanding the multiple musical identities and cultures that a single musician in the community can represent because a pianist, guitarist, or percussionist may choose to engage in various styles, within varied musical settings, for various purposes. This attention by teachers to diversity that exists even within individual artists can help students to understand the complexities of the heterocultural musical influences that surround them, thus emphasizing the vibrant musical space that musicians in communities inhabit. The "liberating ordinariness" thus mitigates against a negative exoticism or neocolonialist elitism, giving voice to the lived and experienced cultures of people from multiple backgrounds.

It is no secret that professional musicians or musical groups playing folk instruments may get pigeon-holed as capable only of performing standardized musical repertoire of the traditional style or genre that is associated with particular instruments. The thought goes that a *guzheng* musician will play only Chinese music. A player of Egyptian *'ud* may be classified as one who plays only Egyptian music, while a Peruvian panpipe musician may be automatically perceived as a player only of Andean genres. A Mexican *mariachi* player may know well the repertoire and techniques on her trumpet, but she may also have an interest and expertise in other styles. Musicians can be ladened with historical, social, and cultural expectations and labeled as "the *guzheng* player", "the *'ud* player", "the Peruvian panpiper", or "the *mariachi* musician". These labels can limit their creative boundaries, particularly if they wish to break out of their mold to explore and play experimental music on their instruments or to creatively modify the sounds of their instruments through extended techniques. How would these musicians and their non-traditional repertoire fit within a critical dialogue about world music? Can players (and singers) switch in and out of their roles as traditional musicians to take on other styles, to innovate, to fuse their music with others with resultant new expressions? Why does stereotyping exist, and how might school-community projects in music help to break the biases of this sort?

With conviviality as a working framework for dealing with cultural difference, another key element for teachers to consider is the development of an open, active, and responsive listening way through a process of "dialogic empathy". In attending to the needs and perceptions of others, listening can be usefully enacted, embodied, and enhanced within school music programs. Sociologist Richard Sennett clarifies the advantage of empathy over sympathy by asserting that empathy focuses attention on people in their own terms and that the listener is pushed to get outside him or herself. As a result, empathy becomes intertwined with dialogic exchange in which cooperation, imagination, and the exploration of wide-ranging possibilities are evoked (Sennett, 2012). In arts education programs that deal with cultural difference, such as through world music engagements that connect closely with a given musical community, this quality of "getting outside the self" in order to "listen attentively" has great potential in expanding cultural inclusion through artistic dialogue (Dolby, 2012).

Musicians are typically curious about other musical genres, styles, and instruments. Many enjoy collaborating with musicians from different cultural experiences to learn from one another and to create new sound spaces. These creative collaborative fusions can spread across an array of possibilities. Consider these musically collaborative practices: (1) Using popular music as a conduit, creating arrangements for different configurations of folk instruments, and giving popular music tunes a fresh twist by playing with the musical characteristics of traditional music genres and the unique timbres of the varied folk instruments; (2) Taking on the spirit of improvisation through a fixed structure, such as a group's performance of the main melody or "head" and allowing musicians to have musical dialogue with each other while also having moments of "togetherness"; (3) Coming into a musical encounter with an open mind and a readiness to work with a "blank slate" while exploring and experimenting with sound sources in order to build a cohesive musical piece together; and (4) Having a composer write specifically for a unique combination of folk instruments in completely experimental ways while building on concepts and elements of music that are significant in the genres represented by the musicians and their instruments. Listeners to these musical innovations can be drawn into the sound-worlds of these musicians who work at the edge of their music traditions—who preserve, change, and redefine their creative intentions. An insight into the creative musical collaborations of musicians thus drives at the acceptance of ambiguity, of accepting the messiness of authenticity, and of acknowledging the dangers of stereotyping particular musical expressions.

From the perspective of music in communities, which aims at the development of people's general well-being in and through music, group music activities can help musicians and music learners of all types share experiences and grow in an understanding of each other. Group music activities can be directed to collective creativity as well as self-expression in developing artistic abilities and probing more deeply into issues of individual (and collective) identity. Sociologist Anita Harris (2013) observes that youth cultures, in bringing a productive mix of people together through collaborative activities, can sometimes transcend "ethnicised difference" to create cultural expressions that are expansive "beyond singular cultural categories" (p. 46). Thus, a mixed population of children, youth, or adults who come together from varied multicultural experiences and identities can experience opportunities for knowing one another through the process of creating something musically or artistically cohesive—together. Music educators, and educators in all the arts, can be highly effective in encouraging student expression of multiple artistic perspectives to emerge. Certainly, teaching musicians have the means for facilitating critical expression while examining meaning, value, and artistry in the process.

A cautionary note should be sounded about diversity as a double-edged sword. Even with open minds, music teachers and teaching musicians can swing too far to the left and end up marginalizing and even ostracizing the majority. Teachers need to acknowledge that while striving to find a balancing point in the slippery slope of diversity, there will always be a tipping point to consider. The key to diversity is inclusion. While teachers try to increasingly include everyone into the fold of their arms, and their safe spaces, there is the looming need to be mindful of who is outside these warmth and comfort zones, too. To be certain, teachers need to remind themselves that they are subjective beings who are constantly choosing who to include and exclude in the curricular plan. In the increasing diversity of musical styles that students are exposed to and will encounter, teachers need to facilitate links to community, allowing students to connect their everyday musical spaces in meaningful and critical ways. It is vital that teachers guide students toward conviviality through dialogic empathy (using the music and the arts as a vital bridge and the community as contextual frame), building agency for students to create critical safeguards in dealing with current complex and challenging narratives of multiperspectival lives.

Community Musicians and Culture-Bearers

Within the realm of school programs where teachers are convinced of the merit of school-community intersections, the presence of community musicians and culture-bearers is felt in the programs they provide, the skills they help students to hone, the musical and cultural knowledge they share, and the broadening of values and meanings of music in diverse segments of human life. Across city or town, but also in the school's surrounding neighborhood, there are musicians who are engaged in various musical activities both professionally and informally. They may be violinists, violists, flutists, and trombonists in the local symphony; jazz and popular musicians; and pianists who play solo, in chamber groups, and as accompanists to singers and instrumentalists. They may be musicians who teach—piano, the orchestral instruments, guitar, singing, and any other known instruments. Widening the lens to any of the world's musical cultures that may be present and available for school involvement, community musicians may be singers of folk songs from Nicaragua and Nigeria, Poland and Peru, and players of Venezuelan harp and Vietnamese *dan tranh* (zither). By nature of their cultural identity, they may play Chinese *er hu* (fiddle), Russian *balalaika, kora* (harp) from the Malinke of Mali, *tar* (lute) from Iran, *bodhran* (hand drum) from Ireland, and *sitar* (lute) from North India. Community musicians can be found at performances in concert halls, at gigs in the local pub, and in their homes as they practice, perform, and teach. They may be engaging seniors in music-making activities in a multiservice center, working in the capacity of artist-in-residence in a middle school, or teaching in a drum circle at the local community club. They may be more evident than it would initially seem; through person-to-person conversations, newspaper notices, and internet announcements, community musicians are identifiable. Community musicians are often actively engaged within different "pockets" of the local community, sharing the love of their musical traditions and music-making activities for the purposes of connecting and collaborating, allowing for wide opportunities of participation (from audience listening behavior to joining in songs and on simple instruments). It's note-worthy that many community musicians are empowering change through the music they make and facilitate in others, even as they continue to evolve what they do in context with the local time and space. On invitation from teachers, community musicians can expand and enrich the musical experience and study that happens in schools.

Culture-bearers are evident everywhere, and many culture-bearers are also musicians living locally in the community. They carry their culture and consciously embody cultural values in a variety of ways, including through language and dialect, food, dress, traditional crafts, the arts, and music. Many (but by no means all) culture-bearers are community musicians, working as preservers, transmitters, and innovators of a particular musical tradition. Some may be at home with children or elderly family members, engaged in various professional positions, or employed across a wide spectrum of the service sector. On the side, they may knit, weave, carve, bead, bake, and make musical instruments. They may also tell stories, sing songs of their heritage, play instruments, and dance. Culture-bearers are the authority and port of call when musicians, teachers, and students hope to connect more deeply with the cultural knowledge of the musical tradition. Culture-bearers may have deeply imbibed and embodied the musical culture not just in musical terms but in understanding the particular music from an historical, social, and cultural context. Schools that claim an interest in cultural heritage can make possible a budget for inviting culture-bearers to work within the school as they share music, stories about music, and a full range of cultural riches. Likewise, students can be brought to the cultural spaces of the

Figure 1.2   Sustaining music traditions through the efforts of community musician Kedmon Mapana and Wagogo villagers of Central Tanzania

culture-bearers so that they can experience firsthand the environment with which the culture-bearers live out their traditional practices even as they make work to fuse them with contemporary expressions, improve upon them, or otherwise change them. For those culture-bearers who carry the music of their heritage, students can join them in making music or in contributing to a dialogue on music in a culture and of a community. The roles of community musicians and culture-bearers are sometimes separate, but they can also be beautifully intertwined.

A Lens on Ethnomusicology

In the field of ethnomusicology, musical diversity is defined, discussed, and dissected in remarkable detail. The interests of musicologists and anthropologists merged in the making of the discipline so that ethnomusicology developed as the study of music in culture and as culture, with attention to how people of the world's cultures make music meaningful and useful in their lives (Wade, 2004). Ethnomusicologists study music as sound, behavior, and value. They offer musical and sociomusical analyses and descriptions (and, more rarely, transcriptions of sound to notation), and they aim their lens on the musicians, the functions and contexts of their musical involvement, and the meanings that they make of the music. Because music is present wherever there is human life, all cultures are potential subjects for ethnomusicological study. Thus, there are ethnomusicological studies of music in urban and rural areas, in secular and sacred surrounds, in courts and cathedrals, in cafes and clubs, in parks and playgrounds. Some of the most profound understandings of music as cultural reflection emanate from classic ethnomusicological studies of gagaku court music of Japan by Robert Garfias; the everyday and elevated functions of music among the Flathead and Blackfoot people of Montana by Alan P. Merriam and Bruno Nettl, respectively; Bonnie C. Wade's analysis of the relationships among music, art, and culture during the Mughal Empire of India; Timothy Rice's dissection of the music learning process for Bulgarian pipes and bagpipes; and Anthony Seeger's probings of singing among the Suya, an indigenous group living in the Amazon River region. Cultural and social histories of music have come out more recently, including studies of mass media music in Turkey (by Martin Stokes); antinuclear music of protest in Japan (by Noriko Manabe); the cultural politics of popular "light music" in Albania (by Nicholas Tochka); and the rise of South African electronic *kwaito*, an urban black musical form by Gavin Steingo. The ethnomusicological lens for these works is fixed on the nature of people's interactions with music as they perform it, create it, respond to it, learn it, sustain it, and transmit it to others.

In ethnomusicology, where sensitivity to community members has always been at the forefront of fieldwork, growing attention has been given to applied ethnomusicology (Pettan & Titon, 2015). Grounded in principles of social responsibility, ethnomusicologists are applying their understandings to practice through music-centered interventions into communities. They are involved in education, cultural policy, medicine and healthcare, peace-building efforts, museums, archives, and festivals and in projects that intersect technology, media, and marketing, all the while working on grant-funded projects to facilitate musical experiences for people of local and global communities. As they work beyond the standard academic contexts, applied ethnomusicology has grown into the use of ethnomusicological perspectives in developing human relationships and locating music at the center of activist projects that support minority groups, the marginalized, and the oppressed.

Ethnomusicologists have been collaborating with educators for decades in identifying and developing music curricular materials, particularly at the university level but also for use with children and youth in school and community settings. In their research as well as in their applied projects, ethnomusicologists have argued for a recognition of human musicality, asserting that every individual is musical, if only their society would listen (and provide the necessary frameworks for their musical development, education, and training). Ethnomusicologists have demonstrated the critical importance of the music learning process over the final (performance) product and of wrapping the music that is shared in schools with the traditional ways in which music is learned within the culture. Critical to World Music Pedagogy, ethnomusicologists have given their attention to the presence of orality/aurality in the transmission of music, the complete (or partial) absence of a notational system, and the extent to which many musical practices are at their core creative processes that are spontaneously expressed, or adjusted impromptu, in the instant of the performance act. For teachers in schools and communities, then, ethnomusicology paves the way out of mere "material-grabs" and over to acknowledging music as a human phenomenon, as core cultural expression, as an aural and creative endeavor, and as a means of knowing the splendors (and intricacies) of musical and cultural diversity.

Defining World Music Pedagogy

World Music Pedagogy (WMP) springs from a belief in the principles of democracy, both cultural and musical, as a driving force for the steady presence of musical diversity in school music classrooms and rehearsal halls (Campbell, 2018). WMP suggests that the exclusion of musical styles for study is inherently the exclusion of the people whose music it is, and that music of all cultures are worthy of study—regardless of the class or ensemble. Democratically speaking, it maintains that the principles of equity and inclusion need to be present in the design of the curriculum, the selection of the repertoire, and the full play-out of regular encounters with the world's musical expressions. It considers the complexities of diversifying the musical content of the curriculum, the multicultural-intercultural facets of the teaching-learning interface, and the myriad ways in which social justice is achieved through a transformative design of an equitable education in and through music. World Music Pedagogy provides a pathway for fashioning powerful experiences in knowing diverse musical practices, systems, and cultures and upholds music as the multicultural-intercultural and international phenomenon that it truly is.

With the growth of multicultural awareness in society and its schools, World Music Pedagogy has emerged from earlier efforts by educators, ethnomusicologists, and artist-musicians to seek effective means for teaching and learning the beauty and logic of the world's musical cultures. For well over a half century, various programs and projects have come forward to multiculturalize and globalize school music studies. Across North America, and internationally, declarations have been issued; textbooks have been revised and expanded; and conferences, symposia, and a steady stream of workshops have given focus to methods and materials that address issues of cultural diversity in music education. Schools and their communities can boast exceptional programs for children and the youth of West African drum-and-dance troupes, Trinidadian *steelbands*, African American Gospel choirs, "Zimarimbas" (Zimbabwean *marimba* ensembles), and Mexican *mariachis*. There are exemplary study modules or curricular units of "music in the Americas" and "music of the African diaspora" that are in practice in various elementary and secondary schools—some that feature visits by culture-bearing heritage musicians who perform, facilitate participatory experiences, and otherwise highlight or extend studies of a particular people and place in the world. Noteworthy programs in music education, including those that maintain long-standing band, choir, and orchestra programs, have taken on the occasional song from South Africa or Samoa or an instrumental arrangement from Senegal or the Sioux Nation to experience and study.

While previous efforts of teaching world music are categorically commendable, they are also somewhat isolated or irregular instances. They are at times pedagogically unsystematic, incomplete, even superficial, and often incapable of meeting aims of musical and cultural understanding that are timely and necessary, and entirely achievable. World Music Pedagogy offers a systematic and substantive approach to the experience and study of the world's musical cultures for students of all ages and in various educational contexts. It reaches beyond questions of "why (world music)?" and "what (music from which culture)?" to questions of "what (meaning does the music hold within the culture?)" and "how (can the music best fit into systems and situations of musical education and training)?" It presses on the manner in which music is taught/transmitted and received/learned within cultures and how best the processes that are included in significant ways within these cultures can be preserved or at least partially retained in classrooms and rehearsal halls. It assumes the expansion of possibilities for repertoire as it also considers those culture-specific instructional techniques with which the repertoire is associated. Importantly, WMP pays tribute to the critical importance of learning by listening and of repeated listening in increasingly active and interactive ways. It underscores the logic of making sense of music as an aural art, a channel of creative practice, and a means of personal and communal human expression. As such, it is relevant to learners of every age and stage of musical development.

There are five dimensions of World Music Pedagogy that can be applied to any selection of music, from anywhere on earth (see Figure 1.3). Since music specialist teachers frequently go it alone in their classrooms and rehearsal settings and do not typically have the wherewithal to work with culture-bearers from the community nor to have instruments from every corner of the world, the WMP process acknowledges

---

Figure 1.3:   Five Dimensions of World Music Pedagogy

- Attentive Listening
  (Multiple directed listening experiences)
- Engaged Listening
  (Participatory musicking; Active participation while listening)
- Enactive Listening
  (Performance through continued oral-aural listening)
- Creating World Music
  (Inventions in the style of a studied selection)
- Integrating World Music
  (Connections of music to disciplines, fields, topics)

the importance of recordings to initiate and advance the learning of the world's musical expressions. With the use of historic recordings of folk and traditional music in their rustic surrounds as well as contemporary productions of current performers who mix older and newer layers of music into newly fused forms, teachers can facilitate learning through the phases, offering students opportunities to grow more widely and deeply musical, as well as more culturally compassionate, over time.

Three listen-to-learn dimensions are core to the process of World Music Pedagogy: (1) *Attentive Listening*, directed and focused on musical elements and structures, and guided by specific points of attention; (2) *Engaged Listening*, participatory listening, or the active participation by a listener in some extent of music-making (by singing a melody, patting a rhythm, playing a percussion part, moving to a dance pattern); and (3) *Enactive Listening*, the performance of a work in which, through intensive listening to every musical nuance, the music is re-created in as stylistically accurate a way as possible. These listening dimensions may sit as separate entities within a class session, or they may be linked in a sequence in which attentive listening leads to participation (Engaged Listening) and performance (Enactive Listening). The recorded segments that are selected for these listening phases are typically brief, for example, just 30–45 seconds, so that concentrated attention can be given to learning the musical excerpt well and in all thoroughness. The listening experiences flow in a sequence and require many repetitions. In fact, it's likely that 10, 20, or many more opportunities are necessary for learners to listen with attention for the discovery of elemental features of a selection and style, with another 10 or 20 listenings leading to the contribution by listeners of one or more vocal or instrumental parts to the music, and with at least another 20 listenings necessary for enabling learners to perform the music close to the manner in which it sounds on the source recording. These three core dimensions may double back on each other, too, so that students may be directed by their teachers to return (back) to the first phase (Attentive Listening) so that they can check themselves as they are striving to match the musical style and substance of a recording in a performance of the music (Enactive Listening).

To these three listening phases come also two more essential dimensions: (4) *Creating World Music*, the invention by students of new music in the style of a musical model through composition, improvisation, songwriting, and even the act of extending a piece just "a bit" beyond what is represented of it on a recording and (5) *Integrating World Music*, the examination of music as it connects to culture and as it illuminates a prism-like grasp of integrated topics and interdisciplinary subjects as varied as history; geography; language and literature; the sciences; and the visual arts, dance, and drama. These dimensions may quite naturally seep in between and around the listening dimensions, rather than to be reserved chronologically for end-points in the process. Of course, creativity in the style of the musical model requires considerable familiarity with the music's structures, and listening leads to this familiarity. As students are enactive in recreating the music precisely as they hear it, such re-creative experience can also dovetail with occasions to try something new, to advance an interesting invention atop or aside from the way it sounds on the recording. Such creative work offers students an opportunity to honor the source music while also opening up to the making of a musical experience that recognizes their innovative selves.

A curiosity of music's functions, uses, and meanings often comes earlier on, too. While engaged in participatory musicking (Engaged Listening), for example, students may wonder aloud about the musicians they are listening to, what the purpose of the music may be, whether there are particular places and times for the music, why some instruments are featured and others are not, or what the words mean. These "student wonderings" are teaching moments that allow for the integration of ideas about music and culture that need not be left to "the end" of the process.

While listening inherently evolves and proceeds across the three phases, the dimensions are not lockstep but rather there to be used with a balance of logic, flexibility, and relevance to the teaching-learning situation. Altogether, these five WMP ways of knowing can feature in a teacher's facilitation for her students of music as sound, behavior, and values. The dimensions do not preclude the possibilities for co-teaching with culture-bearers, heritage musicians, or with teachers of other subject areas (especially language arts or the social sciences), but, as assembled, they do suggest that a thorough-going understanding of music cultures can happen through the course of these phases. World Music Pedagogy offers a practical course for honoring those whose music it is by listening and learning it well enough to participate in it, to enact it through performance, to fashion it in creative new ways (without losing site of the stylistic essentials), and to understand its meaning in culture.

A Pedagogical Road Map for Community-Conscious Musicians

Musicians who can, teach. Regardless of the instrument they play, the repertoires they know, and whether or not they are explicitly trained to teach, musicians almost always find themselves in a position to give back, to share, to model, and to articulate the techniques of their expressive musical art. Opportunities for musicians to teach run parallel to opportunities to perform, and few musicians live their lives removed from occasions to shape the musical skill sets of those who aspire to make music. Many musicians are drawn to teaching as a vocation, following the track to become state certified (or certified by governing bodies in their city, province, or nation) in the pedagogical methods that fit the contexts of students in elementary and secondary schools. Or they may enroll in specific pedagogy courses in piano, voice, the orchestral instruments, and jazz and thus become involved in honing particular skills that are well-aligned with specific teaching pieces for students of various levels of learning. Teaching artists, and community musicians, too, learn the arts of social interaction, of facilitation, of negotiation in weaving their musical art into the experiences of their students as well as in drawing the musical potential from individual students in developing a community-owned musical experience. Pedagogy is a discipline that entails a deep understanding of the subject matter, as well as knowledge of the learners, including their interests and needs, the teaching-learning context, and the circumstances in which the learning will be applied. For the music teacher (or teaching musician), knowing the music is critical, as is understanding the social skills, the cultural norms, and the prior musical experiences of their students and the families, neighborhoods, and communities to which they belong.

Since the rise of multiculturalism in many modern nation states, musicians have become aware of and somewhat attuned to a diversity of music practices. The term "world music" became common parlance in the 1980s, first in the recording industry and then among musicians and music listeners, in denoting musical styles and genres in cultures everywhere in the world, from remote rural communities to urban neighborhoods, of old-culture and "pure" origins or of a variety of multiculturally mixed fusion expressions. The familiar label encompasses "high-art" music and "low-art" forms, as well as vernacular genres of folk music and popular music, music for listening, and music for performance by highly skilled musicians as well as for full-group participation by music learners. Archived recordings and films, including those available through Smithsonian Folkways Recordings and the archive of the Association for Cultural Equity, document the music of the world's cultures, and older historic recordings of fading traditions have been preserved and brought technologically up to date through digitization processes and audio engineering techniques that sharpen the musical features (while reducing the static, the hisses, and the pops). The earlier, even "first", layers of a world music culture—be it from people in the Amazonian rainforest, at the Javanese court, or in a Slavic peasant village—are valued and revered, and professional musicians as well as casual listeners are intrigued with music that is frozen in time and conceivably uncontaminated with other cultural influences. For many, world music has meant historic folk and traditional expressions, with little attention to popular or hybrid expressions.

Yet the act of teaching world music need not be confined to old-world traditions, and contemporary musical expressions should not go unrecognized. Popular music is rampant in the world and in the recording industry that invites, packages, and sells the music. Teaching world music encompasses "world pop", "Afro-pop", "hip-hop", and the great variety of culture-specific popular expressions, and samplings of popular music can effectively counterbalance the high-art or long-standing traditional musics. For example, Tanzania's *musiki wa danzi* can be nicely counterbalanced with *bongo flava*, even as Bulgarian *chalga* or folk-pop music can be learned alongside traditional Bulgarian *gaida* music.

Certainly, musical fusion is real and requires attention. The substance of musical styles in many cultures today can be traced to the traveling of musicians, musical instruments, techniques, and repertoires so that new music is arising from these journeys that invite blended expressions. This calls attention to the phenomenon of changing musical contexts and of the importance of recognizing the musical ethnographies of individual musicians (both professional and amateur); musical families; and communities of musicians, listeners, consumers, and "users". Some musicians remain true to their "pure" musical culture while others are drawn to the possibilities of intermingling music with their first culture, experience or training with newer experiences, switching between musical styles, or forging a commingled musical expression. The harnessing of expertise of musicians and members in the community becomes crucial in connecting living, changing, and fused musical styles with the teaching and learning of music in schools, and music teachers and students need to be aware of the fluidity of musical processes and repertoire between classrooms and community settings. The integration of world music cultures in education can happen by way of honoring traditions while also allowing opportunities for musicians, music teachers, and students to work together to evolve authentic learning experiences with attention to the realities of our time and place—and the many musical influences that permeate our lives. Teaching and learning music of the Burmese, the Brazilians, or the Bulgarians may in the end be challenging not only because there are choices to make given the many subcultures within each national group but also because musicians of a culture may choose to abandon old traditions for new expressions—or at least combine old and new musical features in yet another form. The question of selection looms large, then, as one wonders which world music, musical genre, or musician is the best, most authentic, and representative choice to listen to, to teach, and to learn. With an understanding that music and musicians are in flux, and that the musical art is subject to change, teachers are challenged but also fortified in knowing that many musical works are open for listening, participation, performance, exploring in newly creative ways, and understanding for its cultural meanings. In fact, nearly any musical selection can stand for itself and can be featured for experience and study.

Within schools and communities, World Music Pedagogy arrives as a road map for looping together the threads of music, community, and diversity for effecting change in and through music. Through the convergence of theories and practices within ethnomusicology, music education, and performance studies, World Music Pedagogy is a method for developing musical and cultural understanding. From ethnomusicologists who study music in and as culture comes the music itself, which is present in their field recordings of art, traditional, tribal, and popular musical cultures of nearby neighborhoods as well as those of remote and far-flung locales across the globe. Ethnomusicologists not only offer the perspective that music is far more than its sonic features alone but also offer insights as to what the music means, how it functions, how it is learned, and the myriad ways in which music reflects the lives of people who make the music and own the music as a component of their cultural identity. Music educators, whether in the schools or on university faculties, bring a depth of understanding on techniques and sequences that are developmentally and contextually appropriate for students of various ages and in classes of an assortment of settings, aims, and functions. Because they are musically trained (although still chiefly in the performance and analysis of music that is overwhelmingly European or Euro-American in style), music educators are able to configure curriculum and instruction that is highly effective in honing the musical knowledge and skills of their students vocally and on instruments. Coming from the realm of performance studies, the expertise of singers and instrumentalists of many musical practices serves well the pedagogical aims of presenting strong musical models for students to follow, opening their ears to musical possibilities, and whetting their appetites to know more of the music and cultures from which it comes. Residencies or even fleeting "cameo" appearances of a violinist; accordionist; bagpiper; or player of jazz-style trumpet, *djembe*, or *koto* can make for powerful and long-lasting experiences. World Music Pedagogy, then, results from the combined insights and practical contributions of ethnomusicologists, educators, and performing musicians, and the "WMP (World Music Pedagogy) strategies" respond well to the changing demographics, societal forces, and multicultural mandates that are everywhere evident in the schools.

Beyond the theoretical understandings of music in and as culture, and the aim for global expansion of repertoire in vocal and instrumental music, the pedagogy of world music strives to involve but also to reach beyond queries of "what music?" to the question of "how shall teachers bring the music into the lives of students?" World Music Pedagogy concerns itself with the ways in which music is taught/transmitted and received/learned within cultures and how best the processes that are included in significant ways within these cultures can be preserved or at least partially retained in classrooms and rehearsal halls. Many of those working to evolve the WMP method have studied music with expert musicians and culture-bearers and have come to know that music is understood through experience with the cultural mode and manner in which it is taught and learned. Thus, selecting a song to sing from the Akan of Ghana is only the first step of a teacher's responsibility, while there are then the critical dimensions of ensuring a comprehensive experiencing in understanding the song as sound, behavior, and values. The WMP process suggests that the post-selection challenge for teachers is in figuring ways to present the song, to allow directed attention to the way the music sounds, to facilitate participation in singing (and moving) it, to advance students to opportunities to perform the song, and then to engage in creative expression by improvising upon it or composing something new within the style of the original song. Beyond these sonic-centric pedagogical elements, there is in World Music Pedagogy the critical element of integration by which the music is studied for its uses, functions, and meanings to the people from whom it has come. By integrating bits and pieces of the humanistic social sciences, for example, history, geography, literature, and language arts, music can be known for its cultural significance as much as a culture can be known through study of the music.

As authors of this book, we welcome the opportunity to share our experience as musicians and educators in schools and communities, working as we have with children, youth, and adult learners and with teachers of music and the arts. We each have been immersed in a diversity of musical cultures globally and within our local spaces and are keen to teach "all the world's music"; to work with community musicians, artists, and culture-bearers in schools and out in the community; and to foster music-making communities in our classrooms. We care deeply about the flow of music from schools to communities and from communities into schools. We briefly share thoughts here concerning our positionality so that our beliefs about music, education, and culture can be known up front and ahead of our journey into World Music Pedagogy.

Patricia Shehan Campbell: *My work in education and ethnomusicology tells me that we have dedicated more than a half century of efforts to bringing the world's musical cultures to our elementary and secondary school students. We moved only gradually from offering them "the exotic" in music cultures (from across the African continent, the Asian court cultures, the European peasant villages, the Pacific Islands, the little-known music of the Americas) to music of people anywhere, on any day, for any reason. Since the turn into the 21st century, greater attention has been given to the music of the families of the students whom we teach and of the local neighborhood musicians who gather to groove and to celebrate, to strum, pick, fiddle, blow, tap, shake, and drum. Now an interest is surfacing in music education practice on how to balance global and local musical strands in our curricular work, how to cover the bases of so many musical expressions, how to invite and entice students to become more broadly musical and to develop friendship, trust, and true community through the music they experience. The challenges are there for music educators, teaching musicians, community music activists, ethnomusicologists, and various others within the realm of music, the arts, and education, and our efforts are shaped by the contexts in which we teach and by the education and training we bring to the classrooms. I wonder:*

- *Can music professionals work together to provide students with genuine experience and study in music that is alive and well in the world, including right under our very noses, in the community?*

- *How can music teachers, community musicians, and culture-bearers embrace the natural flow of music from communities to schools, and back again, so that students can be (quite naturally) fully immersed in the riches of people making music because they must?!*
- *Will students be not only educated in music but empowered by music to "find their voice" and make a difference in the community and in the world in music and through music?*

We need to recognize the coming together of visions in what was once-separate identities as performing artists (only), music teachers (only), and music scholars (only). We observe that music educators are becoming more culturally conscious, that community musicians and culture-bearers are often keen to connect with young listeners and learners in schools to share their artistic and cultural practices, and that many ethnomusicologists have gone from research-only academic scholarship to thoughtfully crafted applied ethnomusicology that reaches to communities, schools, museums, the media, and beyond. We can explore how World Music Pedagogy, shaped for school music education programs of every sort, can call out to the community for musicians, music devotees, and culture-bearers (some with more stories than songs to bear but who do well to contextualize the music of their heritage through their reminiscences) for their contributions to the education of students in music. We can look to fieldwork recordings, commercial recordings, and all the media as windows to worlds beyond our immediate reach, allowing students to "travel" via music into communities from distant times and places. Importantly, we can bring students into the musical circle that envelops us, if only we will listen and facilitate these possibilities.

Chee-Hoo Lum: *As a music educator and researcher who is always keen to challenge and advocate for a diverse range of musics to be included into the formal space of the school curriculum, I was struck by a few glaring observations as I conversed with musicians and thought about the current state of music repertoire inclusions in the general music classroom. Within school music textbooks and many school music programs, world music genres are often portrayed as distinct and insular, i.e., having specific instruments and "basic/fundamental" characteristics of melodic and rhythmic structures. Music teachers introducing these musics in the general music classroom often tap on these "basic/fundamentals" in superficial ways, getting students to listen and experience the music often devoid of the musicians who embody the music in its current contexts and manifestations. In my observations, even when particular musicians are invited to perform and workshop with students, music teachers or school authorities often dictate what they want the musicians to play and do, which oftentimes mean a stereotypical showcase of "representative" repertoire (for example, Jasmine Flower [Mo Li Hua] for Chinese music; or perhaps Arirang or Doraji for Korean music) and getting musicians to talk to students about the "ethnic" instruments they play. Rarely do school music programs steer toward an interest or even a cursory glance at the musicians, their original repertoire, what and where they play as musicians in the local scene, or their creative processes. It is as if the musicians* *only exist in a music box, waiting to be wound up to play this representative repertoire over and over again. I wonder:*

- *Will we ever talk to students about musical fusion and the real work that these world musicians do in their professional lives?*
- *When will we get past the "basics and fundamentals" when we decide to introduce new musical genres of the world to students? Or do they often remain "exotic" and trapped in some representative bubble?*
- *Do we and should we as music educators get into the social/cultural/ historical/economic/ political dialogues and discussions with students that surround world music genres and musical fusion?*

In our work as music educators, we need to caution against a "silo" mentality. We need to bring in the ambiguous, the fusion that is happening in the current contexts of musicians. We need to provide lived and living examples of music and the musicians that engage deeply with what they do, perhaps even bringing students into the musicians' living, rehearsal, and performing spaces to further their musical and contextual understanding. Music educators should also work collaboratively (not unilaterally) with musicians to come up with helpful guides and facilitative possibilities that would encourage active listening and music making with students in the classroom. This will then truly begin a process of bridging the great divide between the fictional world of world music that exists only within the four walls of the music classroom and the lived realities of practicing musicians. The key is to keep an open mind and engage enthusiastically with the wonderful world of musics that surrounds us, allowing students to enter and interweave into the fold of our daily and professional musical encounters.

Advancing the Mission

The chapters ahead give rise to ways in which key issues of our time—music, community, diversity, equity, and inclusion—can be brought into clear definition in schools and their surrounds. The roles of musicians who teach, with particular attention to certified school music educators, are played out in illustrations, scenarios, and pedagogical bytes by way of "episodes" that are meant to show sequential teaching-learning interactions along the path to learning music. Listening will be foregrounded in the pedagogical discussion, as WMP begins with and continues through listening as the central avenue for knowing a specific musical selection, a wide-angled style, a neighborhood's musical identity, or more broadly the essence of a world's musical culture. So, too, will participation, performance, and creative encounters in improvisation and composition figure significantly in descriptions and illustrations, where listening is key to learning, providing the model in all of its cultural nuances to attend to, engage in, and "enact", that is, to make the music with and without the recording by using the ear as a guide to the music's meta-structures and nuances.

With full attention to the volume's theme of "music and community", the chapters will give prominence to a host of education-relevant people, places, settings, and circumstances: Community artists and their short- and long-term interactivities with teachers and students in schools; teachers and their students who engage in on-site learning via field trips to the locales of community musicians; students whose self-motivation, or encouragement from teachers, can involve them in virtual community engagements in online learning (and performing); music teachers and teaching musicians whose interest is their own personal musical growth by way of studies with community artist-teachers of instruments and musical styles; and teachers whose involvement in outside-school music-making situations land them in a community's amateur and professional ensembles and in recreational and social music settings. The approach taken in this volume is to crisscross from global to local cultures for music that is worthy of a single experience, a full lesson, a unit of lessons, or a public performance. As well, the chapters take the journey from communities to schools, thus pointing to the fluidity between the two contexts as well as to the movement by teachers and their students to and fro in coming to understand music in community—in all of its diversity, and music as community—where individual musicians from entry-level students to professionals can experience music in the group, as a collaborative, and in a genuinely communal process with musical as well as social and cultural outcomes.

The task, then, is in recognizing the in-flow and out-go of artist-musicians, culture-bearing community musicians, and music educators and teaching musicians, all of whom can contribute to the musical learning of students in schools and community settings. The pedagogical points are meant to draw attention to resonances between people in growing an understanding of local and global musical identities and cultural heritage in all of its musical diversity. We believe that the way to a "compleat", comprehensive, contemporary, and highly effective musical education for learners of every age is through a collective effort of musicians who are keen on "passing it on", giving back, and stitching together the necessary learning pathways for their students.

References

Ansdell, G. (2004). Rethinking music and community: Theoretical perspectives in support of community music therapy. In M. Pavlicevic & G. Ansdell (Eds.), *Community music therapy* (pp. 65–90). London: Jessica Kingsley Publishers.

Campbell, P. S. (2018). *Music, education, and diversity: Bridging cultures and communities*. New York: Teachers College Press.

Dolby, N. (2012). *Rethinking multicultural education for the next generation: A new empathy and social justice*. New York: Routledge.

Gilroy, P. (2005). *Postcolonial Melancholia*. New York: Columbia University Press.

Grant, C. A., & Sleeter, E. (2011). *Doing multicultural education for achievement and equity* (2nd ed.). New York: Routledge.

Harris, A. (2013). *Young people and everyday multiculturalism*. New York: Routledge.

Higgins, L. (2012). *Community music in theory and in practice*. New York: Oxford University Press.

Higgins, L., & Bartleet, B. (2018). *Oxford handbook of community music*. New York: Oxford University Press.

Jorgensen, E. R. (1995). Music education as community. *Journal of Aesthetic Education, 29*(3), 71–84.

Pettan, S., & Titon, J. T. (Eds.). (2015). *The Oxford handbook of applied ethnomusicology*. New York: Oxford University Press.

Prensky, M. (2001). Digital natives, digital immigrants. *On the Horizon, 9*(5), 1–6.

Robinson, K. (2001). *Out of Our Minds: Learning to be Creative*. Chichester: Capstone Publishing Limited.

Sarath, E. W., Myers, D. E., & Campbell, P. S. (2017). *Redefining music studies in an age of change: Creativity, diversity and integration*. New York: Routledge.

Sennett, R. (2012). *Together: The rituals, pleasures and politics of cooperation*. New Haven: Yale University Press.

Stige, B. (2004). Community music therapy: Culture, care and welfare. In M. Pavlicevic, & G. Ansdell (Eds.), *Community music therapy* (pp. 91–113). London: Jessica Kingsley Publishers.

Wade, B. C. (2004). *Thinking musically*. New York: Oxford University Press.

2

Attentive Listening for Cultural Awakenings

February 2, John Adams Middle School. All 32 eighth grade students were settled in their assigned seats when the guest musician arrived to their mandatory first period music class. This was that early morning class that some students regularly arrived to with sleepy eyes, all set to slump into their seats and tune out of the teacher's expected focus, especially when there was too much talk and too little music. But this morning there was this slim and sinewy fellow standing up at the front next to Ms. Johnson, their music teacher, and he was dressed in a bright green and black paisley short-sleeved tunic and pants, his thick dreadlocks framing his wide and handsome face. "Luis" had just arrived in the room at the sound of the school bell, made his way to the front of the room, turned to the class, and without introduction began quietly tapping his cuica *(drum). He asked the students to "listen up". They did, several of them straightening their bodies into an alert and receptive position. Luis then stopped and invited students to talk about what they heard. "Sounds like squeaks", offered one boy, and another boy added "Yeah, squeaks from a monkey in some tropical forest somewhere". A girl suggested that "it's African music" then turned and, in a stage whisper, explained to her friend that "it's got to be, look at him, and listen" (possibly putting together the sound of the syncopated rhythms with the musician's dark skin and "African" print). The Afro-Brazilian guest introduced the instrument, asking students to "say kuwee-kah", and they joined in after him. As he adeptly hooked up his iPod to the music room's sound system, Luis challenged them: "I want you to listen to these tracks and tell me what you can about the music of this* cuica *drum". There were six short excerpts featuring the* cuica, *each running about 20–30 seconds in length. Luis stopped and started the music and preceded each track with a question ("Can you hear the* cuica? *" "Is it playing rhythm or melody, or both?" "Are the sounds high or low?" "What other instruments are playing with the* cuica?"). *Luis followed each musical excerpt with a brief discussion that highlighted the correct answer. The students were more attentive than was usual in the early morning class, and this Afro-Brazilian musician was making his way into their hearts (and ears). The repeated listening bytes were followed by the guest musician's playing of his own* cuica, *to which he invited students to keep the beat on their desks and chairs and to try tapping out some of the rhythms in imitation of his* cuica.

February 12, Centro de cultura em brazileiro. The students of John Adams Middle School were invited to a musical event at the local Brazilian Cultural Center. The event was scheduled for Thursday; immediately after school, a school bus was made available to transport those interested students and Ms. Johnson to the Center for a 90-minute experience in live music as performed by several Brazilian groups: A guitar and drum duo; a samba band of tamborims, *snare drums,* pandeiros, surdos, *cowbells and shakers; and a popular music group featuring guitars, keyboard, and percussion. More than a dozen from the first period music class were on board, and several of their friends, too, along with the music teacher. The host of the session was none other than their Afro-Brazilian guest musician, Luis, who introduced the groups, played* cuica, *and led the* samba *band. He opened with a directive to all to "listen up". Rather than to silence the audience of school students and community members, however, he invited them to "feel the rhythm". As the bands played, a sea of heads nodded, some were clapping and tapping in motion, and bodies swayed from the hips to the shoulders to the recurring groove. The groups played on, and the host provided interludes between the music that encouraged careful listening: "Watch what the guitars are doing—chords, or melody, or bassline?", "The* cuica *is working off the keyboard: Can you hear how?", "If you're getting the beat, find new ways to show it". With a broad smile, Luis welcomed the John Adams Middle School students from the mic and then followed them out to their bus at the close of the event to thank them for their participation.*

March 25, Starbridge Center: A Juvenile Safe Space. Luis made further visits to Ms. Johnson's first period music class. The students listened repeatedly to the same six cuica *recordings (in the music of Jorge Ben, Trio Mocoto, Os Mutantes, and Seu Jorge) and then listened for the drum in Paul Simon's "Me and Julio Down by the Schoolyard" and "Locked Out of Heaven" by Bruno Mars. Luis continued to direct their attention to rhythms they could decipher, and Ms. Johnson followed up on his admonitions to "listen up", to keep the beat, to find the rhythms. Students were encouraged to focus on the rhythms that they would eventually learn to play. Over five more weeks, Luis offered using further experiences with the* cuica *and adjoining instruments of a* samba *percussion ensemble. Still, they listened to recordings of Jorge Ben and Raul Seixas, while they also played parts on classroom drums, cowbells, shakers, and a hand-made* cuica *that Luis had loaned them. With Ms. Johnson's help, students of the first period music class began to sound like the samba band selection that Luis had offered as model for a first performance piece. The finale came with an invitation by Luis to perform at a "juvenile safe space", Starbridge Center, in the neighborhood one Thursday evening in late March, to which families and friends were invited. There the first period music students played and paraded at the outer edge of the audience area of chairs, their bodies moving in time. Luis was visibly pleased with the feel that was coming out of the eighth grade students and delighted to receive the comment from one of his band members: "They sound like a Rio band".*

The Art of Listening: A Pedagogical Priority

The act of listening is an art. As a powerful sensory experience, the art of listening is developed through training and experience. In schools, when teaching musicians (including certified music educators and community musicians) perform music *live*, the vibrant sound travels the very short distance from their voices or instruments to the ears of their students. Such live music by experienced musicians can excite and enhance learning. Collective listening to recordings by students can be strong and stimulating sensory experiences, too, and the thrill of such listening increases when the sound equipment is of sufficient quality to allow a full musical sound in which even the nuances of melody, rhythm, and timbre are in plain reach of listening ears. Listening is a pedagogical priority for those who teach music, and both audio and video recordings do well to convey music as performed by masters of their musical cultures. For many music teachers, teaching musicians, and culture-bearing community musicians, encounters with music through live and recorded performances are key to learning music.

We acknowledge in this volume the critical attention that accomplished musicians give to the art of listening and maintain that music is learned by ear rather than by eye in most of the world's musical cultures (Campbell, 1991; McLucas, 2010). Notation is a useful tool, but it is never vital for knowing music because the listening ear is the core means of learning to sing melodies and rhythms and to play them on instruments. While musicians of some practices—for example, Western European Art Music—understand that music can be read and written via notation, musicians of other practices—for example, Hindustani classical music of North India; Maori *waiata*; Mexican *son jarocho*; Javanese *gamelan*; Shoshone social songs; and popular forms such as hip-hop, *reggaeton*, and *bongo flava*—have learned their music through a careful honing of their listening ears. Most musicians in the world have no need for notation in learning melodies, rhythms, intersections of instruments, and voices in particular organized forms, as they "get the tunes" (or grooves) by ear. Across a wide array of genres and styles, every pitch and duration, and all their approaches, attacks and decays, their elaborations and embellishments, are learned by listening.

The term "oral tradition" has been applied by scholars to musical forms that are learned by listening. Folklorists have a long history of documenting folk tunes from people in such regions as the American Appalachian Mountains, the Scottish Highlands, the Iberian Peninsula, the Canadian Maritime Provinces, and the Balkans of southeastern Europe. There's a considerably wider span of oral tradition cultures, too, as the fact is that most of the world's people learn music by listening, such that most art, folk and traditional, and popular forms of music are transmitted and acquired by ear, *sans notation*. Oral transmission and aural reception, referred also as orality and aurality, are the two components of the oral/aural process that are common practices in knowing music. Where written notation is available, still the learning of music may be a free mix of notation with oral/aural techniques. Everywhere, listening is critical to learning music.

Children learn music quite naturally by ear. Even as they learn language by listening to it in their infancy, as they also did prenatally, so do they learn songs and rhythms through an immersion in the sounds that surround them. They require no notation to learn rhythms and rhymes, songs and singing games, symphonic themes, and musical phrases that emerge from their being in the world. Likewise, adolescents continue to store in their mind's ear their personal storehouses of "audio tunes", including popular music, songs of holiday seasons, and every other music that they've grown into over the course of their 12, 15, or 18 years of life. By listening, they have acquired the music, which is clearly evident when they sing it and play it on preferred or available instruments. At home, in various social settings, and through the music that they channel through their earbuds and headphones, children learn by ear their musical repertoire (Bickford, 2017).

Notational literacy becomes important in school music curricular programs. If not in preschool, then certainly by kindergarten and first grade, children are learning to read standard Western staff notation. Beginning with vocalization exercises in imitating pulses and their subdivisions via syllables such as "ta" and "ti-ti", children learn to match what they hear to what is written. Melodic notation follows, frequently beginning in the primary grades with a modified staff of just two lines for learning (in C-Major) "so" and "mi", and the full diatonic scale pitches are laid out over the course of several years of children singing and eventually playing on recorders, xylophones, and keyboards the pitches they see on the staff. The point, of course, is to enable young students to read Western staff notation to assist them in learning choral and instrumental music that features in school bands, choirs, and orchestras. As learners hone their performance techniques vocally and on strings, wind, brass, and percussion instruments, they become capable readers of Western standard staff notation.

Somewhere in the course of their musical education, then, children's capacity to learn by ear may be subordinated or abandoned, and certainly not prioritized. The emphasis on notational literacy in Western-styled music education sends a clear message to students as to the importance of the eye over the ear in learning music, and teachers often press their students to pay attention to the notation so as to learn by eye the various works that will comprise their studied repertoire. There is still plenty of music outside the school that students may "get" by listening, but the oral tradition and oral/aural techniques are not so widely exercised in school music programs. The art of listening may be lost or at least is not developed further in most curricular programs in music.

What of oral tradition music in school settings? With the advent of multicultural music education and the increased presence of musical examples from the world's cultures in elementary and secondary schools, music from orally based cultures would seem quite naturally to be the repertoire in which to foster a process of learning music by ear. This does not typically happen, however, as the prominent school music goal of literacy frequently influences teachers to seek out the notation that publishers provide. Thus, oral tradition music such as Irish airs, jigs, and reels; Akan, Ewe, and Ga percussion music from Ghana; Hawaiian hula chants; Cantonese folk songs from China; and African American singing games are frequently converted to notation in service of the curricular goal of notational literacy. The intent of the notation is explained as a means of cutting the time it could take to learn the music so that listening is downplayed or ignored in the learning process. Is it any wonder why university music majors who play and sing well struggle with musicianship classes that feature aural skills when their school music programs were keyed to eye training over ear training? Perhaps more importantly, the cultural valuing of learning by ear that is evident in oral tradition music is disregarded when music is transcribed to notation. In a very real sense, a critical cultural component is negated when the oral transmission system is abandoned, when tribute is paid to the eye rather than the ear and to writing and reading music rather than to learning by listening.

Core to the process of World Music Pedagogy is the art of listening. The aural/ oral art of music is celebrated through the application of multiple listenings that reach progressively deeper into the music and that lead learners from an initial stage of deciphering musical features, through partial participation in the act of recreating the music, and on to a fully informed performance with all the musical nuances that no system of music notation could ever represent. The ear catches what notation simply cannot represent; with every opportunity to listen and every invitation to sing or play the music, the connection between listening and musical expression becomes evident. In particular, the initial three WMP dimensions rely on repeated listening encounters so that learners can experience the musical features by ear (Attentive Listening) as they graduate to participatory musicking (Engaged Listening) and then full-out performance of the music precisely as it sounds (Enactive Listening). In the ever-important experience of creative composition and improvisation, all of the prior (and continuing) opportunities to listen provide students with a vocabulary of sonorous possibilities for their spontaneous or deliberately fashioned expressions. These new creations are thus musically informed by the logic and beauty of works they've experienced by ear and by the musical features that they have derived from listening.

The World Music Pedagogy process acknowledges not only the importance of teaching more of the world's musical cultures from earliest childhood through elementary and secondary school music education, and in university-level studies as well, but also the cultural behaviors associated with the music. Once again, listening to initially unfamiliar, "strange", and "new" (to them) instruments and vocal styles results in curiosity by students to understand why the music sounds the way it does by people in a particular place. Here then comes the integration of ideas that fills out the stories behind the music and that fosters cultural understanding that was first initiated through the musical sound. From a pedagogical standpoint, WMP plays to a set of dimensions that help music educators and community musicians to bring the music to students through the oral tradition, into the ear, "the bloodstream", the brain and the body. Understanding music of the world's cultures begins with listening, as the art of listening is front and center in a process that is applicable to any and all musical cultures, genres, and pieces.

A Journey Into Attentive Listening

Listening to music transfers to listening at large. In every aspect of life, careful listening is important to communication. The result of listening to others is an understanding of people and their predicaments, perspectives, and purposes. While hearing is a human trait and a physical ability, the act of listening is an artistic endeavor all its own. Listening with close attention, especially to details beyond the sensory surface, allows a person to understand others and to grasp what is meant by not only what they say but how they say it. Listening has the potential to bring about a cultural awakening in students, with their ears leading them to all sorts of questions about the people, place, and time in which this music is situated. In a world replete with visual stimulation, listening (especially when without images) can be challenging, yet the rewards are very real.

As the first of the five dimensions of World Music Pedagogy, Attentive Listening is the gateway into the musical experience. Without notational symbols or visual icons of any sort, listeners still acquire sound, speech, and music. When the music plays, listeners turn their ears to matters of timbre (tone quality), melody, and rhythm and to the manner in which musical elements are organized. With the guidance of music teachers and community musicians, the listening student presses more deeply into the musical elements and structures that comprise the music—no matter what the musical style or genre.

The listener achieves Attentive Listening by following the teacher's questions, challenges, and cues to listen to an instrument or voice, the relationships between instruments (and/or voices); the pulse, metric pattern, or rhythmic cell; the melody's pitch, contour, range and register; and the music's expressive qualities. The listening student is drawn into various facets and features of the music through multiple directed listening experiences. Repeated listening opportunities are vital to the discovery of musical elements and structures and to developing familiarity with the music so as to enable the listener to anticipate and expect certain sonic features. When suggestions flow from both music educators and community musicians, their collaborative teaching fortifies while also reiterating selected facets and extends and elaborates key features.

For a single selection of moderately complex and unfamiliar music, for example, the Bulgarian song "Lenorije Chaje" (Episode 2.6), it may be necessary to facilitate student listening a dozen times or more, over several lessons, sessions, or days, to enable listeners the opportunities to sort through instrumentation, melodic, rhythmic, and formal elements and to begin to create a kind a memory for the piece. The listening selection is often only a short excerpt of a minute or less, from a longer work, yet it will be long enough to make musical sense. It is through teacher-directed listening, supported by questions to focus the Attentive Listening, that student listeners develop the knowledge and confidence to enable them to move forward to the dimensions of Engaged and Enactive Listening and to the further dimensions of Creating World Music and Integrating World Music.

There follows a set of six episodes that offers sequential steps for initial encounters that first-time listeners of any age or experience can follow in growing to know culturally unfamiliar music. These episodes are exemplar of Attentive Listening, all of which are united by the intent to open ears and minds to musical sounds; their origins; the musicians whose music it is; and their languages, cultural priorities, and values. These Attentive Listening episodes serve the purpose of cultural awakenings, allowing curious listeners to imagine and then to discover why musical expressions sound the way they do by musicians living locally or globally. The first three episodes (2.1, 2.2, and 2.3) bear noticing here, too, as these musical selections will re-appear in all dimensions of World Music Pedagogy, here in this chapter as well as in Chapters 3, 5, and 6, and in this way can be seen as evolving through the comprehensive WMP process. These three selections will also appear in Appendix I as full-fledged learning pathways so that they can be viewed in their entirety across all five dimensions. The last three episodes (2.4, 2.5, and 2.6) offer three further Attentive Listening experiences, featuring three more musical selections; these musical selections do not appear again, but there is every reason to expect that they can be carried through the five WMP dimensions by thoughtful music educators and community musicians.

Romance in East L.A.

A series of pedagogical steps anchored in the act of Attentive Listening is displayed in a ballad called "Todo lo que Tengo" (All That I Want). The Spanish-language song is performed by Quetzal, a band of Mexican-heritage (Chicano) musicians from East

Los Angeles (or "East L.A.", as it is widely known). This neighborhood is known for its Latinx population which, at 97%, is the highest density of Latin Americans in a greatly Latinized American city. While unincorporated, East L.A. has its own cultural character; its Independence Day Parade and Festival, Farmers Market, Latino Walk of Fame; and schools, playgrounds, and parks. Episode 2.1 opens students to their first encounters with this Chicano-inspired ballad.

The band's name is traced not to the colorful bird, "quetzal", but to the name of the band's founder, Quetzal Flores. They are committed to music for social change and have been inspired by global grassroots movements in the topics they address in

---

Episode 2.1: Romance in East L.A.
"Todo lo que Tengo"
(Learning Pathway #1)

Specific Use: Elementary Music Education, Secondary Music Innovations, Instrumental Ensembles

Materials:

- "Todo lo que Tengo", from the album *Imaginaries,* by Quetzal

Procedure:

1. "What instruments do you hear and in what order?"
2. Play track to 1'53".
3. Discuss answers (guitar, *pandeiro*, violin, voice).
4. Play track up to 1'53" to check answers.
5. "Can you pretend play one of the instruments?"
6. Play track to 1'53".
7. Respond to the pretend-play gestures, noting, for example, that they were rhythmic, in-sync with the sound, continuous.
8. "This is a love song. Raise your hand when you hear 'todo lo que quiero' (all that I want) and 'todo lo que tengo' (everything I have)."
9. Play track to 1'53".
10. "Given what you hear, where in the world might the musicians be living?" (Given the Spanish language and the instrumentation, Mexico or a Mexican American community)
11. Invite a musician of Mexican-heritage music to visit, to listen with the students, to exchange with students on the meaning of this music, to play or sing with the recording, or to offer a live rendition of the song.

their songs. The group consists of six musicians, including Martha Gonzalez, a dynamic singer and composer and a published scholar on music, feminism, and Chicana identity. Quetzal's music mixes Mexican and Afro-Cuban sensibilities alongside rhythm and blues and rock styles. Some of the music bears traces of *son jarocho*, the community music and dance form of Veracruz, Mexico, that blends together indigenous, African, and Spanish flavors for purposes of social activism and the ultimate struggle for human dignity (and artistic and communal expression). Quetzal's album, *Imaginaries*, won the Grammy for Latin rock, urban, or alternative music, and the sounds of guitar and bass guitar blend with *jarana, requinto, bajo sexto*, violin, keyboard, vocals, and various percussion instruments such as *cajon, conga, shekere*, and the tapping sound of hard-soled dancing shoes on a raised platform known as *tarima*.

In the way of Attentive Listening, the pedagogical approach is to provide opportunities for collective listening to all or part of the selection (in this case, 1'53", or one minute and 53 seconds). In a classroom setting, it may take many listening experiences to develop a familiarity with the selection. In Episode 2.1, there are just four opportunities to listen while in reality the teacher may want to provide ten and many more opportunities at a single sitting or across several classes or group sessions. The questions are meant for teachers to ask and they can be used in focusing the attention of listeners; each question can be provided just prior to an actual listening experience so that listeners can "discover" the answer. Note that there is no invitation or expectation to participate in or perform the music, although it would not be surprising if listeners begin to nod their head, tap their fingers, or even hum along; participatory listening comes later. This episode runs about 12 minutes in all but can easily be extended or reduced and saved for a later time.

Kecuh! Riuh! Gemuruh!

"Kecuh! Riuh! Gemuruh!" (Ruckus! Chaos! Thunderous!) is the spirited Malay percussion piece featured in Episode 2.2, music that is at once virtuosic and technical yet also enticing to students at early stages of skill development. This is an emblematic piece for the 50-member strong NADI Singapura, a Malay percussion group from the Southeast Asian nation of Singapore. NADI refers to "pulse" or "flow of consciousness". Singapore's multicultural population of Chinese, Malay, Indian, and other cultural groups has resulted in a goldmine of musically diverse expressions, both intact and unique unto their own particular traditions as well as in fused practices that mix instruments and musical features. In the Malay-inspired music, there are hand drums known as *kompang*, which are frequently played at wedding celebrations and are known for the intricate interlocking rhythms they perform with one another; there is also a tambourine known as *rebana* and double-headed drums made of cowhides or buffalo hides known as *gendang*. Riduan Zalani, the creative director of NADI, seeks to understand and use the capability of percussion instruments in performative ways through the creation of contemporary repertoire to promote the traditional playing of Malay drums. He and his group have fashioned vibrant and dynamic music that draws audiences to grand concert halls and more intimate performance spaces to experience traditional music in transformation in the hands of innovative and expressive artists.

This half-minute experience in Attentive Listening serves to deepen aural awareness to differences in timbre, allowing opportunities for listeners to pay close attention to how instruments can sound differently depending on where, how, and with what

Episode 2.2: "Kecuh! Riuh! Gemuruh!"
(Learning Pathway #2)

Specific Use: Early Childhood, Elementary Music Education, Secondary Music Innovations, Instrumental Ensembles

Materials:

- Track 4, from the album, *Kata Kita Kota* by NADI Singapura

Procedure:

1. "What instrument do you hear at the beginning, and how do you think the instrument is being played?"
2. Play track up to 0'30".
3. Discuss answers. (*Gong.* Note that instead of a hanging *gong* that is played by striking with a mallet, this piece features a *gong* that is laid on the ground and played with two wooden rulers on the ground.)
4. "Can you find out more about the origins of this instrument (*gong*) and how it is normally being played?"
5. Discuss answers. Provide students with information about *gongs*—their composite material (bronze, metals), places of origin and use (especially in Southeast Asia), various sizes and shapes (flat or knobbed, thin or thick), types of beaters (wood, metal, wrapped with cloth, yarn or twine).
6. "Can you hear a constant pulsation throughout the track? Can you pretend play this pulsation on your lap or any other part of your body?"
7. Play track up to 0'30", modeling the pulse keeping, observing the steady rhythm.
8. "How does the pulsation make you feel?"
9. Discuss answers. Consider responses of mood made by the music and make note of those students who find it easy or difficult to keep up with the pulsation.
10. "Given what you hear, are you able to identify where in the world the music might have come from?"
11. Discuss answers, which may include continents (such as Africa, Asia) and countries (such as the Philippines, Japan), and draw out their reasons for these responses. (Note that Singapore, in Southeast Asia's "*gong* region", is the origin place of this music.)
12. Host a community musician who plays percussion in the local symphony orchestra or Chinese orchestra, and request a session on orchestral *gongs*, or host a community musician or culture-bearer aligned with a local temple of Buddhist or Taoist practice, for which East Asian or Southeast Asian *gongs* may be available for show and tell, focusing on their variety, their timbral qualities, and their cultural significance.

the instruments are sounded. It serves to develop a beginning recognition of how current musicians are creatively using their instruments and reshaping their musical genres to work out new contemporary repertoire. Episode 2.2, as is, can run about four minutes. It can also span an entire class period in exploring with students the intricacies of timbral possibilities in percussion instruments, or it can quite naturally find its way into a succession of classes to allow students to thoroughly experience the varied timbres and how they complement one another in this selection. The questions from teachers precede the listening experiences, which lead to student responses, and the three listening experiences are exemplar of further listenings that can be offered to familiarize students with the work. Learners can also be drawn into a cultural awakening as they sort through the phenomenon of "traveling" instruments that find their way into music from their origin place to other places on the globe.

Sub-Saharan Collective Song

The power of song comes shining through in the experiences in Attentive Listening that are outlined in Episode 2.3. "Nange" is a song of the Wagogo (or Gogo) people of Central Tanzania; it is also known as "Yange". The translation is "my plate, it is my plate, and it is shining", but the deeper meaning of this older male initiation song, which is now a widely shared song sung by all Wagogo, is that life is good, happiness is here, and there is hope for the Wagogo people—especially once the initiation has healed them and brought them to maturity. (Another interpretation is that when a man sings the song, he is publicly and proudly declaring the beauty of his wife.) The song's pentatonic melody and duple meter form the basis of a song that is known by the Wagogo people in their villages of farmers and herders. It is sung by men, women, and children and features a proclamation of *mukumbi* (the initiation ritual) by a solo voice, followed by a group's choral response.

In many Wagogo villages, musicians hold political power, as do hunters, medicine men, collectors of honey, and weapon makers. Musicians sing; play instruments; and dance at weddings, funerals, initiation ceremonies, and harvest celebrations. The Wagogo welcome newborns into society with music, send men off to hunting expeditions with music, and honor cattle raisers with music. They use music to express social positions on domestic abuse, drugs and alcohol, and education. Theirs is a choral music that is danced with the group in full alignment with one another. Songs are sung a capella or can be accompanied by metal-pronged thumb pianos known as *ilimba*, double-headed *muheme* drums, a two-stringed fiddle known as *sese*, and a rattle made of flattened metal cans filled with pebbles, called *kayamba*. They sing in unison at times and polyphonically at other times, and parallel singing is common, in which two vocal parts sound simultaneous melodies a fourth apart.

In Episode 2.3, Attentive Listening to "Nange" features just 29 seconds from a longer selection. There are four questions posed by the teacher to students, each one meant to be immediately followed by an opportunity to listen in order for students to seek a response. The questions are straightforward, directing attention to instrumentation (voices only), words or syllables, and differentiation between solo and choral voices, with an invitation to "rock gently" to the pulse. As is, the 12 pedagogical steps may time out to 5–6 minutes in total in a classroom setting, but these steps can be repeated and extended, and the episode itself may appear in multiple lessons and sessions. The recording can be played past the initial 29 seconds, too, at which point students can hear the brilliant polyphonic imitation of Wagogo choral music.

Episode 2.3: Sub-Saharan Collective Song "Nange" ["Yange"] (Learning Pathway #3)

Specific Use: Early Childhood, Elementary Music Education, Choral Ensembles

Materials:

- Track 18, "Nange" [or "Yange"] from the album, *Tanzania—Tanzanie: Chants*

Procedure:

1. "What instruments do you hear and in what order?"
2. Play track to 0'29".
3. Discuss answers. (Voices, solo and group, children, some women; also claps)
4. Play track to 0'29" to check answers.
5. "Can you hear any of the sung words or syllables?"
6. Play track to 0'29".
7. Respond, fielding out "Yange", "Yange Yange" (sounding "yahn-gah yahn-GAY"), "Hedukila" (sounding "heh-DOO-kee-lah"), "Tanzania" (sounding "Tahn-zan-nee-YAH").

    [Note: At times, "nange" may sound as "yange".]

8. "Can you follow the solo and group voices? Raise your right hand when you hear the solo voice, your left hand when you hear the group voices, and both hands when you hear the solo and group voices together. Feel welcome to rock gently to the pulse you hear".
9. Play track to 0'29".
10. Discuss the song's independent vocal parts, call-and-response features, the imitation of short lines in quick succession, and the threading of solo and group singing in between and around each other.
11. "Given what you hear, where in the world might the musicians be living?"
12. Discuss answers, which may include Africa (due to the full and open tone quality, the imitative voices, the claps).
13. Make time and space in the program for a visit from community musicians or culture-bearers who are Wagogo or from Tanzania, East Africa (Kenya, Uganda, Rwanda), or sub-Saharan Africa. Ask that they share their vocal music, particularly a selection that may feature several parts that together create harmony, and request that the visitors tell a little of the presence of music in their "African childhood and youth".

High Flute in the Andean Highlands

The soaring sound of a cane flute is featured in Episode 2.4, whose melody is referred to as "La Pastora" (The Shepherdess). The band of musicians call themselves Jatari, which translates from their indigenous language of Quechua as "stand up" or "rise up", signifying that the performers do more than just play the folk songs of their native Ecuador and neighboring Andean countries. They collect and compose songs and use music to express social injustices of the urban poor and peasants of rural villages. Their songs include testimonies to workers, tributes to the landless, and a dance to freedom, and they articulate the class inequities that continue to exist in Ecuador and across the Andean region despite reforms promised by industrialization.

"La Pastora" reflects Ecuador's mainstream culture of a Hispanic mestizo population of Spanish heritage mixed with indigenous Indians. The combination of flutes and pipes (often multiple pipes collected together, or panpipes called *sikú* or *zampoña*) with plucked guitar-like instruments comprise folk and folkloric groups, especially in the mountainous areas. The most well-known lute is the *charango*, a ten-stringed guitar whose body was originally made from an armadillo but is now often carved wood. The rhythmic strumming of the *charango* sets a strong and solid ostinato that is contrasted by melodic instruments that include flutes and pipes and, in some places, violins, too. Barrel-shaped *bomba* drums are also played in Andean regions, and percussion instruments such as maracas and tambourines are sometimes heard.

Even in a brief half-minute selection, listeners can enter into the experience of musical tones and textures of the Andean *sierra* (mountains and highlands). Episode 2.4 offers four questions as a focus for listening four times for the instruments, the melodic contour of the flute, and the steady pulsive strumming that accompanies it. Students can be challenged to apply their Attentive Listening skills to the formal properties of the music while also wondering as to the source of the music: Whose music is this? Where does it come from? (and perhaps also Why does it sound the way it does?). Such questions reflect a kind of cultural awakening that occurs even in these initial experiences. There is good reason to want to increase the listening opportunities to ten or more times, and to spread the listening over multiple sessions, so that the music becomes embedded in the mind's ear.

Episode 2.4: High Flute in the Andean Highlands
"La Pastora"

Specific Use: Early Childhood, Elementary Music Education, Instrumental Ensembles

Materials:

- "La Pastora" (The Shepherdess), from the album *El Grupo Jatari: Folk Music of Argentina, Bolivia, Chile, Ecuador, Peru and Venezuela*

Procedure:

1. "What instruments do you hear and in what order?"
2. Play track to 0'30".
3. Discuss answers (High-pitched lute, tambourine, low-pitched lute with flute)
4. Play track to 0'30" to check answers.
5. "Tap the pulse while listening to the strums of the lutes and the melody of the flute".
6. Play track to 0'30".
7. "In the air, use the pointer finger to 'draw' the rising and falling pitches of the flute's melody. Show discrete pitches as well as any slides between pitches".
8. Play track to 0'30".
9. "Listen again while tapping the pulse in the left hand and drawing the melody's rise-and-fall contour with the right hand".
10. "Given what you hear, where in the world might the musicians be living?" (Because of the timbral quality of the flute and the fast strumming of the high-pitched lute, the music is Andean, from Bolivia but not far from what might be heard in Peru, Ecuador, and the high mountainous areas of northern Chile and Argentina and parts of Columbia and Venezuela.)
11. Invite a community musician or culture-bearer to share aspects of Andean music, stories, clothing, and food. Opportunities are invaluable for students to hear a live performance of one or more of the traditional Andean instruments and to hear Spanish sung in a song or spoken in short colloquial phrases.

A Country Ballad

There are only 200 words in the ballad "Jolene", the focus of Attentive Listening in Episode 2.5, but there is plenty of power packed into the story behind the music and the progression of three chords that cycles through the song. The song's story itself is ageless and relates emotionally to listeners who have known feelings of inadequacy in their relationships. A beautiful woman, Jolene, appears to be catching the attention of the singer's husband (or "special friend"), so the singer worries herself sick over the possible threat of this flirtation to her relationship. As a narrative form of song that describes an event, this ballad rises from the style of US-based country music, and the haunting melody and prominence of guitars, including slide guitar, refer the listener to the "roots music" of the traditional expressions that emanate from the hills and hollers of the Appalachian Mountains.

Episode 2.5: A Country Ballad
"Jolene"

Specific Use: Choral Ensembles

Materials:

- "Jolene", from the album *Ultimate Dolly Parton*

Procedure:

1. "What instruments do you hear?"
2. Play track to 1'40".
3. Discuss answers (acoustic guitars, bass, drumset, metallic shaker, vocal solo and harmony, slide guitar, violins).
4. Play track to 1'40" to check answers.
5. Follow the pulse, tapping every other beat or alternating pats and claps.
6. Play track to 1'40".
7. "Repetition is a technique that provides musical unity. How is repetition manifested in the song?"
8. Play track to 0'30".
10. Discuss the use of repetition in the lyrics in the recurring chorus: "Jolene, Jolene, Jolene, Jolene, I'm begging of you please don't take my man. Jolene, Jolene, Jolene, Jolene, please don't take him just because you can". Note also that the melody, rhythm, and chords, embedded in the chorus, are also repeated.
11. "What is the topic of the song text? Find a line in the lyrics that encapsulates the singer's dilemma".
12. Play track to 1'40".
13. Consider various song texts to describe the singer's dilemma: "I'm begging of you please don't take my man", "You could easily take my man", "My happiness depends on you and whatever you decide to do".
11. "Given what you hear, how might you describe this musical style?" (Given the instrumentation, country music)
12. Listen to another rendition of Jolene, featuring Dolly Parton and Pentatonix, https://itunes.apple.com/us/album/jolene-feat-dolly-parton-single/1151582560 and compare the arrangement to the original recording.
13. Arrange for a visit from a singer-guitarist who specializes in country music and in related styles referred to as "old time", "folk", and even "bluegrass". Recommend a short performance of several songs, including "Jolene".

Country singer Dolly Parton is both a singer and songwriter, with many popular country-styled songs in the form of colorful verses and the returning chorus section. She released "Jolene" in 1973, and it continues to be one of the most recorded songs of her career. It soared to the top of the Billboard charts and was also high on the listening lists in the United Kingdom, Ireland, Sweden, and Denmark at the time. "Jolene" has been covered by more than 30 singers and in several languages. It was rendered by Olivia Newton-John as a disco song in the later 1970s and was later given a Goth rendition by the post-punk band The Sisters of Mercy. The 2016 all-vocal version by Dolly Parton with the a cappella group Pentatonix returned to its original rendering, and the vocally produced harmonies and rhythms offer a fresh yet faithful rendering to the ballad.

A song so popular as "Jolene" may already have settled into the listening ears of students, yet the questions (and responses) provided in Episode 2.5 start into a deeper and more-focused listening than students may have had with the song. Even if the song itself is unfamiliar to listeners, the sonic mix of country and popular elements make for a least path of resistance among students who know these styles. At a length of 1'40", the selection embraces the chorus as well as some of the singer's imagined dialogue with the woman who she fears is threatening her relationship with "my man". The instrumental tracks are laid down in one of the focusing-questions; in others, the technique of repetition and the song text or lyrics are noted. The dimension of Attentive Listening is reinforced through the four plays of the selection, even as additional listening will quite naturally lead to a further perking of the ears to the story's situation, the chord progression (D-minor, F-Major, C-Major), and the rising melody's emotive appeal to the flirtatious woman. The episode may run only ten minutes in a class but can be brought back again, using an extended set of questions, in later class sessions.

Bulgarian Beat

On first hearing the music of Bulgaria, listeners may well catch the emotional energy of a joyful celebration, a life of frenzied activity, an unrequited love relationship, or even the loss of a loved one from the world. When it is as vibrant and kinetic as the featured music in Episode 2.6, there is no question that it must be music for weddings. Ivo Papasov, clarinet, and Yuri Yunakov, saxophone, are the reigning stars of wedding music, and few musicians have reached the heights of their high-speed tempos, melodic flourishes, and improvisational inventions, as they are the innovators who go beyond standard tunes for dancing, dining, and socializing with families and friends who join forces to celebrate the union of the bride and groom and to give wishes to them for their long lives together. Two other musicians contribute further musical energy on accordion and drum set, filling out the Bulgarian band.

Weddings are important to Bulgarians, and people all over the Balkan region of southeastern Europe view wedding celebrations as joyous gatherings over a day, or even several days, to make merry with the married couple. Long ago, Bulgarian wedding celebrations ran for five days of village festivities; after World War II, the socialist regime disapproved of wedding music because of its mix of Bulgarian with elements of Jazz and music from Greece, Turkey Macedonia, Serbia, and Roma (Gypsy) culture. With the end of the People's Republic of Bulgaria in 1989, wedding music returned with gusto, especially when it was amped up and played by skilled

Episode 2.6: Bulgarian Beat
"Lenorije Chaje"

Specific Use: Instrumental Ensembles

Materials:

- "Lenorije Chaje", from the album *Together Again* (Ivo Papasov/Yuri Yunakov)

Procedure:

1. "What instruments do you hear and in what order?"
2. Play track to 0'18".
3. Discuss answers (clarinet, saxophone, drum set, accordion)
4. Play track to 0'18" to check answers.
5. "Listen for a short repeated melodic figure of just seven pitches, and trace in the air the four-pitch rise and then three-pitch fall".
6. Play track to 0'18".
7. "Pretend-play the melody on an imaginary clarinet or saxophone".
8. Play track to 0'18".
9. "Listen to the instruments, followed by the singer, on the same melodic figure, and pretend play the same melody".
10. Play track to 0'38".
11. "Given what you hear, where in the world might the musicians be living?" (Direct them to a Slavic language, but not Russian, and to the mix of instruments found in wedding bands.)
12. Listen to another rendition of Lenorije Chaje, featuring the Raka Balkan band of wind, brass, and percussion instruments; a violin; and a singer. Note also the bassline of the tuba player, the improvisational escapades, and the general groove that the musicians cannot resist showing in their performance of this favorite tune. https://soundcloud.com/rakabalkanband/leno
13. Invite a community musician who plays clarinet or saxophone, symphonic-style or jazz, to perform a few short selections that demonstrate the timbre, technique, and range of the instruments. Recommend advance listening of "Lenorije Chaje" to the visitor so that he (or she) might play along with the recording or demonstrate a phrase or two alone and without the recording. A culture-bearing visitor, from a Bulgarian orthodox church (or other community), could provide some insight as to Bulgarian culture.

improvisors. The clarinetist Ivo Papazov, a Bulgarian Gypsy, is credited with the creation of the kinetic wedding band style, and Yuri Yunakov, a Turkish-Bulgarian Roma musician, plays saxophone and introduced Bulgarian wedding music to the United States. Bulgarian wedding music is played at the time of the exchange of gifts, at the banquets, and for dancing many hours into the night.

Episode 2.6 is based on just the first 18 seconds of the song "Leonrije Chaje" (Lenorije Charged). The song's melody repeats four times in just this brief excerpt, and it is all the more contagious because of the opportunity to become familiar with it through its repetitions. Despite the brief length, however, there are chromaticisms in the melody that may challenge those who are unaccustomed to the minor melody that starts and ends on the seventh degree of the scale. Suggestions for Attentive Listening highlight the naming and "pretend-playing" of the instruments, gesturing in the air in the position of fingers moving across the keys of an imaginary clarinet or saxophone. Following several listening opportunities of the instruments alone, a later step recommends that listening continues to a little over twice the length of the initial excerpt to hear the doubling by the singer of the instrumental melody. In all,

Figure 2.1   Ana Borisova Ganeva, Bulgarian keeper of traditional song, in the process of "passing it on" to the children

this episode may run about six minutes, longer with the addition of the video recording or if additional listenings are desired.

Listening as a Gateway to Cultural Understanding

Attentive Listening requires considerable effort on the part of teachers, community musicians, and culture-bearers. Students need to develop focus on the music (and on the musicians and their cultures) as there are so many distractions in their lives and continuous reminders and reinforcements of what they might be listening for. They need teachers who can provide them with continuous reminders and reinforcements of what they might be listening for. Music educators can prompt students to channel their attention to particular musical elements and events, respond to their curiosities, and encourage their continued attention. Community musicians can help the effort to listen attentively, too, especially since they know the musical style and instruments well enough to be able to point students in the direction of an instrumental or vocal timbre or technique, how it is handled and produced, and why the music must sound the way it does. Students are drawn to a musical sound, but without some exchange about the music and the circumstances of its sound and function, their interest can rapidly fade.

With the musical experience can come an awakening to the culture. In a brief musical excerpt, and in the opening few seconds of a musical selection, can come the questions: "Who's playing (or singing)?" (and there are the requests for details as to their age, their gender, their overall physical appearance); "Where are they from?" (and the wondering leads to whether they are close by or a world apart from the students and whether the music is urban or rural, at home in the village, the bush, the court, or the church); "How do they make that sound?" (of a vocal yodel or a glottal stop or of tinny-sounding strings or a very breathy flute or horn); and "Why would they make that music?" (which initiates a conversation, highlighted by photos, videos, and stories, as to the music's meaning and function to those who value it). Attentive Listening opens ears to culturally unfamiliar music and paves the way to insights on equally unfamiliar people and cultures. These questions lead to opportunities for Integrating World Music into the broader interdisciplinary potential for knowing the music in culture and as culture, more of which is featured in Chapter 6. This need to know about the music underscores the nature of WMP as mostly sequential with regard to the first three or four dimensions, but which goes off the sequential track when it comes to students wanting to know early on the cultural significance of the music through integrated and interdisciplinary study.

The varied nature of music causes some pieces and styles to draw students more immediately than others to the music and its cultural location. Music at fast tempos, at considerable volume, of very high (or very low) pitch, of resonant timbres (such as the bronze xylophones of Bali), or unusual vocal qualities (such as the nasalized voice of an Egyptian singer) with striking differentiations of dynamic levels (or timbral groups)—these sonic envelopes will attract the attention of learners of every age and experience. Music with repeated phrases, whether melodic or rhythmic, is enticing, and music with a prominent pulse sets listeners into a groove that is often irresistible. With the teacher's careful framing, so, too, can slower, softer, more subtle music appeal to listeners, such as challenging students to think about the context of the music and for what reasons the music is performed. The appearance of community musicians and culture-bearers who know the music well, and who may have a story to tell about it, can reel in students who may be as curious about the musician as about the music itself.

Listening on one's own, outside of school, can be lighthearted, casual and carefree, amusing, and entertaining. In music classrooms, listening activities that are not thoughtfully planned can result in lightweight, somewhat out-of-focus, and decidedly superficial experiences. Attentive Listening, on the other hand, involves a deeper look into the musical composite, its nature and essence, through thoughtfully prepared questions. This initial dimension of World Music Pedagogy requires focus, accepts curiosity, and offers opportunities for students to reflect upon sonic and sociocultural meanings. The goal is a deeper listening, or what American composer Pauline Oliveros called "deep listening", a willingness to receive new ideas in sound and to think musically as the ideas unfold.

The musical world is out there, awaiting discovery. Listening happens alone and together, in many different settings and circumstances, and is greatly facilitated through the efforts of music educators and community musicians. Since one of the aims of a solid musical education is the development of thoughtful analytical listeners, then responsible teachers will take the time to shepherd their students into the midst of a musical selection from Kenya and Korea, Ireland and India, Venezuela and Vietnam. They will work with community musicians at school and in the field, offering students multiple opportunities to gauge the beauty and logic of a musical selection. At the start of a class; in transitions between class segments; or as a break from performing in a school or community band, choir, bluegrass group, or African drum-dance session, teachers who take time out to listen are guiding their students through the gateway to musical and cultural understanding.

Eduardo Mendonça, Brazilian "Mestre" Musician

Community Musician Eduardo Mendonça Modeling the Stick Technique of Brazilian Samba

Photo by Susie Fitzhugh

Eduardo Mendonça is a culture-bearing community musician, a master percussionist who performs (guitar, percussion, and vocals), composes, and teaches various genres of Brazilian popular music in the United States, Canada, and Brazil. A native of Salvador, Bahia, Brazil, Eduardo Mendonça has shared international stages with legendary Brazilian musicians Geraldo Azevedo, Alcione, Olodum, and Jorge Ben Jor. Eduardo has performed for many notable personalities, including the 14th Dalai Lama, Pope John Paul II, and former South Africa President Nelson Mandela, and he was featured in the PBS American Masters documentary *Paul Simon: Born at the Right Time*. He enjoys the creation of musical fusions throughout and between the Americas, which can be heard on his five CDs: *Steps* (2016), *Brazil and Me* (2009), *Dois em 1* (2009), *Brazil in Washington* (2003), and *Show Brazil* (1997). He is much sought after as an artist-in-residence and master class instructor and gives workshops, lectures, and school assemblies. Eduardo Mendonça traces his lineage to a royal African family bearing the hereditary title of Mamabeka ("prophet of the royal court"), as documented by the Instituto Geográfico e Histórico da Bahia. Eduardo is the co-director for Brazil Arts & Education, DBA: Show Brazil!, music director for iBuildBridges Foundation, and director of creative youth development for Arts Corps. Eduardo's performances never fail to enlighten and entertain multigenerational audiences, as the "mestre" ("master", in Portuguese) musician that he is.

Q: Can you talk about your early entry into musical life?
A: I am the seventh child born to a family of eight kids altogether. All of them, except my mother and my younger sister, play an instrument. Every Sunday, my folks got together to play and harmonize incredible originals and Brazilian popular songs. I was fascinated to hear them playing and singing while my mother was preparing her delicious food. I always wanted to play guitar, but due to my hyper behavior, my siblings really wanted to see me very far away from their well-cared-for instruments. I paid very close attention to the fingers of my brothers and sisters on one particular song, and thought, "I can learn to do that!" So, while my older siblings were at school, I "borrowed" one of the guitars and started to work my fingers on the frets as they had done. It was very hard, and the steel strings hurt my fingers, making them bleed, so I put adhesive plasters on the tips of my fingers and then continued to play. After several weeks of quietly practicing, when my brothers and sisters started to play their Brazilian song, I interrupted them, asking to let me play. I surprised my family and received applause, many kisses, and their promises to show me more chords, melodies, and other stuff.

Q: How did you learn music? Who were your influences?
A: I learned first by ear and observation and only later learned music theory. I had teachers who mentored me, such as Ademar Andrade, a community musician, Neyde de Aquino Borges, a music and arts educator. I also studied classical guitar at a local university. I learned by ear an eclectic mix of music by Antônio Carlos Jobim, Vinícius de Moraes, Baden Powell, Dorival Caymmi, Milton Nascimento, Roberto Carlos, Villa-Lobos, The Beatles, Pepeu Gomes, Caetano Veloso, Gilberto Gil, and Luiz Gonzaga.

Q: Do you think that children/youth should know music of people and places throughout the world?
A: Definitely. We expand our minds when we travel or through experiences with locally available cultural communities. We extend our knowledge when we learn from people who are different from us. I teach music of Brazil such as samba percussion and bossa nova, although I'm also interested in learning music of many of the world's cultures.

Q: Who learns music from you?
A: I work with children, teens, and adults. I'm drawn to working with people from low-income communities and students of color who are not typically receiving arts education in schools. My goal is to close the gaps in race, social class, and gender and to work with children who are otherwise left out of artistic and musical opportunities. I go to where the needs are in schools, community centers, communities at large, and at festivals.

Q: How do you teach music?
A: Since my traditional music in Brazil was and is orally passed on, my approach to teaching is organic, orally delivered, and hands-on. Music notation and theory come later. I use "box rhythms", with x's that mark actual sounds in a horizontal string of boxes that stand for pulses. Western staff notation may follow. I use games to teach music, and I use music to meet emotional and social goals. I mix my drums with plastic buckets, mallets made with tennis balls, and other unusual instruments to prove that sonic diversity can be very beautiful.

Q: Can you share one of your stories in teaching music to children?
A: This year, I was teaching my Creative Rhythms course in a community program. We experience some of my Brazilian rhythms, and I invite students to share rhythms that are personally creative. We listen to the many rhythms and join in with each and every rhythm that comes up. There was a piano at the building's cafeteria, and I saw a young student from the class playing melodies with his right hand. I went to him and began reproducing his melody while also adding chords. His eyes popped open wide, and he asked where the music came from. I replied, "It's your song, I just added chords, but you're the composer!" I recorded his song on my phone and played it to him. He was back at the piano over the days ahead, adding a beginning, an ending, and continuing to match the iPhone recording while adding a beginning and ending to the music. Totally by ear, he learned the music, then he created the music, and it sounded a little like me and a little like him, too.

Listening With Purpose

School music programs are almost always about full-tilt musical involvement, the act of musical doing. Indeed, learners (especially young learners) typically prefer to perform music rather than to sit still and listen to it. Yet listening is a precious experience, as well as a necessary one, particularly in coming to terms with culturally unfamiliar music. In the manner of World Music Pedagogy, listening with purpose paves the way to participation and performance. Teachers who facilitate small steps to listening with focus, through the provision of specific questions, can show learners the way into a thoughtful understanding of the music. For best results, the listening selection may be brief (often within one minute in length), the selection may be repeated multiple times (with a new question or directive offered for each listening segment), and the talk (by teachers, in particular) can be kept to a minimum to make room for more listening. When music teachers join with community musicians and culture-bearers, listening can become that much more meaningful. Listening is an art, as it is also the way forward into understanding musical humanity.

References

Bickford, T. (2017). *Schooling new media*. New York: Oxford University Press.

Campbell, P. S. (1991). *Lessons from the world*. New York: Schirmer Books.

McLucas, A. D. (2010). *The musical ear: Oral tradition in the USA*. Farnham: Ashgate Publishing Limited.

Listening Episodes

"Jolene", Dolly Parton, https://itunes.apple.com/us/album/jolene-single-version/282883573?i=282883578

"Kecuh! Riuh! Gemuruh!", Riduan Zalani and NADI Singapura, https://itunes.apple.com/sg/album/kata-kita-kota/id924288831

"La Pastora", El Grupo Jatari, www.folkways.si.edu/el-grupo-jatari/la-pastora-the-shepherdess/latin-world/music/track/smithsonian

"Lenorije Chaje", Ivo Papasov and Yuri Yunakov, https://itunes.apple.com/us/album/together-again-legends-of-bulgarian-wedding-music/74364531

"Nange" ["Yange"], Tanzanian Wagogo musicians, https://itunes.apple.com/us/album/tanzania-tanzanie-chants-wagogo/424221991

"Todo lo que Tengo", Quetzal, www.folkways.si.edu/quetzal/imaginaries/latin/music/album/smithsonian

3
Participatory Musicking

The five members of the bluegrass band called Winter Wheat have honed their skills over many years, playing the lutes and fiddles that comprise their music. Some began as children, learning to sing with a mother or a grandfather, picking up the guitar because their uncle played and could teach them on weekend visits. Others took up an instrument in school, choosing to stay in at lunch recess in order to take the once-weekly violin class, joining the elementary school orchestra, and later continuing to play in school or community youth symphonies as middle and high school students. Now, the five musicians, all millennials, are a group, coming from formal and informal experiences, learning skills and repertoire, and shaping a lively sound in their band of bluegrass, "Irish", and old-time music. For six years, Winter Wheat has been playing in restaurants and clubs on weekends, touring up and down the American west coast and twice along the eastern corridor to cities like Boston, Philly, Washington DC, New York, and Providence, Rhode Island. They've produced three recordings, and they're making a modest living as performing musicians (even as they also give lessons on their instrument(s); one member is also a coffee shop barista on weekday mornings, another has part-time work at the local radio station, and still another does landscaping in a seasonal arrangement).

Meghan Hughes wanted something more for the group, something "other". A fiddler, mandolin player, and singer, she wanted to "give back", so she spearheaded a plan to bring her band into the lives of children and their families. She went to the principals of a local elementary school and middle school, met with a group of teachers (of history, language arts, and music) and several "all-subjects" elementary school teachers, and worked collaboratively to forge a plan. She worked with several teachers in crafting a successful grant proposal, which they sent to the school district administration, the community arts council, and the PTA councils of the two schools. For a period of three years, they are now funded for monthly school assemblies (at each of the two schools; classroom visits for more intimate performances; Tuesday and Thursday after-school group lessons on bluegrass guitar and "vocals";

occasional Saturday morning workshops on bluegrass fiddle; and three annual "old-time events" that feature bluegrass performances, potlucks, and contra-dances in the middle school gym). The community was already oriented toward bluegrass, country, and old-time music, located as they are in southern Illinois, and the playlists of parents and students alike include Ricky Skaggs, Emmylou Harris, Alison Krauss and Union Station, and legendary artists such as Bill Monroe, Ralph Stanley, and Flatt and Scruggs. But these events with Winter Wheat have sparked many in the community to recognize that the music goes beyond the presentational programs to the participatory possibilities for all.

Meghan serves as the liaison to both the school teachers and the bluegrass musicians. She works especially well with the music teachers at the two schools, as there are opportunities in the music classes for their students to listen, sing, and play guitar for standard tunes like "Roanoke", "Wildwood Flower", "Old Joe Clark", "Rocky Top", "I'll Fly Away", and "Will that Circle Be Unbroken". Students are listening hard, too, to the melodies, harmonies, rhythms, and lyrics for these classic bluegrass songs through the class sessions that their music teachers provide. Although neither of the school music teachers knows how to play fiddle or banjo, they are teaching their students the tunes and guitar chords "by ear", providing collective listening altogether to selected recordings in attentive, engaged, and enactive ways. When they visit the two schools, the Winter Wheat band members add the sounds of their own instruments atop what the students can already sing and chord. Students are invited to perform with the band at their various school visits; at the annual "old time events", some of students' own family members are joining in with their instruments and voices (and contra-dancing selves) to make the most of Winter Wheat's residencies. Thanks to Meghan Hughes, her band, and the teachers of music and other subjects, bluegrass has grown its own following among students and their families. Through mediated listening experiences, live encounters with bluegrass music and musicians, in-school and after-school "lessons", workshop sessions, and special family events, bluegrass has found its niche as a vital (and revitalized) community art form.

Participatory Musicking in Engaged and Enactive Modes

Following on the path of World Music Pedagogy, experiences in musical cultures that initiate as episodes in Attentive Listening develop further in drawing learners into particular selections and overall styles. With their ears exercised, students are thus awakened to the sonic features of the music (even as they are also edging toward the need to know something more of the context, function, and social meaning of the music). In the WMP process, students are encouraged to continue onward into the music via the mode of Engaged Listening and then further to a gradual shift into the mode of Enactive Listening. Both modes invite learners into the act of making the music to which they are listening, proceeding in small steps to join with the music, refining the musical expression with repeated attempts to sing it or play it, adding further parts to multipart music, and advancing to more nuanced expressions that match the musical selection. Students are invited by teachers to continue listening to the origin source—typically, the recording or video recording as they become increasingly active participants in singing and playing the music. With every iteration of the music, in every further listening experience, learners become ever more familiar with the music, ever

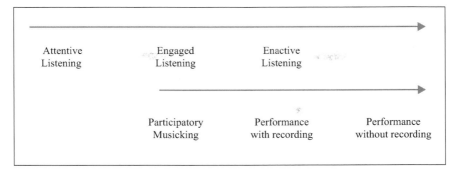

Figure 3.1   Continuum of Participatory Musicking via Engaged Listening and Enactive Listening

more confident in themselves as participants in the music, and ever more aware of the elemental features of the music as they are also producing them.

Imagine listening as it appears on a horizontal continuum (Figure 3.1), in which initial listening (Attentive Listening) leads to listening in a participatory manner to the origin-source recording (Engaged Listening). Moving from ground zero and from left to right on the continuum, the listening continues as the entirety of the musical work is learned by listening, singing, and/or playing all the musical components in all of its nuanced ways (Enactive Listening). From the first listening experiences comes the gradual involvement of learners in contributing partly to the recording's music, to fully performing along with the recording, until the time comes when the music is learned and the recording is no longer necessary. This listening continuum comprises the first three dimensions of World Music Pedagogy, in which the ear leads the way in a thorough-going learning of the music.

The "listen-to-learn" theme goes into full swing as "Participatory Musicking" comes into play (Campbell, 2018). This term refers to the invitation by teachers and community musicians to students to be musically active in a performative manner in the moment of listening to "new" music—that is, music that is musically unfamiliar and possibly culturally unfamiliar as well. Students are invited to combine their listening even as they sing a little, move a little, play a little—and then a little more with each ensuing listening opportunity. The Participatory Musicking process is beneficial in multiple ways in that it calls on students to actively "do something" as they listen; to join together their receptive (listening) and expressive (performance-based) potentials; and to combine what they hear and can musically comprehend with what they can musically make happen vocally, on instruments, or in kinesthetic response in a manner that fits with the recorded music. Students increase their involvement as they are challenged by music teachers and community musicians to extend the phrases they sing, play, or move; as they are invited to layer in multiple parts that may comprise polyphonic (or homophonic) musical selections; and as they are directed to listen and match the nuances of pitch, rhythm, and timbre over the course of successive listening experiences. This increased involvement of students quite naturally moves them along the continuum from Engaged Listening to Enactive Listening as the Participatory Musicking gradually shifts to a full performance with the recording and eventually to performance of the recorded piece without the recording.

Participatory Musicking is buoyed by the scholarship of Christopher Small, Charles Keil, and Thomas Turino, ethnomusicologists with a directed interest in human musicality, in the position that musicality is innately present from birth onward and throughout life and that music is an essential human behavior. The term "musicking" was coined by Christopher Small (1998) as a means of clarifying that music is an activity, a human process, and not an inanimate thing. It is a verb, as in "to music", that describes human musical action, rather than a noun that denotes physical objects such as instruments, music scores, and music notation. Musicking encompasses involvement via listening, performing (rehearsing, practicing, singing, or playing in full or in part), composing or improvising, and dancing. (By extension, Small sees that all who join in the ritual of a performance, including those who write the program notes, set up the chairs, or take the tickets at the door, are also within the realm of the musicking process, but this is beyond the scope of our interest here.) Charles Keil's interest in participation is legion, as he declares the conversation among musicians *in the act of making music* as central to the human spirit (Keil & Feld, 1994). The essence of music, Keil declares, whether jazz, popular, or music from any place (or time) in the world, is in the interplay of singers, players, and dancers who contribute their expressive parts to the musical whole and who co-create the musical groove. In a view of music as social life, Thomas Turino (2007) outlines participation in the music-making process as a profound personal and social experience. A musical act can be about the presentation of it, which is judged by audience members as to the musical quality of the performance or by the participatory nature of it, in which the social interaction among participants is the primary focus. While both realms are performance-based, presentational performance separates performers from their audience while participatory performance envelops all present in the activity of "doing the music" and of bonding the participants to one another in the participatory process.

Participatory Musicking is common in some musical cultures, particularly when communal activity is valued. Such is the case in much of sub-Saharan Africa (from Ghana and Senegal to Kenya and Zimbabwe) and in diasporic African communities such as those in Brazil, Columbia, Cuba, in many of the coastal communities throughout Latin America, and within the worship services of many African American churches. In these communities, everyone is "in" and accepted as part of the musicking community; no one is intentionally left out; and singing, playing, and dancing are all acceptable contributions to the musical act. Indigenous groups in North America, Australia, New Zealand, and across the Arctic region are likewise prone to the musical involvement of all who gather for a ritual of celebration or of mourning so that singing, dancing, and playing (and sometimes all three together) are expected rather than optional behavior. In children's musical cultures, too, there is an inherent inclusivity in their musical play, too, in singing games, jump rope songs and chants, and handclapping routines. Music at weddings, in the villages of eastern Europe, and in the social halls of North America function to bring guests to the floor to dance in circles, lines, and couples. There, the band plays on as social interaction is evident in the ways that people amusingly exchange conversational items with one another even as they step, skip, and whirl around.

In the rollout of the World Music Pedagogy process, Participatory Musicking may seem to be the ultimate culminating event in which music is experienced by ear, gradually learned, and finally produced. While we would argue for creating opportunities and integrative interdisciplinary studies, too, the involvement of students in

Figure 3.2 Little ones at high alert in listening and trying out the songs of a visiting musician

making music is a centering point in the pedagogy. To be sure, an obvious outcome of students' expenditure of energy to "learn the music" is to perform it, although students need not take every musical work they learn into a public performance. Learning can lead to such a performance, teachers and community musicians can work with students in organizing a program in school or out in community venues and functions (see Chapter 4). Via the engaged and enactive modes of experience, however, students can know the music deeply as they make their way as participants into the midst of singing, playing, and dancing it.

Engaged Listening as Initial Musicking

The WMP dimension of Engaged Listening is the interactive involvement of learners with the music so that they actively enter into the musicking process while the music is sounding. For many listeners, they need no invitation to move and groove to a Puerto Rican *bomba* sound, a Hindustani folk melody in a *dadra* (six-beat) *tala*, or a praise song from Uganda. Listening alone at home or in the car, with friends at a restaurant or a coffee shop, in the midst of a live concert, they may hum along to a melody from Norway, drum along to the beat of an Irish *bodhran*, join in singing the chorus section of an old-time Appalachian tune or to adding a harmony part to a Mexican *ranchera*. The music moves them, literally and figuratively, and an instrumental timbre, an ostinato rhythm, or a contagious melody may attract them to contributing to the music as it plays. These engagements will typically match the music they hear (although sometimes they may be inspired to add a musical complement to the recorded (or live) musical sound). For teachers and community musicians, the WMP task of Engaged Listening is to invite students into initial musicking experiences, shaping their participatory contributions to match what they hear.

Engaged Listening requires careful and conscious listening, with expectations for students to upgrade their involvement from a more passive listening status to possibilities for singing and playing along with the music and moving eurhythmically to it or in an actual dance pattern. The aim is to develop an understanding of musical features by identifying them by ear as sounded on a recording or as performed by a culture-bearing community musician, and then reflecting them in movement, in the voice, and/or on instruments. With the sound of a *pow-wow* song, students can be invited to play the rhythm of the *pow-wow* drum—in their laps, on their desk top, into the floor, or on drums. As they track the melody of a French-Canadian fiddler, they can be led into tracing the melody's rise and fall by drawing an imaginary contour in the air and then by singing it softly (on "dee" or "loo" or other syllable), even under their breaths until, over multiple listenings, they gain the confidence to sing it aloud. Students can be encouraged to sing or play drone-tones they hear on a recording of a *dulcimer*, a *sitar*, a bagpipe, or a *hurdy gurdy* and to follow the chord progression (or bassline) of a gospel song vocally or on instruments. As learners listen to a *klezmer* tune on violin and clarinet, they can be challenged to play the melody on whatever instruments may be available; plainly at first and then through continued attempts, they add in the scoops and slurs, the ornaments, the push-and-pull of the ensemble. (Of course, students will appreciate disclosure by the teacher of a melody's starting pitch, or a home tone or "the key", and they will be grateful as well for the provision of enough time to figure out the melody, "get the rhythm", or practice a figure without the recording so that they may practice it and ready themselves for playing it at proper tempo with the recording.)

The following scenarios provide exemplary illustrations of ways in which Engaged Listening can transpire in school settings, beginning with the same three learning pathway selections (Episodes 3.1, 3.2, and 3.3) that were featured in Chapter 2 and extending to other recorded selections of the world's musical expressions. While these episodes provide sequential steps for musical engagement while listening, they do not represent the extent of repetition that is typically needed by learners to get to the point of playing or singing a part with accuracy. Nor do these episodes build in the steps that may be necessary to correct parts that go awry and that need a reboot. The time allotment for an Engaged Listening experience may vary, depending upon the musical selection and the student group; often, the best way forward is to spread out this WMP dimension across several class sessions, mixing in other musical selections and activities within these sessions, returning to the WMP work regularly or at least on occasion, and thus allowing days and even weeks for the full immersion of students into the selected musical work. While the episodes are centered on recordings, the presence of a community musician performing the music "live", or performing with the recording, or offering insights to learners into the musical work, are ideal strategies to strive for.

Romance in East L.A.

Recall "Romance in East L.A." as one of three learning pathway selections within this volume that are intended to illustrate all five dimensions of World Music Pedagogy. (See Appendix I for the complete five-part learning pathway for each of the three musical selections.) Episode 3.1 offers ten steps in Engaged Listening that provides discovery of the three-chord harmonic progression, the rhythm of the *pandeiro* (drum), and the melody and text of the piece. The sequence is designed for use by music teachers and community musicians with the intent of drawing students ever closer to the essence of the song, "Todo lo que Tengo", and of the sound of the Chicano group, Quetzal, whose message is the maintenance of personal identity even in the midst of a romantic relationship. The steps of this episode invite learners to become increasingly involved by gauging the guitar's straightforward harmonic accompaniment, tapping out the prominent repeating rhythm on hand drum, and singing the soulful melody of this emotionally powerful song. A performance demonstration by a community musician who knows this style of Mexican-flavored music can reinforce the techniques necessary to contribute these musical parts. With every step of Engaged Listening (each of which may be repeated), students are further familiarized with the music so that they may comfortably enter into the process of Participatory Musicking as the recording plays on. This episode may run about ten minutes in length or longer, depending upon the repetition of some steps.

Episode 3.1: Romance in East L.A.
"Todo lo que Tengo"
(Learning Pathway #1)

Specific Use: Elementary Music Education, Secondary Music Innovations, Instrumental Ensembles

Materials:

- "Todo lo que Tengo", Quetzal (from *Imaginaries*), Smithsonian Folkways Recordings
- Guitar, *pandeiro* (hand drum, or other drum)

Procedure:

1. "Listen and show fingers for the chord numbers I, IV, V (G-C-D)".
2. Play track to 1'53".
3. Discuss duration of the chords (I/G-four beats, IV/C-two beats, V/D-two beats)
4. Play track to check answers.
5. "Tap the rhythm of the *pandeiro* (drum)".
6. Play track to 1'53".
7. Demonstrate and discuss the continuing eighth-note rhythms, two taps per beat.

8. "Hum along with the sung melody. Listen for sung words like 'mundo', 'tiempo', 'quiero', 'amor', and 'corazon'.

9. Play track to 1'53".

10. Call for students to translate the words they hear: "mundo" (world), "tiempo" (time), "quiero" (I wish or I want), "amor" (love), and "corazon" (heart).

11. Play track to 1'53", while listening for the words, humming the melody, and tapping the rhythm of the *pandeiro*.

12. Arrange for the visit of a Mexican-heritage musician who might perform the piece with and without the recording, demonstrate the *pandeiro* rhythm and the guitar's chord changes (in various strumming patterns), and inspire language learning through the use of occasional Spanish words.

Kecuh! Riuh! Gemuruh!

This Engaged Listening activity is a continuation from Episode 2.2, Chapter 2's Attentive Listening activities that first introduced listeners to the work. In this Engaged Listening encounter of about ten minutes of experience (which could easily be accomplished in one session or in multiple sessions), the focus is on playing discernible rhythmic patterns that are identified by students through a series of repeated listenings to the music track. The teacher's own leadership in playing the patterns can be enhanced through the efforts of a community musician who is invited in to demonstrate the rhythm and to play along with the students while listening collectively to the recording. In Malay music, there are traditional rhythmic dance patterns that are common and recognizable, and they are referred to as the *Masri, Inang, Joget, Zapin*, and *Asli* rhythms. The *Inang* and *Asli* patterns are considered indigenous to the Malay Archipelago, while the *Joget* (influenced by the Portuguese) and *Zapin* (traced to the influences of Arab traders to the region) are later arrivals to the region. These common rhythms are expressed in their fundamental forms, or they may be embellished and made more complicated by experienced musicians. As an example, the fundamental *Inang* pattern features a syncopated pattern within a duple four-beat meter, which can be played on the *kompang* or a hand drum (as substitute). In a classroom setting, the fundamental rhythm can be chanted on mnemonic syllables using "dum" and "ta", while also playing it on an available percussion instrument or sounding it as body percussion that feature pats, claps, and slaps. As performed by experienced musicians, this *Inang* pattern can sound on the three accented durations (on "1", "3+", and "4"), and be given embellishment on durations "2" and the first part of "3".

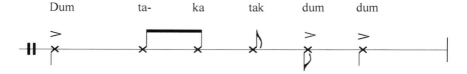

Basic Inang rhythm

Episode 3.2: "Kecuh! Riuh! Gemuruh!"
(Learning Pathway #2)

Specific Use: Elementary Music Education, Secondary Music Innovations, Instrumental Ensembles

Materials:

* Track 4, from the album, *Kata Kita Kota* by NADI Singapura

Procedure:

1. "Listen and identify one distinct repeated rhythmic pattern in the track" (there are at least three distinct rhythm patterns that can be identified, all in distinct eight-beat patterns).

2. Play track from 1'00" to 2'00".

3. "Listen again and confirm what you hear. Try to notate this rhythm pattern in simple notation".

4. Play track from 1'00" to 2'00".

5. "Share and compare notation of the rhythm pattern with your classmates".

6. "Play this rhythm pattern with body percussion, choosing to use pats, claps, or slaps".

7. Play track from 1'00" to 2'00", and have students play their rhythmic patterns along with the track.

8. Encourage students to use the internet to source out the other four fundamental Malay rhythms (*Masri, Joget, Zapin*, and *Asli*), and check if any of the rhythms match their identified rhythm pattern.

9. Host a Malay musician with full knowledge of the rhythms and techniques for playing them on percussion instruments to provide a live performance and demonstration. Consider also inviting a percussionist to learn the work, demonstrate fundamental playing technique, and help to shape the participatory musicking of the students.

Sub-Saharan Collective Song

The vocal-choral sound of Tanzania's Wagogo people is featured in Episode 3.3, in which a sequence of Engaged Listening experiences is applied in the further involvement of listeners in the sub-Saharan Collective Song called "Nange" (or "Yange"). As the third of three selections that illustrate the five dimensions of the WMP learning pathway, the multiple steps continue the course of listening that began with questions to focus the ear in Attentive Listening and that graduate to an invitation to physically trace the melodic contour of individual sung phrases, to physically tap the rhythms of the melodic phrases, to hum the melody, and to voice the melody corresponding to the title of the song. While not explicitly indicated in the sequence, it's no surprise on hearing the song to realize that the music may call listeners into a groove that further engages them in nodding their heads or showing other kinds of regularly recurring movement. Without repetition, this episode may require up to eight minutes. The episode can be extended through repetition and can also be split up across multiple class sessions, thus allowing students to grow familiar with the song and style as they continue their participation as listeners and doers.

Episode 3.3: Sub-Saharan Collective Song "Nange" ["Yange"] (Learning Pathway #3)

Specific Use: Early Childhood, Elementary Music Education, Choral Ensembles, Secondary School Innovations

Materials:

- "Nange" [or "Yange"], from the album, *Tanzania—Tanzanie: Chants*
- Whiteboard

Procedure:

1. "Listen and track the contour of the melody: With the index finger, trace the descending, slightly ascending, and undulating melodic lines".
2. Play track to 0'29".
3. Discuss the melodic directions of the four short phrases: Phrases 1 and 2 descend, Phrase 3 ascends and then descends, and Phrase 4 descends (repeating the descending melody of Phase 2).
4. On whiteboard or other screen device, visually depict the four phrases as four independent lines that descend or ascend. Place them one under the other so that the four lines appear as rising, falling, and wavering lines.
5. Play track to 0'29" to check answers, tracing the lines in the air with the finger.
6. "Tap out the rhythm of the melodic lines while 'singing inside'".
7. Play track to 0'29".
8. Demonstrate and discuss, noting that every syllable is a rhythmic unit requiring a separate tap. Suggest that given the speed of the melody, tapping the leg with alternate hands may work better than tapping with just one hand.
9. "Hum along to the melody while tracing the pitches or tapping the rhythm".
10. Play track to 0'29".
11. Clarify the meaning of the text: "Yange Yange" (it is shining), or "Sahani Yangu" (My plate), "Hedukila" (it is mine). [Note: "Yange Yange" may sound as "Nange Nange"]. Note that this direct word-for-word translation can be taken further to the song's true meaning, which is meant to

communicate happiness of a husband and wife together, of "being Wagogo", and of being alive and healthy.

12. "Sing 'Yange yange' when it appears, humming all other components of the melody".

13. Play track to 0'29".

14. Bring in a community musician, especially from sub-Saharan Africa, if not East Africa specifically, or from Tanzania or Wagogo culture in particular. As the recording plays, it may be intriguing for students to observe not only that this visiting musician may know the song (if from Wagogo culture) but also that he or she will be likely to learn the song quickly by ear and will be inclined to "dance" with the music or to move to its rhythm.

Enactive Listening as the Road to Performance

Enactive Listening moves the listener onward to the brink of performance. It is through the earlier dimension of Engaged Listening that students are drawn little-by-little into the music. As active participants, and with repeated opportunities to contribute one part or another to the recorded music, they engage in Participatory Musicking. This repeated musical engagement paves the way to Enactive Listening, the point at which learners can "enact", or fully realize, the music, putting the parts together and paying tribute to the musical details. They can carry the music into performance with the help of the recording, and they can arrive to the point that they can perform it fully without the recording. In fact, there is a back-and-forth set of experiences that transpire in this dimension in which students perform with the recording, then without it, then with it again to check what may have been missing or that requires a tune-up, and then again without the recording. The teacher may start the students to perform with the recording and switch the volume off and on, with the students continuing to sing and play all along the way. With the presence of a community musician, there is a live music model to follow, sometimes enhanced by a recording (or not), with students performing along with and then without the community musician's model.

As in the case of the earlier dimensions, the ear guides the learning in Enactive Listening. Notation is absent (or is secondary to learning by ear, and functions as a road map to acquiring aspects of pitch and rhythm), as the listening ear is the true guide to the musical essence that can never be thoroughly captured in iconic symbols. Perhaps a score is available for a listening selection, but can it portray the timbral effects, the discrepancies of pitch, the push or the pull of the rhythm? Should music from a cultural practice continue to be separated from its culturally valued learning process? Do students really need to learn a musical work from notation when in fact it may derive from the oral tradition? How can learning by ear deepen the understanding of oral cultures? By all means, music can be transcribed by the teacher to assist visual learners, and an assignment to students to transcribe sound to symbol can be instructive and even enlightening. Still, it is not necessary to move from the oral tradition to notation in order to learn music, and ear-training can be greatly enhanced when there is a challenge to learn by listening. Consider the three Learning Pathways that were introduced in Chapter 2 as Episodes 2.1, 2.2, and 2.3, and which were revisited above in Episodes 3.1, 3.2, and 3.3. They appear again in Episodes 3.4, 3.5, and 3.6 to exemplify the continuing progress of Participatory Musicking from Engaged Listening to Enactive Listening.

Romance in East L.A.

Earlier opportunities through Engaged Listening to try out one part and then another brings on the capacity to perform Quetzal's Chicano-styled song "Todo lo que Tengo". Listeners who were guided through experiences in Attentive Listening (Episode 2.1) and Engaged Listening (Episode 3.1) to recognize formal aspects of the song and to the timing of the chord changes are now, in Enactive Listening, challenged to play these chord changes on guitar. (In fact, prior to starting this episode, students may have been asked to learn basic chord configurations so as to enable quick changing of these chords in time with the music.) Likewise, earlier experiences in playing the rhythm of the *pandeiro* drum help students to stabilize the pattern so that it becomes "second nature" to players as they move through Enactive Listening. With multiple sessions behind them, and with what may well be 20, 30, and perhaps many more times to listen to the song, students can recognize and sing familiar words. Students who know Spanish can help to decipher the lyrics more fully, even as the first verse and chorus are also provided in Episode 3.4 (and other verses are available online) to guide their singing. The song is already partly learned by the time students arrive at the Enactive Listening dimension, and musical parts are already falling into place to play and sing, so students can make their way forward to a satisfying experience in Participatory Musicking that stands on the very edge of all-out performance via this third WMP dimension.

Episode 3.4: Romance in East L.A.
"Todo lo que Tengo"
(Learning Pathway #1)

Specific Use: Elementary Music Education, Secondary Music Innovations, Instrumental Ensembles

Materials:

- "Todo lo que Tengo", Quetzal (from *Imaginaries*), Smithsonian Folkways Recordings
- Guitar-*pandeiro* (hand drum, or other percussion)

Procedure:

1. Sing the melody on "loo", occasionally adding some of the words: "mundo", "tanto", "tiempo", "quiero", "amor", "corazon", "vivir". The "text" may sound something like "loo-loo-loo-loo-loo mundo".
2. Assign a Spanish-speaking student to write out the words.
3. Play track to 1'53".
4. "Sing the melody with (and without) the recording". Note: Lyrics are provided for the first verse and chorus; additional lyrics are accessed through

---

https://genius.com/Quetzal-todo-lo-que-tengo-all-that-i-have-by-quetzal-lyrics.

Verse 1:

Dicen, que el mundo, se acerca a su fin
Mi bien, da pena
Que tanto tiempo perdi
Ven, que te quiero
Te quiero decir
Que sin tu amor, no puedo vivir
Te quiero y no niego
Mi Corazon es para ti
Te quiero y da miedo
Que pronto acabe de existir

Chorus:

Todo lo que quiero yo lo hare en la vida
La fe que me nace es por ti mi vida
Todo lo que quiero yo lo hard en la vida
To lo que tengo

5. Repeat #4, singing the melody with (and without) the recording.

6. "Take tambourines and hand-drums (if not *pandeiro* drums), and tap the rhythm of the *pandeiro* (drum)".

7. Play track to 1'53".

8. Repeat #6, #7.

9. "Take guitars and play the chord progressions with (and without) the recording".

    4 X G - - -   C - D -

    2 X Am - - - G/em - - - C - - - G/em - - D - -

    4 X G - - -   C - D -

10. Play track to 1'53".

11. Repeat #9, #10.

12. "Sing and play guitar and *pandeiro* with (and without) the recording".

13. Play track to 1'53".

14. Repeat as necessary, building in practice time as necessary to develop the skills for singing and playing the piece.

15. For advanced guitarists, challenge them to follow the hypnotic broken chord pattern of the small plucked lute known as leona.

16. Challenge a violin student to learn the violin melody.

17. Clarify the meaning of the song's lyrics, which clarifies that to be in love with another person does not require losing your own identity. Share the translation of the chorus: "I love you, and I don't deny it: My heart is for you. I love you, and it scares me that life will soon no longer exist". Explain that this last phrase refers to living life alone, as it has been experienced, and will change, as living life together demands new perspectives.

18. Host a community musician of Mexican heritage, particularly for demonstrating the various instrumental parts and techniques while also singing as well as interpreting the song's lyrics.

Kecuh! Riuh! Gemuruh!

The earlier listening experiences in Episodes 2.2 and 3.2 prepared students to become more fully involved in this Enactive Listening episode with the second of three learning pathway selections. Aural-oral transmission through rhythmic mnemonics is the most common way that music is learned by members of NADI Singapura, so it stands to reason that students should experience the same process of acquiring the music and learning it by ear to the point of performance. Singular or interlocking rhythmic patterns that are individually listened to and learned can subsequently be combined by students to sound like a beautiful stream of edgy, musical pulsations. When combined with dance or martial arts (*silat*) movements, a dynamic performance can be created; such movements can be studied online and expressed in creative ways that fit the musical durations and phrases. Episode 3.5 brings students through this experience by actively working through some of the key rhythmic patterns in Kecuh! Riuh! Gemuruh!

Episode 3.5: "Kecuh! Riuh! Gemuruh!"
(Learning Pathway #2)

Specific Use: Elementary Music Education, Secondary Music Innovations, Instrumental Ensembles

Materials:

- Track 4, from the album, *Kata Kita Kota* by NADI Singapura

Procedure:

1. "Listen and identify" the constant pulsating rhythm from the beginning of the track (this is the same rhythm identified from Episode 2.2); two *jidur* rhythmic patterns (found at 2'20"–2'23", teachers can refer to notation reference provided below [bars 57–58]); and three-part *hadrah* rhythmic patterns (found at 2'25"–2'30", teachers can refer to notation reference provided below [bar 60]. Note that *Hadrah* 1 and 2 play as an interlocking pair).
2. Play track from 2'00" to 2'45".
3. "In small groups, use body percussion to 'play' the identified rhythm and interlocking patterns".
4. Play track from 2'00' to 2'45".
5. "Transfer these rhythm patterns onto drums of different timbral qualities" (regardless of whether or not they are Malay in origin).
6. Play track 2'00" to 2'45"
7. Repeat #5, #6.
8. "Play the piece without the recording".
9. "Play with the recording, checking for accuracy".

10. Play track 2'00 to 2'45".

11. Recommend that students explore the internet for examples of silat movements that they may wish to add to each of the rhythm patterns they perform.

12. Arrange for a percussionist to visit the music class for purposes of facilitating performance techniques on available percussion instruments. While a specialist in Malay music is ideal, a community musician with performance expertise on various percussion instruments can be musically enlightening.

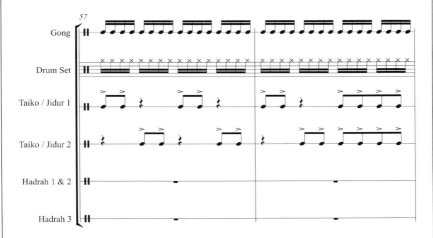

Figure 3.3 Notation reference for Kecuh! Riuh! Gemuruh!

Courtesy of NADI Singapura, transcribed by Riduan Zalani

Sub-Saharan Collective Song

Given the many repetitions they've experienced by listening in response to directed questions, and in the course of learning to sing various components of the song, students can arrive to Enactive Listening with a clear conception of how the song goes. In earlier episodes of Attentive Listening (2.3) and Engaged Listening (3.3), they felt the pulse of the song and moved to it. They also sang short word-length phrases of the song, added other phrases in Engaged Listening, and learned how the phrases are stitched together. In Episode 3.6, students are invited to sing "Nange" ["Yange"] with and without the recording. They may trip up on some of the words, but through the practice of pronouncing them rhythmically, they will gradually come to singing them in the smooth flow that edges in on the actual sound of the Wagogo singers. As students join their voices together in this solid call-and-response form, they can explore how, in the true Wagogo spirit, the music leads to movement that solidifies the experience of "Nange" as a collective song that is intended to be sung and danced simultaneously.

Episode 3.6: Sub-Saharan Collective Song
"Nange" ["Yange"]
(Learning Pathway #3)

Specific Use: Early Childhood, Elementary Music Education, Choral Ensembles

Materials:

- "Nange", from the album, *Tanzania—Tanzanie: Chants*

Procedure:

1. "Sing aloud 'Nange, Nange' each time it occurs in the song". [Note: "Yange Yange" may be substituted.]
2. Play track to 0'29".
3. "Repeat these words: 'Nange Nange', 'sahani yangu', and 'adukila'". Note: These words can be delivered rhythmically only, or as sung phrases.
4. "Sing aloud 'Nange Nange' and 'adukila' as these phrases appear in the song". Note: The second phrase is elongated, even played with, and can only be learned by listening carefully.
5. Play track to 0'29".
6. Divide the group into two parts, one group assigned to sing "Nange Nange" and the other to sing "adukila" with the recording. (In another run, ask the groups to switch parts).
7. Play track to 0'29".

8. "Sing the phrase 'sahana yangu' each time it occurs in the song".

9. Play track to 0'29".

10. "Sing the song—all parts—altogether, with the recording". [Note: Encourage students to feel the rhythm, nodding their heads, swaying to the pulse.]

11. Play track to 0'29".

12. Play track again for opportunities to sing with and without the recording. Select a soloist, or a small group, to sing "Nange Nange" while the remainder of the group sing the "sahana yangu adukila".

13. Listen further to 0'45", clapping the pulse along with the singers and learning by ear to sing the next section of "Nange" in two parts. (This step is well-suited to more experienced singers in upper elementary school and in secondary school choral ensembles.)

14. Arrange for a community musician with choral expertise, ideally with expertise in sub-Saharan African choral music, to lend a hand in shaping a coalescing choral sound while also demonstrating basic movement that supports the musical feel of the piece.

Nange (Yange), melody line

1. Nan - ge Nan - ge (na - in-di-ye) sa-ha-ni Nan - ge a - du-ki - la
2. Ya - ngu Ya - ngu (na - in-di-ye) sa-ha-ni Ya - ngu he-du-ki - la

Nange (Yange), in two parts

Figure 3.4 Notation reference for Nange and Nange (2-part)

Figure 3.4 (Continued)

The Flow From Engaged Listening to Enactive Listening

In learning a new or culturally unfamiliar musical work, World Music Pedagogy centers on a process of continuous and evermore thorough-going listening so that, with each repetition, the work becomes increasingly familiar. Taking two WMP dimensions together, there is a flow that occurs from Engaged Listening to Enactive Listening, as learners can move seamlessly from minimal to maximal participation, from singing a single line or playing a single part to performing all parts right along with the recording (and eventually without need for the recording). The adage "One thing leads to another" is apropos here. The following four episodes illustrate that where the extent of participation grows from contributing one part to the layering in of additional parts, it's only a matter of time (and continued run-throughs) until all the multiple parts are sounding together. Through the listening act, Participatory Musicking evolves until the music is learned inside out and becomes "performance-ready". Afghan, African American file-and-drum, Balinese *gamelan*, and Bluegrass music selections exemplify the flow of Engaged Listening to Enactive Listening, where the ear carries learners all the way in to the music as an act of performance. This Engaged-Enactive Listening continuum suggests that the two dimensions have no boundaries, but that one dimension blurs into the next, as Episodes 3.7 to 3.10 do illustrate. Teachers, all alone or with community musicians, can help to buoy students through the experience of learning to listen—and listening to learn the music all the way to a higher performance level.

Melody in Perpetual Afghan Motion

With the assumption that "Qataghani" has already been introduced through a series of question-directed experiences in Attentive Listening, Episode 3.7 launches into the next two dimensions of World Music Pedagogy that invite participatory musicking. With students already familiarized with the timbre of the *rebab* and the pattering sound of the *tabla* keeping the *tala* in its own intricate rhythms, they are readied for the challenges of Engaged-Enactive Listening. The piece flows in short melodic phrases on the *rubab* that are repeated, sometimes in phrases that are twice as long (and that are also repeated). Depending upon the amount of time available for this experience, just one or two phrases may be learned by listening: Sung silently, then aloud, and then played on various available instruments.

Episode 3.7: Melody in Perpetual Afghan Motion
"Qataghani"

Specific Use: Elementary Music Education, Secondary Music Innovations, Instrumental Ensembles

Materials:

* "Qataghani", from the album, "The Art of Afghan Rubab", featuring Homayoun Sakhi

Procedure:

1. "Listen, tap the pulse, and sing (inside, not aloud) the melodic phrases that are repeated as many as four times and that may return later in subtle variation".
2. Play track to 1'26".
3. "Sing aloud the first phrase, which is repeated four times, while tapping the pulse". (Notice that the third and fourth phrases contain one slightly varied pitch, while otherwise they are the same phrase.)
4. Play track to 0'10".
5. Repeat #3, #4.
6. "Play the first phrase on available instruments: Piano/keyboard, guitar, ukulele, flute, recorder, violin, and other instruments".
7. Play track to 0'10".
8. Repeat #6, #7.
9. "Sing aloud the second phrase, which is twice as long as the first phrase and is repeated only once".
10. Play track from 0'11" to 0'20".
11. Repeat #9, #10.
12. "Play the second phrase on available instruments".
13. Play track from 0'11" to 0'20".
14. Repeat #12, #13.
15. "Sing aloud the third phrase, which may remind you of the first phrase in length and pitch content and is repeated only once".
16. Play track from 0'20" to 0'25".
17. Repeat #16, #17.
18. "Play the third phrase on available instruments".
19. Play track from 0'26 to 0'32".
20. Repeat #19, #20.
21. Continue this pattern of listening and singing phrases and then playing them as time and interest allows.

Figure 3.5 Notation reference for Qataghani

22. Sing and play selected phrases with and without the recording.
23. Challenge students to listen and notate these melodic phrases. Notation follows.
24. Seek out a musician of Afghan musical expertise or of South Asian (Indian or Pakistani) training and experience to visit class in order to perform, demonstrate rabab or other melody instrument from the area, or share insights on playing *tabla* and keeping tala.

Mississippi-Style Fife and Drum

Past the point of first listening experiences that Attentive Listening offers, with directives for students to identify the instrument, feel the pulse, and imagine the possible context, location, and function of the music, Episode 3.8 shifts "Oree" over to Participatory Musicking opportunities. Both Engaged Listening and Enactive Listening are in operation in the episode below, as learners listen and clap and then play on hand drums the repeated rhythm and transfer their sung melodies to flute (or fife or recorder or other available instruments). Pedagogically, there is a progressive flow from clapping and tapping the rhythm to singing the melody to combining sung melody with rhythm to sounding the melody instrumentally. The melody is redundant but vigorous and vibrant; this eases the learning of the melody from 0'10' to 0'25", after which the melody sounds three sustained pitches in closure to the section. Should learners manage to perform a full 22 seconds of this selection, they will have mastered enough music to use for a street parade (or procession down the hall of the school or community center).

Episode 3.8: Mississippi-Style Fife and Drum
"Oree"

Specific Use: Early Childhood, Elementary Music Education, Secondary Music Innovations, Instrumental Ensembles

Materials:

- "Oree", from African American Fife & Drum Music: Mississippi, featuring Ed and Lonnie Young
- Hand drums, flute (fife or recorder)

Procedure:

1. "Listen and clap the clapping pattern (and/or tap/pat the drumming pattern)".
2. Play track to 0'32".
3. Repeat #1, #2.
4. "Listen and hum (or sing on 'loo') the melody".
5. Play track from 0'10" to 0"25".
6. Repeat #4, #5.
7. "Listen and sing on 'loo' the melody while clapping the rhythm (and/or tapping/patting the drumming pattern)". (It may be effective to divide the group into two parts, one of which sings the melody while the other claps or plays the rhythm. The two groups can also be invited to switch parts.)
8. Play track from 0'10" to 0'25".

Figure 3.6 Notation reference for Oree

9. Repeat #7, #8.
10. "On fife, flute, or recorder, play the melody with and without the recording".
11. Play track from 0'10" to 0'25".
12. Repeat #10, #11.
13. Add another brief melodic phrase (of sustained 5, 4, and 1 pitches), from 0'25" to 0'32", to listen to, hum, or sing on "loo" and play on fife-like instruments. Encourage the tapping out of the drum patterns. Build in repeated attempts to listen, sing, and play, as per earlier steps in the sequence.
14. Practice playing on flute (or fife or recording) and hand drum with and without the recording (from 0'10" to 0'32").
15. Arrange for a visit with a community musician who plays flutes, including the reed flutes that are heard in the American South, to show them and share them with students.

Cluster-Sounds From Bali

The brilliance of the Balinese *gamelan angklung* is featured in this example. Initial listening that is directed to the pulse, the periodic sound of the singular *gong*, the undulating melody, and the bright timbre of the bronze xylophones opens up students to the participatory musicking possibilities of this village music. The music is old, if not ancient, and yet it is vibrant and energized. The *gamelan angklung* instruments are coordinated to fit well with each other: metallophones, *gong* chimes, *gongs*, drums, and cymbals. The metallophones come in pairs, and one of them is tuned slightly higher than the other, thus giving off a resonance that beats and shimmers. Double-headed conical drummers are also featured, called *kendang*, and these play the role of conductor to signal starts and stops and dynamic levels. "Godeg Miring" is ceremonial music that is played at a temple festival. The interlocking parts are characteristic of a style known as "kebyar", and the first section can function as a stand-alone piece that provides an exciting introduction to Balinese musical culture. Episode 3.9 assumes earlier experiences in Attentive Listening, and the Engaged-to-Enactive Listening dimensions flow together as students are invited to listen, sing, move, and then play (at a fast tempo) this beautiful music.

Episode 3.9: Cluster-Sounds From Bali "Godeg Miring"

Specific Use: Early Childhood, Elementary Music Education, Secondary Music Innovations, Choral Ensembles

Materials:

- "Godeg Miring", from the album *From Kuno to Kepyar: Balinese Gamelan Angklung*

Procedure:

1. "Listen, sing the melody on 'loo', and pat the gamelan angklung's melodic rhythm, alternating hands due to the fast tempo".

2. Play track to 0'15".

3. Repeat #1, #2.

4. Divide the group into singers and patters. At track 0'15", after three revolutions of the melody, facilitate the switch of parts so that singers are patting and patters are singing.

5. Play track to 0'34".

6. Repeat #4, #5.

7. On metal or bronze xylophones (or classroom xylophones), challenge students to find the melody they've been singing. Note that the starting pitch is approximately "A" and allow students to work out a playing of the melody, encouraging them to sing as they play. Encourage them to use two mallets, which will help them keep up their playing at a very fast tempo.

8. Play the track to 0'34" often so that students can play with and without the Balinese gamelan sound.

9. Repeat #7, #8.

10. Suggest to learners that they add a single-pitch *gong* tone, performing the periodic sound of the tonic pitch, ideally a pitch approximating "A". As well, a drum can be added to sound the melodic rhythm, using two hands in order to keep up with the fast tempo. As before, learners may play with and without the recording.

11. Suggest a form for the composition, performing the melody at louder and softer dynamic levels, allowing the drummer to lead in changing the dynamic level of the melody over eight revolutions: soft-soft-soft-loud-loud-loud-soft-loud.

12. Host a musician or dancer from Bali or neighboring Java, both parts of the nation of Indonesia, to help in rehearsing the phrases and shaping a form for the composition.

Figure 3.7 Notation reference for Godeg Miring

The Grass Is Blue

The well-known old-time and bluegrass tune "May the Circle Be Unbroken" is a favorite for musicians who gather on back porches, in living rooms, in church basements, at picnics and in parks, and on the stages of summer festivals. It may strike some students as vaguely familiar, if only in that the style relates to country (or country western) music that is internationally known through the music industry that permeates the market and perpetuates it. Episode 3.10 is exemplary of the Engaged Listening and Enactive Listening components of World Music Pedagogy and builds from initial experiences in Attentive Listening in which students would have been directed to identify the instruments; sort out the message of the lyrics; and respond to questions of tempo, meter, and form. The melody and its lyrics are learned by listening, singing along with the recording on the chorus, and shifting from listening to the verse to singing the chorus as it comes around again and again. The chordal accompaniment is straightforward in its I-IV-V harmony and is best honed by playing with the recording. Over time and through many listenings, students can learn to sing harmony, trying out one and then another "voice", or part, that they can decipher on the recording.

Episode 3.10: The Grass is Blue
"Let that Circle Be Unbroken"
(Engaged-Enactive Listening)

Specific Use: Elementary Music Education, Secondary Music Innovations, Instrumental Ensembles

Materials:

- "Let That Circle Be Unbroken", from the album "Doc Watson and Clarence Ashley 1960 through 1962"
- Guitars

Procedure:

1. "Listen and sing the melody of the song's chorus".

    Will the circle be unbroken by and by, Lord, by and by.

    There's a better home awaiting in the sky, Lord, in the sky.

    (Note: The chorus may begin with "Will", "Let", or "May".)

2. Play track from start to 1'02", noting that the chorus begins at 0'35".
3. Repeat #1, #2.
4. "Listen to the verses and sing the chorus each time it rolls around".
5. Play track all the way through, noting that the chorus appears three times at 0'35"–1'02", 1'28"–1'55", and 2'48"–3'15".

6. Repeat #5, #6.

7. "Sing the verses of the song, as well as the chorus".

> I was standing by the window on one cold and cloudy day
> When I saw the hearse come rolling for to take my Mother away.
> Chorus
> Hey Undertaker, her Undertaker, Undertaker please drive slow
> For that body you are holding, Lord, I hate, I hate to see her go.
> Chorus
> I went back home my home was lonesome, Missed my mother she was gone
> All my brothers, sister crying in our home so sad and alone.
> Chorus
> Well, I followed close behind her, tried to hold up and be brave
> But I could not hide my sorrow when they laid her in the grave.
> Chorus

8. Play track all the way through, singing along with the recording.

9. Invite students to play the chordal accompaniment on guitars, with and without the recording. The chords are noted below for the chorus, and this progression transfers precisely to the verses.

> D   D   G   D
> Will the circle be unbroken by and by, Lord, by and by,
> D   D   A   A7 D
> There's a better home awaiting in the sky, Lord, in the sky.

10. Encourage students to listen carefully to the recording in learning to sing harmony on the chorus. Repeated listening can assist in learning to harmonize, as well as playing the chords on guitar and vocalizing chord tones above and below the melody (especially thirds and fifths).

11. Invite a guitarist and singer of the bluegrass tradition, or related genres of old-time music and Country, to facilitate the learning of the guitar and singing style.

12. Watch/listen to "The History of Country Music 04 Bluegrass", with attention to the evolving "NewGrass" sound, featuring Ricky Skaggs, Emmylou Harris, the Louvin Brothers, Alison Krauss, and Ralph Stanley: www.youtube.com/watch?v=p0qIUJlhC2g

13. Listen to "May the Circle Be Unbroken" in a rendition by the Virginia Mountain Boys Old Time Bluegrass: www.folkways.si.edu/the-virginia-mountain-boys/old-time-bluegrass-from-grayson-and-carroll-counties-virginia-vol-3/music/album/smithsonian.

Listening Collaboratory: Students-Teachers-Artists-Culture-Bearers

Listening to music can be passive, where the sounds wash over us, traveling "in one ear and out the other". Then we are simply "hearing" the music, having the capacity to sense and perceive its nuances but paying it little mind, or choosing intentionally not to know it. Listening can also be active, concentrated, requiring students to give focus and take hold of the music, particularly as they join in the making of the music.

Through various episodes in Engaged Listening and Enactive Listening, students are invited into Participatory Musicking experiences that ensure their understanding of music that initially may have been culturally unfamiliar to them but which gradually settles in and becomes a part of their musical selves. Their teachers and community musicians are key to their progress as listeners, participants, performers, and eventually creators. When they are guided to tune their ears to the wide array of the world's musical cultures, students come to know more of the musical world, and their musical growth is exponential when they are led to launch from listening into the capacity to contribute as singers and players (dancers, too) to the music as it sounds. Then, with the help of facilitating teachers alone and together with community musicians, students "become the music" by making it, eventually without need of recordings to back them up. At that stage, they have learned the music to be able to perform it, unassisted by recordings any longer.

Schools, and more than a few community sites, too, are places where listening collaboratories are a natural presence. In classrooms and in rehearsal halls, practice studios, and community centers, for example, students, teachers, and artists can listen and learn music together. Because music teachers are musically smart, they can decipher in advance the recorded music they themselves did not study, in preparation for leading their students into remarkable discoveries. Teachers can engage in advance listening in order to prepare and enable themselves to model the music for students vocally and/or on instruments. These instruments may be those from the origin cultures or on readily available instruments that substitute for the Japanese *koto,* Egyptian *'ud,* Swiss alphorn, Irish harp, or Andean *kena* (flute). Community musicians and culture-bearers who visit with students are well-equipped to lead experiences as they perform and demonstrate music of their heritage on various instruments, vocal styles, and musical forms. A listening collaboratory is a space and time in which all present can access the essence of musical cultures through active and interactive experiences in listening and doing. Excursions into Participatory Musicking are grounded experiences, too, such that these meaningful encounters offer new understandings that integrate well with the knowledge base and that provide memories that do not fade.

Quetzal Flores, "Artivista" Activist Musician

Quetzal Flores is on a mission that can only happen with the combination of qualities that he possesses, chiefly a love of music and a desire to connect people in music and through music. He plays a variety of Mexican-flavored "lutes", that is, plucked guitar-like instruments: the *jarana* (a small guitar with double strings), *requinto* (a small and higher-pitched guitar with 4–5 nylon strings that is played with a long

Quetzal Flores (standing), "Artivista" Activist Musician

pick), *bajo sexto* (a 12-string guitar in 6 double courses), as well as electric and acoustic guitars. He has mastered a style known as *son jarocho*, a musical tradition from the coastal area of Veracruz, Mexico, that mixes indigenous, Spanish, and African sounds in songs that tell of love and romance, local Veracruz scenes, and the lives of sailors and cattlemen, and which also occasionally carry messages to convey struggle and protest. Quetzal counts as his major influences the Veracruz musicians Ramón Gutiérrez, Laura Rebolloso, Benito Cortes, Patricio Hidalgo, and Cesar Castro, all who are master musicians of the *son jarocho* style, as well as Dante Pascuzzo, Rocio Marron, and Johnny Marr. He grew up in a family of farmworker-organizer social activists. In the band he started up in Los Angeles in the mid-1990s, called "Quetzal", he was aiming at creating music that could express the stories of people in struggle. In East L.A., in the barrio, he helped to revive the traditional *son jarocho* music of Veracruz and to graft it with the Chicano rock music he knows well. His partner, Martha Gonzalez, is lead singer, percussionist, and songwriter in the group. In 2013, Quetzal, the band, was awarded a Grammy for the Best Latin Pop, Rock, or Album with its recording of *Imaginaries*. Their 2017 recording, "The Eternal Getdown", draws together a mix of sounds that include R&B, rock, *son jarocho*, Japanese *taiko*, and Afro-Cuban flavorings in paying tribute to the power of music among people. Alongside the recordings, the touring, and the teaching, Quetzal Flores and Martha Gonzalez make time to work with disenfranchised youth in their Collective Songwriting projects.

Q: Do you think that children/youth should experience and study music of their local community cultures?
A: Absolutely. Studying local traditional music establishes a platform from which children/youth can catapult. It creates a real sense of belonging, confidence, and power that extends to other facets of their lives. Local practices also help us to understand the interconnectedness of being. The myth of the sole genius emerging from nowhere is ridiculous and untrue. We all emerge from communities of practice and have received information from people who received it from others and so on and so forth down the line.

Q: Do you think that children/youth should experience and study music of people and places throughout the world?
A: Much like language, music offers an insight into the subtle intricacies of a culture. By studying music from around the world, children/youth are creating pathways for the possibilities of knowing their world just a little bit better.

Q: Talk about your teaching of children and youth.
A: I teach in community settings, not in schools. My work is based on building spaces where different forms of learning can happen and where everyone has an important role to play in learning/sharing. People learn the music by spending lots of time together, singing and playing, and through repetition, doing the same basic thing over and over again, they come into the sound. We model the need for simplicity in music and the virtuosity within it. My teaching is mostly by way of oral tradition, modeling, and repeating, using simple chord charts or lead sheets.

Q: Do you ever play recordings of the music you want them to learn?
A: Yes. Listening is just as important as performing the music to develop a deeper understanding of what and where the music is made of.

Q: Do you teach young people to be musically creative?
A: Part of what I teach is something called Collective Songwriting. It's a cultural convening method that puts the work of composition in the hands of a community. Improvisation is also a big part of the traditions I navigate. Bonding is important to the process. Building trust and fluidity in a space where people gather is essential to sustaining their motivation.

Q: Could you share an example of your work with children?
A: My son, who has just turned 13 years old, is a talented composer of many genres. His journey begins in the *son jarocho* tradition that my partner and I belong to. Making sure he understood that he had a role to play at the communal celebrations called *Fandangos* has led him to see music as a normal part of social life. "It's what we do". On any given day we grab a number of traditional instruments and "jam" in our living room. When I ask him if he'd like to be a "professional" musician, he says that it doesn't interest him and that he'd rather continue experiencing music in social settings.

Q: What do you see as the purpose of the music (and music learning) experience?
A: My purpose is to put music into the hands of others in order to provide mobility or pathways towards belonging.

Learning by Ear: The Way of the World's Musicians

While much of Western art music is preserved in notation, most of the world's music is transmitted orally and received aurally. Thus, the teaching-learning process links the source of the sound to the recipient's ear. For performers of popular music and folk music across the world, and of much of the art music and deep heritage music of Asia, the African continent, and the Americas, becoming a musician is an oral-aural adventure. Standard Western staff notation is a clever invention, an early and continuing technology of sorts that grants access to those who have acquired the means of decoding symbols into sounds. So, too, do the multiple notation systems found across time and place, where numbers and characters communicate pitch information and other symbols and spacings convey information on durations, or rhythm. While notation does not fully represent music's sonic complexities, it conveys a hefty bundle of information. Still, so much of the world's art, folk, and popular music is transmitted and received via the oral tradition. Learning music by ear is thorough-going and complete, even when notation is available, for the comprehensive manner in which the sound then travels directly from the source to the ear, and the music that pours into the listener can then be danced, sung, and played.

Participatory Musicking, all the way from early inroads into the music to a fully realized performance, flows well and is enhanced through the oral-aural process. Learning music by ear is neither necessarily easy nor quick, and it is often a time-consuming pathway to learning. However, with a careful sequencing of WMP's Engaged Listening and Enactive Listening procedures, the learner can become the music she or he hopes to make.

References

Campbell, P. S. (2018). *Music, education, and diversity: Bridging cultures and communities*. New York: Teachers College Press.

Keil, C., & Feld, S. (1994). *Music grooves*. Chicago: University of Chicago Press.

Small, C. (1998). *Musicking*. New York: Oxford University Press.

Turino, T. (2007). *Music as social life*. New York: Oxford University Press.

Listening Episodes

"Godeg Miring", Gamelan Angklung, www.folkways.si.edu/gamelan-angklung-mas-village/godeg-miring/sacred-world/music/track/smithsonian

"Kecuh! Riuh! Gemuruh!", Riduan Zalani and NADI Singapura, https://itunes.apple.com/sg/album/kata-kita-kota/id924288831

"Nange" ["Yange"], Tanzanian Wagogo musicians, https://itunes.apple.com/us/album/tanzania-tanzanie-chants-wagogo/424221991

"Oree", Ed and Lonnie Young, www.allmusic.com/album/sounds-of-the-south-4-cds-mw0000619631 (CD4 Track 25)

"Qataghani", Homayoun Sakhi, www.folkways.si.edu/homayun-sakhi/music-of-central-asia-vol-3-the-art-of-the-afghan-rubab/islamica-world/album/smithsonian

"Todo lo que Tengo", Quetzal, www.folkways.si.edu/quetzal/imaginaries/latin/music/album/smithsonian

"Will the Circle be Unbroken", Doc Watson and Clarence Ashley, www.folkways.si.edu/doc-watson-and-clarence-ashley/original-folkways-recordings-1960-1962/american-folk-old-time/music/album/smithsonian

4

Performing World Music

In the basement of a public library is a community space, an airy room with a capacity of 140. This room is used for storytelling sessions, book clubs, author lectures, and even the occasional piano or flute recital. There is a lectern at the front, a raised platform, a screen for films, a long table, moveable chairs, a shiny Yamaha baby grand piano, and a set of high windows that look up and out to the tapered lawn and landscape. When Mrs. Youngman, a high school music teacher, learned of the room, a lightbulb of an idea popped on as she saw a new use for it. She thought that there, in that space, lay the opportunity to bridge school and community groups in a musical way. She talked with the librarians, who were intrigued and open to the greater community use of the space, and then she immediately connected with her music teaching colleagues in the school district and with local performing musicians and private studio-lesson music teachers and performing musicians. Within two months' time, they announced the establishment of a Fortnightly Musical Club in the library's basement, a musical gathering scheduled for the second and fourth Sunday afternoons of each month for the purpose of performing, participating in, and listening to music. "Music of every style, and for every taste", Mrs. Youngman, the club's president, insisted.

Mrs. Youngman now schedules events in the library basement that feature a grand variety of musicians available in the community. Her own "Triple Trio" is one of these features, which consist of an all-girl's vocal consort of nine singers with whom she works after school in performing everything from madrigals to "African music", show tunes, and vocal jazz. Mr. Harmon's Hoover High School jazz group has performed there in the library, too, as have the string quartet, the wind quintet, "Engine Room", a percussion group from Riverview High School; the Westside Christian handbell choir; the North Woods mariachi; the McKinley High School gospel choir; and the "Comp Studio" of student composers working with a local composer-producer. Since the inception of the Fortnightly Music Club, the musical possibilities have widened. Private teachers of piano, flute, violin, saxophone, and guitar vie for time in the basement of the library for their annual student recitals. Across the year, the

Fortnightly Musical Club has featured culture-bearing community musicians, too, who perform music from their homelands: A Balkan dance group (with two violinists, one guitarist, and an accordion-player), a Puerto Rico bomba *drum-and-dance group, a small-sized Chinese "chamber" orchestra, and a Filipino* kulintang *ensemble of many gongs. Audiences of these varied events consist of family and friends of the performing musicians, music fans and curiosity-seekers, and library patrons who are drawn by "the sounds from below" to the basement room.*

To be sure, the Fortnightly Musical Club exists for bringing more varied musical expressions on a regular basis into the public sphere. The events are free, families with children often comprise the audiences, and schoolchildren (and their teachers) have every opportunity to enjoy local and more globally travelled music, music that is popular or more "serious", and music that has students performing with experienced musicians. Librarians are astonished, too, by the number of requests for recordings following club events. When she asked one high school student, Kevin, why he was so feverishly in search of Korean traditional music, Mrs. Youngman learned that he had been drawn by the music of the kayagum *(zither), by the discipline and deportment of the musician, and by the embodied spirit of Korean national heritage—something he had not realized until his musical encounter with the musicians one Sunday afternoon in the basement of the library. Now Kevin wanted an earful of the music, and he ventured to say, too, that "I might just want to take up the* kayagum. *Why not? It's a beautiful thing". For many of the library's concertgoers like Kevin, there is a genuine enthusiasm and a little bit of awe that there could be so many musical riches in their very own community. In her role as a public school music teacher, Mrs. Youngman is successfully redefining music education as having a broad bandwidth that extends from school to community and across a vast range of musically expressive practices. Her Fortnightly Musical Club has opened the door to all manner of performing world music.*

Performance as a Natural Human Need

The human capacity for musical expression is made manifest in the act of performing the music. In every culture, people make music in songs and via instruments and, as some cultures would insist, through dance as well (Wade, 2004). Even young children make music because they simply must, singing it, rhythmicking it in vocalized chants and songs and in various body percussion activities such as clapping, patting, and stamping (Campbell & Wiggins, 2013; Whiteman & Lum, 2012). Their repertoire is shaped by forces before and beyond their formal music education, in the family and through the media, as well as by what musically happens to them in school music classes. Older children and adolescents do not lose the penchant to perform, either (although they may be selective about which music they make). They benefit greatly from opportunities to express their feelings within stylistic parameters with which they are familiar, venting their emotional energy and finding their connections with members of a school or community choir, band, or orchestra or a class of guitarists, keyboard players, song-writers, or *sambanistas* (i.e., samba musicians). Vocally and with instruments of every imaginable type, the world's people are known to express themselves musically on instruments made of skins, woods, and metals, by channeling air through tubes and horns and by plucking, picking, and bowing strings. When they are led, encouraged, or inspired by experienced music educators and community musicians, students can go full tilt in realizing through performance their deeply human musical capacity.

Acts of performing music happen in many settings and circumstances, from community centers to theaters, shopping malls, libraries, streets, places of worship, parks, early childhood centers, hospitals, residences (including homes and apartment complexes), senior centers, and—of course—schools. Live music happens, even in a time of mediated and mobile-channeled music. Performances can be traced to the efforts of experienced musicians, including certified music educators and community musicians, who are committed to developing their students' musical skills and repertoire vocally and on instruments. These same musicians, and particularly school music educators, are well-positioned to open students to music's wide span of expressive practices. Even the "young learners" of preschools and kindergartens, the "first-timers"

Figure 4.1 Burmese harp master U Win Maung (far left) in concert with his community of Saung Kuk students

who are just entering into a new musical culture or genre, and learners who identify as "occasional musicians" (who are casually enrolled in a music course) can know the joy of entering into the performance act. They delight in singing a song's refrain, playing a recurring rhythm, and finding the footwork that sails them around a dancing circle and any of this activity can be upshifted into full-fledged musical works for a public program. Quite reasonably, we can thank a teacher for much of the live music that is present in schools and communities. Of course, acts of performing music can happen nearly anywhere and anytime that people assemble for the purpose of musicking adventures, and it is particularly likely when music teachers and community musicians are working together to organize, facilitate, and inspire the performance.

This chapter describes multiple scenarios and settings in which music is made and offers details of schools and communities engaging separately and together in acts of performing world music. It describes musical diversity as it exists in particular communities, and it visits several stellar programs that involve children and adults alone and together in performance and Participatory Musicking. It considers the musical wealth that is everywhere evident in communities and takes into account the bridges that are being made between schools and communities in performing world music. Thematic content of selected public performances is sampled, and the combined wisdom of teachers and community musicians is noted in descriptions of successful efforts to shape powerful programs that envelop the world's musical cultures. The wisdom of three outstanding community musicians, and their knowledge of the music and pedagogical techniques of their three distinctive cultures, is highlighted as well in order to understand music and learning as a cross-cultural phenomenon. All components lead to an understanding of performance in public programs that feature the world's musical cultures.

Through World Music Pedagogy strategies that support the premise of learning by listening (and learning by "doing the music", too, in engaged and enactive experiences), students are thus readied for performing world music in public venues. Yet questions still abound for teachers who understand that public performances necessitate thoughtful preparations: Who performs? What are the dynamics of the community in which the music is performed? What are the expectations of audience members? Who performs? What music should be performed (and what music should remain outside the scope of a public performance)? What interactions are there among performers and audience members? To what extent is a public performance a "straight-ahead concert"? How do some programs develop participatory moments so that all present in the performance space can join in some way in the musical act? How does one set up for successful performances that both entertain and educate students who perform as well as their audiences, both musically and culturally? World Music Pedagogy is an apt approach to acts of performing world music, and this chapter suggests ways to pull off a musical experience that is treasured by all involved.

For those music teachers and community musicians who are informed by World Music Pedagogy, earlier and continuing exposure, experience, and education are acknowledged and assumed so that the music can be "enacted" and brought to the level of full-out public performance. Music once listened to intently by students (mostly via recordings, although sometimes "live" as well as performed by community musicians) becomes music made by students without the need for recordings anymore and offered as programs for the public. As Chapters 1, 2, and 3 have demonstrated, listening is at the core of learning world music, whether the music is vocal or instrumental, urban or rural in nature, culturally familiar or unfamiliar, current or from a stylistic tradition that hails from a distant place (or historic past). Thus, WMP's Attentive Listening acquaints learners to a musical work, Engaged Listening leads learners to joining in with the music via partial participation, and Enactive Listening invites learners into singing or playing (or dancing, too, as it is culturally appropriate) in a complete and thorough fashion. Even when notated scores are available commercially, or because the music has been transcribed by the teacher or even by students, the point of World Music Pedagogy is to allow learning to be achieved as it is in so many of the world's musical cultures—orally and aurally. Then the listening experiences lead to skills and understandings necessary to ensure the music as "ready for prime time", to be shared in public programs. Performing world music is thus a result of earlier pedagogical dimensions that support learning by ear. The featured music of the three learning pathways, of all the episodes (in Chapters 2, 3, 5, and 6), and for which listening episode links are provided at chapter ends were carefully selected as performance-possible through the recommended strategies that span the WMP dimensions. Through the experiences of the many episodes that are taught and facilitated, students acquire the necessary knowledge and skills to successfully make their way to performing world music.

The Presence of WMP in Public Programs

While it is established that "World Music Pedagogy" is a journey by learners into knowing the world's music, the musicians, and culture, it is also true that the combination of WMP dimensions in the capable hands of teachers and community musicians can contribute in remarkable ways to a successful public performance. Not only are these dimensions aligned with the everyday teaching-learning process, but they can also appear as a presence within public performance programs, thus educating audiences, too, in the music and its cultural meaning.

Attentive Listening

Audience members are there at a musical event to experience music as it is performed live. Yet rather than "taking a sound bath" and tuning out, they can be guided in subtle ways into thoughtful listening by the students, the community musicians, and the teachers. A concert program of live music may offer culturally familiar and unfamiliar musical works and a chance for listeners to open their ears to something other than a typical day's worth of talk and commodified sound. Whether the live performance features a Tex-Mex *conjunto* selection, an Indian *bhangra* song (and dance), a choral piece from Russia, a set of Delta blues songs of African American origin, the Korean *kayagum* (zither), an Afro-Brazilian *maracatu* percussion piece, or a Syrian ensemble of *'ud* (lute), *qanun* (plucked zither), and *darabukka* (goblet drum), audiences may appreciate some assistance in following the music as it unfolds. As the dimension of Attentive Listening is typically applied to recorded music, the teacher could decide to play a brief recorded excerpt of a programed piece before it is performed live by the students, drawing the attention of the audience to the timbre of an instrument or vocal style, to the recurrence of a melodic feature, or to the significance of the text. That recording should be exceedingly brief, about 30–40 seconds, and carried into the audience by way of a high-quality sound system. A comparison of the way that "Todo lo que Tengo" (Learning Pathway #1) sounds on the recording and in live performance by the students can inform audiences of the similarities and distinctions of a piece that is expressed by professional artists (and cultural insiders) and by students who are coming into a Spanish-language Mexican ballad for the very first time. Such a brief listening moment with the original recording can reinforce for audience members the challenge that students have met in learning a musical work some distance from their cultural experience. Another means of offering an experience in Attentive Listening is to arrange for the presence of a community musician (or a full community group), providing time on the program for them and the students to perform the same piece, separately and together. Such a strategy offers the potential for comparison between community and student musicians, a certain cultural validation of the music, and a means of "authenticating" it to "keep it real". The ears of audience members perk up as they find their way into the music, tuning themselves to sonic structures that may otherwise go unnoticed.

Engaged Listening

Audience members want to be "engaged" and to be drawn into the music in one way or another, to be invited to musically participate along with the performers. Sometimes, listening in reverie is ideal, but audiences also appreciate the occasional invitation to join in on a participatory musicking experience, to contribute a rhythm, a "response" to a "call", or a songful phrase in a recurring section (such as a song's chorus). Students may sing "Nange" or "Yange" (Learning Pathway #3) together with the audience who, once hearing the work performed, can be taught to sing just the single word of the song title, on cue, as it appears in the full piece that is performed once by students and a second time for the engagement of the audience. At public performances, a community musician can be present to perform and to model a part for audience members to follow or even join in on; this modeling is a role that students or the teacher can also play, although the appearance of a community musician can add another layer of interest as well as validation. While recordings are often less likely to be of use in the context of a performance, it is conceivable to successfully insert a brief excerpt of a recording into a program as an "audience-extra segment". For example, audiences have found much delight in invitations to join a folk or social dance at the close of the concert, where recordings supply the music as students move from their performance spaces to take their places in the dancing circle to which family and friends have been invited.

Enactive Listening

In World Music Pedagogy, *Enactive Listening is the performance itself* of the music that has been previously learned through a sequence of graduated listening experiences, typically to a source recording. Beyond the actuality of Enactive Listening in the classroom, the benefit of attaining this third WMP dimension is to have attained the capacity of performing world music in the public arena. Recall that the lessons in Engaged Listening accumulate and eventually give way to Enactive Listening, the stage at which learners develop the capacity to perform it with and then without the recording. (See Chapter 3.) As a result of the journey through the episodes of the WMP dimensions, students arrive at the performance of music such as those featured in the Learning Pathways #1, Quetzal's "Todo lo que Tengo", #2 Riduan Zalani's "Kecuh! Riuh! Gemuruh!", and #3 the Wagogo song, "Nange" ["Yange"]. Of course, audiences cannot hope to perform the music as the students will do since it takes many lessons and class sessions to hone skills to the performance level that Enactive Listening represents. But they can appreciate that they are present there at the performance, the place to which the process of Enactive Listening has taken student performers.

Creating World Music

The process of creating a new musical work is another time-intensive experience, especially in the style of a world music selection or genre that is culturally unfamiliar. Composition and improvisation demand high-order knowledge and skills that can only be honed through considerable experience in and study of the music. Thus, it's not so plausible to expect this dimension to appear in full force at a public performance. Of course, the *results* of Creating World Music can be performed by the students, and video clips to document the educational process of learning to compose or improvise (in the style of a musical culture's practice) could be of interest to an audience. More fundamental creative encounters may be slipped in to a performance, too, by way of inviting the audience to sing another new ending of their own creation, on cue and altogether, or to provide rhythmic ostinati of their own invention to accompany the performance of a piece. Of course, a community musician can be called upon to lead a brief creative experience, perhaps demonstrating various musical choices vis-à-vis melody, rhythm, or text. A student performance of "Kecuh! Riuh! Gemuruh!" (Learning Pathway #2) would be likely to perk audience attention of the layering of many rhythms within the piece and could readily progress to a second time around in which audience members are invited to contribute their own layer of body percussion rhythms to add to the pulsive music.

Integrating World Music

Because music is culture, and because audiences are quite naturally interested in the human side of music and of where the music comes from, there is a wide-open expanse of ways to fit music-culture components into a public performance. The very presence of a culture-bearing community musician at a concert may be the impetus for sharing a personal story, a folk tale, a poem, a greeting, or other brief words of wisdom in the original language. This up-front-and-personal highlighting of the culture-bearing community musicians can help to connect people to people, bridging one culture to another, and to make the point of music as not only cultural but also human expression. Slides can offer a glimpse of the place and the people from which the music originates, and a brief video clip can contextualize the music that is sung, played, and danced in places of work and worship, schools, cultural centers, and family homes. Of course, the teacher and students can also be responsible for introducing the musical works and informing the audience of the cultural origin, the function and use, and the meaning of the music (and its language). The music of Andean flutes, Bulgarian bebop, Balinese *gamelan*, Puerto Rican *jibaro*, Chinese opera, and a blue-grass band come from somewhere and someone(s), and brief remarks that integrate bits of history, language, philosophical beliefs, and even scientific principles—for example, telling of the music's acoustic properties or the mechanics of playing a particular instrument—are effective ways in which Integrating World Music can play out in a public performance.

Roles, Models, and Venues for Performing World Music

Community-conscious school music performances are defined and developed by the roles people play, the performance models they choose to follow, and the venues and functions that are available for fostering occasions for performing world music. Diversity emerges not only in the actual musical selections that comprise a program but also through the contexts and purposes of a public performance, the contributions that various people make to preparing the music and fashioning the programs, and the various models that are called upon for framing the extent of the program's formality, duration, and audience expectations.

All WMP-derived performances emanating from school music programs rest upon the efforts of dedicated individuals. Naturally, musically educated and experienced teachers are central to every successful school music performance. They labor over formulating the curricular content and instructional procedures that will suit the students, the performance event, and the eventual audiences. Their expectations for students are that they "learn the music" through the channels and methods provided. Students have tasks, too, to attend regularly scheduled classes, rehearsals, and lessons so to be guided by the pedagogical strategies and sequences their teachers provide. Community musicians can be critical to daily learning and performance events, too. They are called to come forward to make appearances in the classes, the musical performance, and much more, as they offer an all-day Saturday workshop on a musical genre or instrument, a week-long (or a month-long) school residency, regularly scheduled teaching visits, and as they arrange for visits by students to their community locale. Music teachers and community musicians can work together to prepare the public performance, selecting the repertoire that they have modeled and taught and that their students have absorbed and learned. Other community members and culture-bearers (for example, a civic leader, a small business owner, a student's grandmother or uncle) may enter into the process of making more musically and culturally informed students, telling the stories behind the music, sharing language to describe its meaning to them; this they may do in a school visit or at the public performance itself. Teachers of other subjects may help to develop the theme of a public program, such as friendship, food, civic responsibility, global affairs, historic holidays, nature and the environment, and social justice, and can help focus student attention on this theme in their own classroom studies so that a more comprehensive understanding may be had of the programed music. It should not be so surprising, either, that the school administration, the janitorial staff, parents, and whole families are potential contributors to the making of a successful public performance.

WMP experiences lead to performances in school and in the community, allowing for diverse musical expressions to be widely shared. All-school programs in gyms, auditoriums, or cafeterias are effective as an exercise for creating community within the school and showcasing the ensembles for all the faculty and students to enjoy. Performances can happen within individual classrooms, when a student group or visiting artist may perform for a single classroom or a small set of classes gathered together, as in the case of a guitar ensemble performing "La Malagueña" for the

Spanish classes or a choir singing freedom songs for one or more history classes. Performances across schools give older music students a chance to share the world's music and a way to attract younger students to musical study, as in cases of middle school ensembles performing for elementary schools in the same district or high school groups touring "feeder" schools of younger students. Community venues for student performances of WMP-based selections are multiple and can be located in expected and unexpected places—from shopping malls to street corners and from community centers to festival stages. Senior centers and preschools are welcome venues for performances by school groups in combination with community musicians, and the potential is there for performances of the world's musical cultures to be held at house concerts and in apartment lobbies.

Several models of public performance are common in schools, all of which are pertinent to World Music Pedagogy and to school-community intersections. Standard at nearly all schools with music as a curricular subject are the traditional concerts that happen two or three times (or more) across the year. These are formal programs that are meant as end-points to the learning process in which students offer the products of their musical study, their very best expressions of musical repertoire—songs, instrumental works, dances, and sometimes aspects of the dramatic arts when music blends with theater, or dance, or poetry. These traditional performances may appear across the seasons, as in cases of "the winter concert" and "the spring concert", or at times of civic holidays when national heroes or historic events are honored. Formal concerts differ from "informances", those occasions that provide audiences with a glimpse of the music learning process students are experiencing and a chance to observe "musical development in motion" by way of students' evolving skills and knowledge. These informances can be "less-than-perfect" in-progress performance "reports" and sharings, informal windows into the music-educational process (as compared to formal performance events at which rehearsed and final-product pieces are presented). As well, there are the occasional participatory musicking events that are intended to attract onlookers (and onlisteners) to join in the singing, playing, and dancing in a modicum of straightforward and "nonthreatening" ways. Of course, competitive interscholastic performance events such as festivals and contests are the ultimate performance models of how perfectly polished the music may be, and secondary schools in some locations actively seek them out as a prime means of motivating students and projecting school pride. For any of these models, a diversity of the world's musical repertoire can be shared, and community musicians may serve as guest-musicians or models for students in preparation for these public performances.

Performing World Music in the Community:
Two Singaporean Events

Musical performances are alive and well across the multicultural island nation of Singapore, in communities as well as in schools. Located at the southern point of the Malay Peninsula in Southeast Asia, this city state is a crossroads of Chinese, Malay, Indian, and Western cultures and customs. It was no wonder, then, that one pleasant evening, in two separate settings in Singapore, two distinctive musical cultures were in full bloom, one featuring kompang *drums as traditional accompaniment for a Malay wedding celebration and another in a public performance of a community ensemble featuring the noble Chinese* guzheng *(zither). The two musical events were notable, too, for their functions, with one far removed from an educational context but deeply embedded in cultural practice (the wedding music) and another involving student musicians and teachers in a meticulously planned concert (the public performance). At each event, children and youth were present, absorbing but not performing the wedding music and performing in the concert program. The co-existence of traditional and contemporary music practices within the two Singaporean events was remarkable, too, as the musical selections in each of the two settings were diverse and inclusive of all present. Following are two portraits of one evening's events, just hours apart, that captivated those within earshot (including one of the authors), offering a glance at Singaporean musical communities that exist beyond the boundaries of school.*

3:00PM, August 13, at the multipurpose open-air hall of a residential estate in Singapore. We colleagues were all invited to the wedding celebration of our beloved Malay technical officer, Zul. One colleague noted his excitement in that he had never attended a Malay wedding before, but that he understood that kompang would be ushering in the bride and groom. Another colleague was fascinated by the two poles with the glossy colored strips (Bunga Manggar) *that were placed by the side of the bride and groom. The* Bunga Manggar *symbolizes prosperity and expresses the hope that the couple will have many children. As we enjoyed the lavish buffet and chatted with the groom's parents, the sounds of the kompang were heard from a distance, announcing the arrival of the bride and groom. There were about 12 kompang players in procession just behind the bride and groom, and they played their celebratory rhythms. The bride and groom moved forward to greet the guests and then proceeded to the* bersanding, *where they sat on a beautifully decorated throne and were treated as king and queen for the day while friends, relatives, and guests offered up their blessings and congratulatory messages to the newlyweds. There, the blessing ceremony transpired, followed by the photo session with family and friends. The* kompang *players seasoned the celebratory music with occasional contemporary rhythms and offered a beautiful rendition to the newly married couple of a lyrical poem sung in Arabic known as ghazal. This traditional Malay wedding was replete with ritual that was underscored and extended by the presence of the* kompang *players.*

6:00PM, August 13, at the Lee Foundation Theatre of the Nanyang Academy of Fine Arts in Singapore. From the Malay wedding, I made my way into town to an all-guzheng concert by the Guzheng Association *of Singapore. A community group comprised of professional guzheng players, school guzheng instructors, primary and secondary students, and working adults, they gather regularly to further their experiences in guzheng ensemble playing. The group's aim is also to "develop and promote uniquely Singaporean guzheng music compositions, and to promote guzheng music and foster cultural exchange in Singapore and beyond" (from the photo-laden guzheng concert program booklet, 2017). The association had commissioned two new compositions by a local composer, Ernest Thio, and had invited a guest performer, Jeffri Natawate, to play various Malay percussion instruments to accompany the guzheng at this concert. The range of traditional and contemporary guzheng repertoire presented during the concert was an indication of the interest in Chinese traditional music while also embracing diverse music cultures. Ensembles of children, youth, and instructors offered a wide spectrum of musical proficiencies and made the point that the Chinese guzheng plays Chinese music—and more—and that "world music" is possible even within the scope of a so-called "ethnic instrument".*

Program of the Guzheng Association in Singapore

"Guessing Tune" (Yunnan, China)
"The Greening" (Contemporary guzheng composition
by Inoru Miki, Japanese)
"Scenery in Four Sections"(Shandong, China)
"Southern Dialogue" (Contemporary guzheng composition by Ernst Thio,
Singaporean, blending thematic ideas of two musical narrative forms, the
Malay Dondang Sayang and the Chinese PingTan).
"Camel Bells along the Silk Road" (Work based in Middle Eastern modes)
"Sparrow Dance" (Composition by Ernest Thio, featuring guzheng tuned to
the gamelan's seven-tone pelog scale)
"Hundred Flowers" (Shanxi, China)

In a few hours, the two musical events were reinforcement of the presence of Singapore's living musical traditions today and of the penchant by players of traditional instruments to perform a blend of musical influences that are so widely available in a multicultural society. For music in Singapore is kompang *and* guzheng, *and much more, including Western art music, popular music, Indian classical music, and all the music of its local communities, its neighboring countries (such as Indonesia and the Philippines), its visiting artists from everywhere in the world, and the mediated music that is pervasive in everyday life. In that Singaporeans absorb so many diverse musical practices, then, performing world music in Singapore is an experience that potentially offers a wide world of expressive possibilities from the multicultural populations that live nearby.*

Beyond the confines of the classroom, young people such as those present at these events are experiencing music of a grand diversity, across many circumstances. Teachers can make note of the music "out there" in the community and that some of this music is already enculturated and learned by their students and may be ready to be expressed and enhanced through music education programs that can be tailor-made for them.

Performance Rules!

There are practical matters to consider in the making of in-school world music performances. As the act of performing world music tends to serve as a culmination of having learned musical content, it is also a celebration by students of their growth of musical skills and cultural sensitivity. The WMP dimensions guide the learning (and teaching) strategies and sequences that lead to public programs, while the actual performance also demands particular techniques and tactics. From veteran teachers with experience in working with community musicians and culture-bearers, and who have successfully diversified the repertoire they program for their classes and performances, come "rules" to abide by in order to guarantee rewarding experiences for their students and their audiences. They are briefly noted as recommendations to heed on matters of program themes, performer attire, staging, and audience considerations.

Program themes abound. Holidays and seasonal celebrations are common themes of school and community programs, and these fit well with ideas for featuring the fruits of World Music Pedagogy. There are the November–December holidays such as Diwali, Chanukah, Christmas, and Kwanzaa and the February–March celebrations of Chinese New Year, African American History, and St. Patrick's Day. Spring in the northern hemisphere brings more New Year celebrations (for example, Cambodian New Year in April) and Cinco de Mayo, while June opens up into summertime festivals. Rounding the bend into September, October, and November come commemorations of harvest time, Indigenous People's Day, and Thanksgiving. There are national holidays to celebrate, too, each with the potential to perform patriotic music, folk music, and other musical selections that are nationally and regionally embraced. All through the year, programs on holiday and seasonal themes join other themes already mentioned such as the environment, friendship, and peace to appeal to students and their audiences.

Although it's not a critical feature in student performances, performer attire can add flavor. If the performance is geographically or culturally themed, as in an all-Chinese or all-West African music and dance program, a basic style could be created by students and parents so that all students are uniformly outfitted in a way that represents the culture or region. A "Mandarin" collared shirt might suit an all-Chinese program, and a print *dashiki* consisting of a loose-fitting V-necked shirt or draped over-the-shoulder material could suffice in a West African program. Any clothing more involved than this could prove time-consuming and beyond budgetary means. Of course, costuming could turn essentialist, too, in that a complex culture may be too simply stereotyped (especially in view of the varied populations of West Africa and within China's national-political boundaries). With regard to programs that feature diverse cultural traditions, unless students break up into various segments of the program that feature music from here and there in the world (and this manner of dividing up students is not always advisable), then quick changes of attire by all students are probably not so feasible. Despite the appeal of traditional attire for the color and verve it presents, students may find themselves most comfortable in basic garb such as white tops and dark (black or blue) bottoms. Still, it turns out that community musicians and culture-bearers often wear their traditional clothing at school performances, and all is well so long as they themselves deem it of value in representing who they are as musicians and members of particular communities and cultures.

Sound, lighting, and staging are important considerations for enhancing performances for audiences and performers alike. Audiences need to see the performance without obstructions and to hear a performance in as "high fidelity" as possible so that they can feel more fully involved in the music as a rich and memorable event. (Of course, the musicians, too, deserve to be fairly heard and seen.) An acoustical shell helps, as do strategically placed working microphones that do not distort the sound of singers and instrumentalists. Continuing advances in technology provide the possibilities for professional studio loudspeakers (of the sort made by Dynaaudio, Genelect, and Meyer Sound) and new hardware interfaces such as keyboards and mixers that use Musical Instrument Digital Interface (MIDI) to control audio software. Teachers, community musicians, parents, and other adults, as well as students, can master the use of these tools that will provide dynamic experiences in musical sound. Lighting helps, too, and in addition to determining which ceiling lights and area lights may best shine on musicians (and how other lights can be dimmed or switched entirely off), there are emerging technologies for video projection that can add immeasurably to a more professionally oriented school production. Finally, staging is a consideration for performances, and cafeterias, gyms, and multipurpose assembly halls can be set up in ways that are conducive to a performance. If a classic stage is available, use it to full advantage. It is helpful to know the geography of the stage, to place community musicians in the direct sight-line of student musicians, to balance the stage by setting performers at stage right, left, and center, to consider points of stasis and times for onstage movement, and to ensure that performers are facing forward to the audience while performing. Audiences do not enjoy visual monotony, so variation of the physical arrangement of performers ensures greater interest. In performing world music, the presence of dance and choreographed movement in public performances cannot be emphasized enough, particularly in that so many musical cultures of the world value the integration of dance with music. Music and dance can readily be programed as opening and closing features of a performance, at strategic times elsewhere on the program, with some of this activity occurring off-stage and at the sides of the audience seating area.

Audience comfort is important and deserves advance planning. In school auditoriums and theaters where formal performances are produced, chairs may be fixed. They also may be cushioned for comfort, although inexpensive loose pillows and paddings can be made available for wood and metal surfaced seats, especially for elders in attendance. In spaces that allow various formations, semi-circles of chairs may be wrapped 180 degrees at the outside of the performance space. Similarly, a thrust theater stage allows for audiences on three sides of the stage, with the last side serving as a backdrop to the performance. More rarely, seating arranged in full circles can be effective, so long as performers are alert to the need to turn occasionally from one direction to the other around the audience circle. Audience comfort requires the regulation of temperature in the room, including the circulation of cool air in what is sometimes a crowded audience space. In any rearrangement of chairs, it's important to ensure that there are aisles to the restrooms, intermission spaces, and building exits. Audiences will prove far more enthusiastic of world music programs when they are comfortable and fully connected in the place of the performance act.

Performing World Music in Schools: Two North American Events

The North American nations of Canada and the United States boast some of the most diverse populations in the world. They are "nations of immigrants", with waves of newcomers arriving over five centuries to join indigenous populations, integrating yet sometimes also "holding their own" in the way of sustaining the cultural values and practices of the places to which they trace their families. The character of Canada and the United States rests upon immigration and the multiculturalism that resulted—and even some of the tensions that appeared over the honoring of cultural diversity while aiming for a national unity. In schools across North America, themes appear in curricular statements and on school-wide programs on topics of respect, "the culture of kindness", cultural diversity and cultural pluralism, inclusion, bridge-building, and community consciousness. Some schools reach across the world for examples of these qualities and concepts to insert into social studies, languages arts, and the expressive arts, with their teachers striving to shape understandings that are multicultural and intercultural. Other schools embrace the multicultural mission while also recognizing the heritage(s) of their own local populations, in which case curricular content (and at least one annual music program) can reflect these underserved and overlooked local cultural groups. Across several months, one of the authors witnessed public performances in celebration of the pride of heritage, each of which aimed for school-community intersections. While the music teachers in charge were particularly geared to global and local music cultures, their programs highlighted cultural heritage in ways that connected the school to the community and the students to community musicians and culture-bearers.

February 16, at the Martin Luther King Jr. Community Center. "Diaspora: African Arts in the World" is a series of music and dance performances, plays, dramatic readings, and poetry evenings in an African American neighborhood in a major East Coast city. The series runs eight months, with workshops and visual arts exhibits appearing along with performances, all intended to call attention to a myriad of expressions out of the African continent and present in the Americas, and in the Caribbean. At the Martin Luther King Jr. Community Center, a multigenerational celebration was scheduled one Saturday evening in February in commemoration of Black History Month. Local school music teachers were invited to involve their young students, the community choir of 70 adult voices was featured, and several local hip-hop artists were invited to supply their beats and messages at the close of the evening. The program was titled "An Evening of African American Song: Then and Now", and spirituals, gospel music, and children's songs were well-represented in the two-hour program. The adult choir opened with a rousing rendition of the Black national anthem, "Lift Every Voice and Sing", and all present were invited to sing. Children's songs followed, including energetic renditions of "Shortnin' Bread" and "Miss Mary Mack". Two middle school choirs and one high school choir sang an exquisite rendering of "This Little Light of Mine", which was followed by a sampling of historic spirituals: "Zekiel (Ezekiel) Saw the Wheel", "Deep River", "O Mary Don't You Weep", and "Oh Freedom". As transition from an older to a more contemporary style, the mass choir of adults and children performed "Steal Away", first as a spiritual and then again in a gospel version. Supported by a combo of local jazz musicians, including players of keyboard, bass guitar, drum set, and conga drums, the adult choir then offered powerful renditions of gospel standards, including Richard Smallwood's "Total Praise" and Kirk Franklin's "I Need You". There were interspersed commentaries that linked the songs to the social history of African Americans, sometimes with expressive readings of sung verses prior to the performance. The closing song brought everyone to their feet for a rousing performance of the joyous sound of "Oh Happy Day".

May 5 at El Centro de la La Raza. "Viva la Musica Mexicana" was the theme of a program for families that gather at La Raza, a central-city community-based organization grounded in the Latino community. At what was formerly a public-funded middle school, the center provides a bilingual multicultural program for preschool children, after-school homework sessions and arts enrichment programs, youth leadership, college and job readiness workshops, and music, dance, and poetry programs. La Raza is open to all and serves Spanish-speaking families from Mexico as well as Guatemala, Columbia, Peru, Argentina, and other Latin American nations. In celebration of the Mexican Cinco de Mayo holiday, the cafeteria, school hallways, and ground floor classrooms were bursting with bright green, white, and red colors of balloons, banners, and tissue decorations, and the spicy scent of home-made tacos and tamales drew the community to the kitchen and on with their plates to the long cafeteria tables. A low stage overflowed with singers, the girls dressed in white ruffled blouses and frilly folkloric skirts and the boys in their untucked guayabera *shirts. A* mariachi *band outfitted in their Mexican* mariachi traje de charro *suits of black trousers, short jackets, and silver buttons were standing nearby and awaiting their time. (So, too, were two music teachers present from the local public schools, at the invitation of both their students and several community musicians who were performing that evening.) To the accompaniment of four guitarists, the youth choir sang full-voiced in their youthful renderings of a set of Mexican folk songs: "A la rueda de San Miguel", "De Colores", "La Adelita", and "Las Mananitas". The families sounded their approval, and more than a few expressions of joy, or* gritos, *were vocalized in the midst of the songs as encouragement to the young singers. The choir finished their round of songs with "Cielito Lindo", at which point the two music teachers joined in on their violins to fill out the guitar accompaniment. As the young choristers bowed and then took their places with their families,* Mariachi de Costa Azul *then rose to the stage, and their program of* mariachi *favorites ensued: "El Son de la Negra", "Volver, Volver", "Si No Dejan", "El Rey", "Guadalajara", and "Cascabel". The* mariachi *had been working together for many years, sometimes in full ensemble and sometimes in trios and quartets in local Mexican restaurants, so the music (backed by the professional sound equipment they'd set up) was of highest caliber. Now the audience was roaring its approval, the* gritos *were more frequent, and the music's rhythm was visibly evident in the tapping toes, bobbing heads, and approval smiles across the cafeteria audience. The* mariachi *welcomed the two music teachers and five of their violin students up to the stage to join in the final selection. Four young ladies came forward in their flouncy and frilly wide skirts, performing in the manner of* ballet folklorica *as climax to the program. The brilliant music of La Raza's holiday celebration was a genuine declaration of Mexican pride—for every good reason*

Despite the prominence of cultural diversity in North American cities and towns, and the tendency for thoughtful music teachers to lean toward a more globally or multiculturally diverse set of musical selections in the performances of their student groups, there come community programs like these that are vibrant testimonies to a single cultural heritage. In Canada as in the United States, there are many community programs designed to celebrate First Nations groups as well as communities of Chinese, South Asian, Latin American, Southeast Asian, and British- and French-Canadian heritage and histories. Propelled sometimes by a holiday, supported by their family-filled audiences, the traditional music of a gathered community is alive and well. More often than not, students whose families are active in the preservation of heritage also may be actively musical in cultural programs. Teachers do well to stay tuned to such activity and to consider how their very own students may turn out to bear cultures well worth sharing.

Performers Who Teach (and Connect Schools to Communities)

Performing world music can be exhilarating to all concerned—students, teachers, and the musical models in the community who have long lived the music and who bear the culture from which the music emerges. As successful performances are realized through the principles outlined in World Music Pedagogy, it's worth repeating that it is through the efforts of thoughtful music teachers and teaching musicians, alone and together, that these performances are developing in the way of school-community intersections. Students of every experience rightfully should be able to rely upon professionals who provide ample opportunities for growing the necessary skills that enable their musical renderings. Alongside opportunities for students to be guided through collective listening to recorded works, through experiences that hone vital performance techniques, and by way of exploratory and experimental processes to playfully create musical possibilities, there must be these occasions for students to enjoy the presence of performing musicians, live and in person, who provide them with musical (and cultural) insights.

Coming out of three disparate communities, each one geographically distant from the next, the descriptive accounts and interviews of Marisol Berrios-Miranda (on Puerto Rican and Caribbean music), Kedmon Mapana (on music of Tanzania), and Riduan Zalani (on Malay music of Singapore) personify the very best of accomplished performing musicians who care to nurture the performing capacities of student musicians. They are performers of long-standing musical expressions within given traditions, as they also invent, through composition and improvisation, music that is personally and collectively expressive. Their instruments and genres vary, as do the venues in which they perform, from concert halls and ballrooms to restaurants to recreation centers, cafes, clubs, festivals, parks, and plazas. They recognize the importance of "passing it on", that is, of opening the ears and minds of new audiences and new generations of musicians. They speak to their own musical beginnings, their musical models and masters, and their vision of a musical education for students that pays tribute to the oral tradition and the creative impulse. They have honed pedagogical techniques that ensure joy and fulfillment in the learning process, from first experiences to the public performance.

Imagine, if you will, the outcomes of a long-term residency, weekly appearances, or even a single glorious visit by these performing musicians in a kindergarten class or with a group of fourth grade children, middle school band students, a group of high school choral singers, and students of a guitar, keyboard, percussion, or song-writing classes. Magic happens! If the particular three musicians portrayed here are not very easily accessible to the reader, there are other culture-bearing musicians in every community who can be tapped to light up the musical lives of students. As visiting artists in schools, they may teach as well as perform in the kind of public performances that bridge schools and communities.

Marisol Berrios-Miranda, Latina Musician-Educator

Marisol Berrios Miranda, Latina Musician-Educator from Puerto Rico

While she studied music academically—all the way through a PhD program in Ethno-musicology from the University of California at Berkeley, Marisol Berrios-Miranda's first musical education came from childhood spent in her native Puerto Rico. There she was soaked in music, learning from listening to her father's song and rhythms and from her mother's encyclopedic knowledge of Latin rhythm and dance. She studied music at the University of Puerto Rico, including classical piano and choral music, prior to her graduate studies in California. Her dissertation fieldwork took her to Venezuela, and she continues fieldwork projects in Puerto Rico. Dr. Berrios-Miranda is an affili-ate professor of Ethnomusicology at the University of Washington, and she teaches courses in the UW Honors College in Afro-Caribbean music and Community Music. A frequent presenter and performer at universities and in community settings in the United States, the Caribbean, and in Spain, she also has numerous publications on *salsa* and Latino identity. In collaboration with Shannon Dudley and Michelle Habell-Pallan, she published *American Sabor: Latins and Latinas in U.S. Popular Music* (University of Washington Press, 2017).

Q: What was your musical childhood like?
A: I was born in Santurce, Puerto Rico, where I was surrounded by music in the neigh-borhood, both live music and on the radio. I've danced since I can remember: *Salsa*, merengue, twist, cha cha cha, boleros, guarachas, mash potatoes, a-Go Go, and rock and roll. We sang all the time to music on the radio and on LP recordings. At Christmas time, there were the *aguinaldos* (songs) with the *parrandas* (Puerto Rican players of guitar, *cuatro*, claves, güiro, maracas, congas, bongos, trumpet, and saxophone).

Q: What are some of your favorite performers of Puerto Rican music, including those who influenced your own musical development?
A: I like pianist Ricardo (Richie) Ray for his combination of "sabor" and the virtuosity in his piano *montunos* and his amazing improvisations. Richie plays a combination of classical piano, especially Chopin, with *montunos* that are rich in rhythm harmony and melody. I was studying classical piano when I began listening to him, and he was an inspiration. I said to myself "there, you have this *salsa* pianist that integrates classical piano licks from the Western art musical repertoire, but he still plays with such *sabor* and feeling. And what divine rhythms he plays in "Aguzate" and "Sonido Bestial"!" As you hear these two pieces, you will understand.

Eddie Palmieri, pianist, composer, and arranger, is outstanding, too, as he has taken the rhythms, melodies, and harmonies of *salsa* arrangements to a higher level. He expanded the *son guaracha* format by playing longer selections with many improvised musical breaks, especially in the percussion section. He is inspiring, too, for what he has written about social justice and freedom for the Puerto Rican people.

Ismael (Maelo) Rivera, is the "Sonero Mayor". A *sonero* is the *trovadour*, one who improvises between the call and response format in *salsa* and African derived musical practices. Maelo was named "Sonero Mayor" by the great Cuban singer-composer Benny Moré in the mid-1960s because of his way of improvising lyrics in between choruses that hardly ever sound on the first beat. Instead, he sings in between the notes of the beat, floating melodies without losing his way ("amarre" or "afinque"). There are hundreds of Maelo songs that I love, but for starters I would recommend having a listen to "Las Caras Lindas de mi Gente Negra", "La Tía María", "Aguinaldo a Puerto Rico", "El Nazarene", and "Mi Negrita me Espera".

El Gran Combo de Puerto Rico, a branch from *Rafael Corijo y su combo con Ismael Rivera*, took all the musicians from Cortijo and has been playing *salsa* for 55 years. Their repertoire is vast and is some of the best *salsa* for dancing. They always kept the concept of dancing as their primary endeavor. In many interviews with Rafael Ithier Nadel and his musicians, they express their emphasis on tunes that always lit up the dancers, and that emphasis has kept them playing all over the world for more than a half century. The band is nicknamed "The University of Salsa".

Q: What salsa *recordings would you recommend for listening with selections to learn?*
A: I highly recommend listening to Eddie Palmieri's *Unfinished Masterpiece, the Sun of Latin Music*, and *Live at the University of Puerto Rico*, along with Richie Ray's *Sonido Bestial* and *Aguzate, Ismael Rivera and Cortijo y Su Combo*, and many of the recordings from the 55-year-old group known as El Gran Combo de Puerto Rico (especially "Acángana", "Arroz con Habichuelas", and "La Salsa de Hoy"—and their performance anniversary compilations: 35, 45, 50, and 55 years.)

Q: Please recommend a song that children could learn to sing and play that is distinctly Puerto Rican or Caribbean of some sort.
A: "Guantanamera" is Cuban in origin and is wonderful for its *son montuno* rhythm, the presence of just three chords, and lyrics that repeat in the chorus section. Young learners can play the rhythm on clave, conga, and piano. "Los Carreteros" is a Puerto Rican song by Rafael Hernandez, with a beautiful melody and call-and-response lyrics.

Students as young as kindergarten age and all the way through secondary school love this song.

Q: What pedagogical secrets can you share as to how you ensure that your students learn Caribbean music?
A: When I teach children and youth, the first thing I always do is to have them mark the beat (1-2-3-4) with their feet. It's important that they learn to control their bodies by concentrating on the rhythm they hear (and feel) in their feet. The key is in keeping the beat so we can then layer rhythms above the beat. We create a polyrhythmic texture by playing the patterns of the clave, the *cáscara* (timbales pattern), the conga, the *güiro*, the baseline of *salsa*, and the *montuno* patterns on the piano. There must be lots of repetition of these rhythms, and when they are solid, we learn to sing simple melodies (but with challenging phrasings).

Q: How do you use listening in the learning that you foster?
A: I always play recordings to illustrate the musical styles and forms and to illustrate different musical concepts. For example, I play a cha-cha-cha recording to illustrate a notable Caribbean rhythm that features in so many songs, which then leads to teaching students how to dance a cha-cha-cha. I play *salsa* music recordings of all sorts—not only to illustrate polyrhythms but to have students play along with the instruments on the recordings. Of course, I also teach students how to dance the *salsa* as we listen to the recordings.

Q: Can you describe your approach to learning rhythms?
A: In my lessons for children (and their teachers), I model for them the marking of the beat with their feet, moving from right to left, and they imitate me. We learn a simple rhythm to clap over the steady beat of their stepping, and next comes a song that they learn to sing while stepping and clapping. Then it's time to introduce the basic clave rhythm, which brings on a polyrhythm that many children may find challenging at first. We may sing the melody of a song like "La Cucaracha", but in *salsa* rhythm, and I may soon add the rhythms of the *güiro* and the conga, but in simplified form. Some children learn more quickly than others, and of course I'm there to help them to listen and feel, to take the rhythms apart, and to repeat them again and again. It helps to be able to demonstrate the rhythms, the singing, and the dance movements and to dance with the children.

Kedmon Mapana, Wagogo Teaching Musician of Tanzania

A singer, a dancer, and a player of many instruments of the Wagogo culture of central Tanzania, Kedmon Elisha Mapana is also a professor and head of the Department of Creative Arts at the University of Dar es Salaam. He performs and gives music and dance workshops at schools, universities, churches, and community centers in Bulgaria, Denmark, Germany, the Philippines, Poland, Sweden, South Africa, the United Kingdom, the United States, and Zimbabwe. He was a visiting artist at the University of Washington, Seattle, USA, while also teaching at Seattle Pacific University during the time of his doctoral studies there. He earned his Ph.D. in Education and has since published book chapters and journal articles, especially on topics of Wagogo music,

Kedmon Mapana, Wagogo Teaching Musician of Tanzania

children's musical culture, musical enculturation, and education. He is recipient of awards for his teaching and community music engagements, from Jubilation Foundation and AIRS (Advancing Interdisciplinary Research in Singing) and has served on the faculty of the World Music Pedagogy course at the University of Washington. He is founding director of the Wagogo Annual Music Festival in his hometown, Chamwino, in the Dodoma region of central Tanzania.

Q: Were you involved in musical performance as a child?
A: I remember that when I was attending primary school at the age of 9 years (grade one) up to the age of 16 years (grade 7), I used to lead the songs we would sing during school assembly. My singing was appreciated by my teachers and fellow students. They used to call me a cassette player, meaning that when I began to lead songs, we'd go from one song to another, up to ten songs that we would sing, non-stop. At 11 years of age, I joined a church choir at St. Peter's church (formally called Maduma Church), the youngest singer within a group of grown-up people. People in the church used to point to me, saying "Mtoto Yule mwimbaji!!" (or "that young person is a really fine singer!")

Q: Did you make music during your adolescence?
A: I was initiated to manhood at the age of 13 through a ritual of boys' circumcision. Music was the tool for imparting knowledge, and so we sang, clapped hands, played

rhythmic sticks. Over a period of six weeks, there was intensive music-making in the process of leaving childhood for adult life. Beyond that, I grew up in a place where music was practiced daily in the community, especially for cultivation, harvesting, fetching water, finding firewood, sweeping the ground at home, and entertaining ourselves and others. In Wagogo culture, when you graduate from school, you do not become only a wise adult but also a great singer.

Q: Did you learn Western art music?
A: While studying for a teaching certificate in mathematics at Korogwe Teacher's College, I joined the college choir and was soon appointed as the choir director. I was conducting and also teaching the choir songs in four-part harmony, apparently well enough, so I was recommended to Butimba Teacher's College to pursue a two year's music education certificate. There I started to learn Western art music, including how to play a B-flat trumpet. I was interested in learning music from everywhere.

Q: Do you perform music other than Wagogo and Western art music?
A: Yes. My best course while a student at the University of Dar es Salaam was called a "music ensemble". In this course, we students were encouraged to share with each other the songs of our separate villages. I had the opportunity to teach my fellow students Wagogo music who were not from my ethnic cultural group.

Q: Who are some of your major musical influences?
A: My musical upbringing was communally based, so I learned from all the community and not from an individual.

Q: Do you think that children and youth should experience and study music of their local community cultures?
A: Yes. In the Wagogo community I come from, music is part of the culture, and for various functions, even for walking long distances, for criticizing bad behavior, for drinking local beer, and for protecting yourself. Knowing this music is key to knowing who you are and where you came from. If children and youth do not learn their musical cultures, they end up losing their identities.

Q: When you teach children/youth, how do you help them to come close to recreating the music of your expertise? How do you help them to sound stylistically accurate?
A: I insist that my students listen, observe, practice, and overcome any fears of doing so. They must connect to the sounds and to the movements and gestures that express the musical sounds. If the musical culture does not utilize notation, then I do not use notation or theory, either. Anyone can learn notation, of course, but it's not necessary or appropriate to use notation in some cultures.

Q: Is listening important, then?
A: Yes, listening is important, and I do feature it in my own learning experience. I may play recordings, and when I'm teaching, this recorded music is helpful in allowing students a way to warm up, to get focused, and to sink in to the language of the musical cultures.

Q: In teaching people to sing, dance, and play, what advice can you offer those who wish to learn Wagogo or other music?
A: These are important pieces of advice: Listen carefully, observe carefully, and try to develop vocal, instrumental, and dance techniques. Young musicians learn by listening and then repeating after their teacher, who can demonstrate the appropriate sounds. It's important to "just do it" and to practice hard.

Q: Do you seek to musically educate children/youth or to use the music/music learning experience for purposes other than music? Please explain.
A: Once music is learned, it can be used in various ways. It is always heartening to see a student who has taken both knowledge and skills of music and is using it not only to generate personal income but also to support community development (culturally, economic, and morally).

Riduan Zalani, Global Musician With Malay Roots

Riduan Zalani is a musician, educator, producer, and artistic director in Singapore. He began his musical journey at a tender age, initially influenced by his uncle who is a musician of Malay traditional art forms. As a young boy, Riduan was constantly

Riduan Zalani, Global Musician with Malay Roots

Photo courtesy of NADI Singapura

surrounded by Malay cultural art forms like the *silat* (martial art form), *kompang* (Malay frame drum), *gamelan*, and the *tarian* (a Malay traditional dance form). By the age of 14 years, he focused his studies on the drums of the Malay Archipelago, particularly *rebana, rebana (ibu/anak), kompang, hadrah,* and *jidur*. He learned the music by attending rehearsals in a community center and eventually organizing arts-related events for the community. He performed in *Gentarasa*, the first performance showcase commissioned by the Singapore government to highlight Malay traditional art forms and their local practitioners, and this led him to an invitation to be a member of the Singapore Malay Orchestra as the percussion section leader. Riduan subsequently enrolled himself locally in a diploma in world music, which widened his exposure to a range of musical genres from Western classical to Afro-Cuban and Afro-Brazilian percussion music. Now in his early thirties, his dedication to his music and the Malay community has won him accolades, including the Goh Chok Tong Youth Promise Award (2006), Singapore Youth Award (2013), ASEAN Youth Award (2013), and the Singapore Young Artist Award (2015). (Learning Pathway #2 features Riduan Zalani and the group, NADI Singapura, and Chapter 5 features a creative experience that is central to his compositional approach.)

Q: Can you describe the outcome of your chance meeting with Wicked Aura Batucada, the local Afro-Brazilian percussion group?
A: I met them as they were busking in the shopping district on Orchard Road and began to play with them. I ended up joining the group and touring with them to London. Wicked Aura was the band that brought me to London and that was the day I realized that . . . I'm going to do this till I die. I want to see [myself] on stage and be a good entertainer, and it will be an added bonus and dimension if I could represent my own (Malay) community.

Q: Why do you feel strongly about representing the Malay community through the music you are making?
A: I want to represent the Malay community because I felt . . . we are oppressed, the Malays. . . . There's no foundation or a structure to empower the Malays in the arts sector. I have wanted to bring my drum, my *rebana*, and I want people to know the *rebana*. I just wanted to. I feel that there is a need to promote Malay arts and the heritage and culture.

Q: What is motivating your sense of the need to revitalize Malay music in Singapore (and elsewhere in the world)?
A: I feel that Malay music has lost its drive, and the icons that are heading it are leaving us slowly one by one. Musical icons such as M. Nasir, S. Atan, even Ramli Sarip . . . whose [musical] forms exist in both folk tradition and pop (are leaving us).

Q: Can you tell us about the professional Malay group that you and your colleague, Yaziz Hassan (another prominent rebana artisan), have established?
A: NADI Singapura is a contemporary group of around 50 members that promotes the traditional playing of drums . . . and the performance is unique to where we come from, that we do not sound like the Malaysians or our Brunei or Indonesian counterparts. (In Behasa Melayu, NADI refers to "pulse" or "flow of consciousness".)

Figure 4.2   NADI Singapura

Photo courtesy of NADI Singapura

Q: What sort of music does NADI Singapura perform?
A: We seek to feature Malay instruments in a performative way. Musicians play a pandemonium of rhythms on Malay percussion instruments while also dancing and performing *silat* movements and/or other dramatic elements. Performance by NADI Singapura becomes more than just playing the instruments, which is often the case in Malay music performance settings.

Q: Would you describe your music as preserving traditions or inventing brand-new expressions?
A: Tradition and culture are inseparable to artists, so the artist is unique to his or her point of origin and to the era in which he lives. We start with where we come from and make music that resonates with the community and that is driven by traditional values, elements, and artistic meanings. Still, we make music with elements of electronica, rock, punk, jazz, house music, drum, and bass (as well as with folk, traditional, and classical features).

Performance at the Core

Central to the musical education of students is performance by them, with them, and for them. World Music Pedagogy encompasses all manner of experience in music of the world's cultures, even as the act of performing world music stands, for many musicians and music teachers, as a prime goal of all the pedagogical energy that goes into daily teaching and learning experiences. Listening that is attentive, engaged, and enactive is a means to performance that is musically accurate and sensitive to nuances that notation can never fully capture, while Creating World Music supports the voices of students in stretching the music they know into new personal and collective expressions (see Chapter 5). Of course, in and out of these sonic experiences with the music is the way in which Integrating World Music can offer an immeasurable depth of cultural understanding to the music under study (see Chapter 6). The beauty of performing world music is that students, teachers, and community musicians can join together in public performance, which is then when the potential for peak experiences in music as a human need (and a global phenomenon) is maximized.

References

Campbell, P. S., & Wiggins, T. (2013). *The Oxford handbook of children's musical cultures*. New York: Oxford University Press.

Wade, B. C. (2004). *Thinking musically*. New York: Oxford University Press.

Whiteman, P., & Lum, C. H. (Eds.). (2012). *Musical childhoods of Asia and the Pacific*. Charlotte, NC: Information Age Publishing.

5
Creating World Music

Martin Wong, the middle school all-music teacher, met Dylan Marche at the Heritage House, an apartment for seniors in a medium-sized city in the American Midwest. He was visiting his grandmother, who had taken up residence there just a few months earlier, in order to catch her up on family activities, read to her, talk with her, and share a meal with her. Dylan had just finished his performance on "flutes and whistles of the world", and Martin's grandmother was delighted with the many shapes and sizes of flutes from Asia, Africa, and the Americas and the myriad of sounds she had heard them produce. In fact, Dylan had just begun a three-month residency at Heritage House, where he would be involved as a "hospital musician", performing for the residents, engaging them in music-making and stimulating them through his performances, and their participation vocally and on instruments. Many residents who had seemed somewhat subdued, with low energy and a bit dazed and distant, had come alive, like Martin's grandmother, with the sounds of the instruments of wood, bamboo, metal, tin, and clay. Dylan knew his wind instruments, and he was not only adept at playing them but also personable, full of wit and humor, and at the ready for telling origin stories of the sources of flutes and whistles.

Martin was intrigued with the prospects for introducing his middle school students to so many of the world's musical instruments. He invited Dylan as a contract musician to his suburban middle school. Dylan was enthusiastic about the opportunity to share the program he had honed for senior citizens with the assembly of young adolescents, and he was successful in adjusting his presentational rhythm and tone to fit the nature of his audience. His performance led to an offer by Martin's principal to take on an extended residency there at the school. Dylan came in twice weekly to teach in Martin's final period of the day and in an after-school program for the students. As he played, he motivated the students to want to learn various kinds of ocarinas, the Irish pennywhistle, the double flute of the Dalmatian Coast, the Chinese transverse flute of bamboo called the dizi and the vertically played xiao flute, the Andean flute known as kena, and a number of wood flutes from East Africa for which he had no names. *He shared the flutes he had (since he had multiples of many of them, including a dozen pennywhistles and about as many each of the ocarinas and the bamboo and wood flutes) and then turned to recordings and video recordings in the sessions so that students could listen together and then play what they could with the recordings. He demonstrated fingerings on the various flutes and drew out a few phrases from the recordings that he thought the students could perform. Dylan assigned some home-listening and viewing, and students returned with curiosity and with questions of their own for him. Together with Martin, Dylan then challenged them to compose their own flute music, and they gathered in duos and trios to create new musical expressions that mixed Andean-like melodies on pennywhistles and Chinese-like tunes on wood flutes. The ideas for their musical inventions belonged to the students, even as they had arisen from earlier listening and playing experiences, too. Students were visibly pleased with their "songs" as they'd graduated from basic skill building to the point of making the music their very own.*

At about four months into the school residency, when Martin and Dylan both deemed the middle school students to be sufficiently skilled, they prepared them for an excursion to the community. At Heritage House, students performed their "covers" for the residents, bits and pieces of the music of selected recordings, and played alone and together some of the student-composed original songs. The young students had found themselves a supportive and approving audience; as they played, some seniors clapped, nodded their heads, and tapped their feet to the tunes. Several students were seen after the performance, talking with their avid fans, showing them how to finger an ocarina and a bamboo flute. Martin's grandmother was beaming: She knew well what had uniquely transpired through the facilitation of her grandson and his colleague for the sakes of their young students and her own senior friends, and she was clearly proud of what had been accomplished in the lives of many through this community-school plan.

In Pursuit of the Creative Human Impulse

Creativity is a human attribute awaiting development in students of all ages. It shows itself in every human endeavor and in all the arts as well as in science, technology, engineering, and mathematics. Within considerations of the need that individuals have for self-expression, creativity is viewed as a universal quality that permeates the human spirit and extends from knowledge and experience to expressions that are new and original in nature. Creativity is not unpredictable, nor is it mysterious, as the creative process has been the subject of systematic study by specialists in philosophy, education, cognition, and neurology, as well as by the very artists and scientists who manifest "the creative trait". Can creativity be "taught"? It surely can be nurtured, modeled, inspired, and facilitated by caring teachers and community musicians.

Music, and all the arts, have been deemed the home base of the creative human impulse, both at large and in the education of children and youth in schools. An array of images depict creativity at work: The lone composer toiling at the piano, the painter with canvas and easel in an idyllic park-like setting, the on-stage producer of a play headed for its premiere, and the modern dancer dressed in skin-tight garb moving fluidly into many angles and positions. All these images are soloistic, yet creativity in a school curriculum is necessarily group oriented, particularly in the way of work in music classes and ensembles. Collective creativity may be more to the point within schools, and group-work in creative artistic expression can be gratifying to students. While it can be challenging to ensure that all students, in every group, are working together toward the creation of something beautiful, the creative process and its artistic (and social) outcomes for students who take it seriously can offer them experiences that last a lifetime.

Music in schools has often remained re-creative rather than creative in that the ultimate aim of school music programs has often tended toward the notion of performing music, that is, realistically re-creating music as the composer had crafted it. All too seldom is there a progression forward by teachers to provide time and space for students to make something musically original (and expressive, even beautiful); to create music starting from "ground zero"; or to launch an expression from the music that was learned, listened to, and performed into a new way of playing or singing it. In Thailand, the contemporary dancer-choreographer Pichet Klunchun has designed artistic works that have long been at the forefront of challenging staunch preservers of (Thai) traditions. He claims that the responsibility of musicians, dancers, visual artists, and creative writers is to innovate so as not to repeat what has been expressed before (Ketbungkan, 2017). While his frame of reference is professional musicians, his wisdom is relevant for music in schools, too, and for students who can be guided by music teachers and community musicians in their composition, improvisation, and song-writing ventures. Experiences in musical creativity can be exploratory and without many pre-arranged parameters, or they can be somewhat shaped by particular features such as a given pitch set, rhythmic phrases, meter, or form. Students can be entirely free to be musical, or they can be guided by a tradition, a genre, or a style (Higgins & Campbell, 2010). They can be drawn into occasions to play with possibilities for creative musical expressions that are steeped in repetition and imitation, call-and-response structures, interlocking parts, motives, meters, and modes. They can launch their new music from the music they have previously experienced and studied. The creative human impulse can advance when circumstances support it and when teachers set the scene and nurture the creative impulse.

The Potential of Innovation by Community Artist-Musicians

Professional musicians who play traditional instruments, or sing in traditional styles, enjoy working with tradition and change in mind to create new musical identities for themselves, situating themselves as eclectic musicians within their geographical and cultural contexts. At the same time, these musicians may choose to represent the traditional repertoire that is emblematic of their particular cultural community. Zakir Hussain, John-Carlos Perea, Souad Massi, Oumane Sangare, Rahim Alhaj, Loreena McKennit, Homayoun Sakhi, Michael Doucet, and Tarek Yamami are among many artist-musicians worldwide who recognize the need for music to re-create tradition while also giving way to renewal, variation, experimentation, and "sea-change". The spirit of locally living musicians is present in every community to model both creating and re-creating processes, and these very musicians make effective collaborators who can work well with music teachers to provide students with opportunities to likewise create and re-create music that is meaningful to them. Altogether, students can learn through creative musical experiences to question sustainability, renewal, and attempts at fusion and hybridity so that they themselves can map their further musical journey of exploration and experimentation.

Creating new music can appeal to musicians and students of music for various good reasons. Musicians who are versed in more than one musical genre or who frequently collaborate with other musicians across varied musical styles often engage in the creation of composed or improvised new musical expressions in the form of fusion repertoire. Their intentions could simply be the enjoyment of playing together as an eclectic group, to further musical knowledge of other musical cultures, or to attempt to find a unique musical voice that they feel has not been explored.

Certainly, for many artist-musicians in the community, their work is often about recreating and performing old, traditional, or continuing repertoire. Yet they also have the license to create something outside of their traditional heritage music, including music that is based in familiar cultural expressions but which may take on new twists and turns melodically and rhythmically. Composing and improvising musicians may choose to preserve all that has come before while also furthering their own artistic intentions, building from the music they have experienced and studied to an expression that is both true to traditional forms and yet also newly expressive. There are also musicians in the community who create new musical expressions for the sheer joy of experimenting with sounds. These musicians who may be steeped in particular musical traditions want to free themselves from their musical frames, explore extended techniques with their own instruments through acoustic or electronic means, engage in soundscape or experimental music approaches, or extract musical ideas from varied musical genres to plug into their exploration.

Many musicians in the community work closely with schools to provide educational programs that range from one-off performances to long-term residencies. As they collaborate with music teachers to consider learning aims, objectives, and sequences that encompass a greater diversity of musical possibilities, the topic of Creating World Music frequently arises. There is genuine fascination for the creative potential of students to make something new from their understandings of the elemental features of a Caribbean dance form, a flute melody from the Eastern Mediterranean, a percussion piece of sticks and drums from Samoa, or an African American children's song with rigorous stamping and clapping rhythms. There is a coalescence among teachers and community musicians for wanting to tap into the imaginations of children and youth and for combining what students know and wish to know into something innovative and original. They are in general agreement that the creative musical work of students may also lead to their fuller understanding of why musicians create their own sound, how their compositions (songs, and improvisations) connect to earlier musical experience, and why new musical works are meaningful and useful to artists and their cultural communities.

Creating World Music via World Music Pedagogy

Creating World Music is the dimension of World Music Pedagogy that typically follows deep and thoughtful listening. It comes on the heels of Attentive Listening, Engaged Listening, and Enactive Listening in that these experiences prepare students for their own songs, rhythms, sound pieces, and full-on musical works. It happens that when the music seeps into the psyche, when that music "becomes" us through many opportunities to listen, to participate, and to perform the music, that the human penchant arises to create something fresh and new—yet often still related to the music that came before. Musical creativity then emerges through improvising or composing "in the style of" music that is already known so that even culturally unfamiliar music can become familiar and function as the base of a creative musical expression. Musical creativity is not meant as just a pretty "end-result" of a pedagogical process; rather, it is a valuable experience in getting to know the sonic principles of the music, working (and playing) with this musical material, and fashioning it in ways that make fresh musical sense. The creative product, as well as the creative process, requires careful musical thinking. It is informed by, and results in, ideals of logic and beauty that creators have, which in turn is rooted in their music experience and study.

In World Music Pedagogy, composing and improvising in the style of world music models can enhance the skills and understandings of a strong musicianship. Enroute to the musical understanding of students is the capacity to personalize the music they have learned, to cull through components of it (aspects of its melodic content, rhythmic components, or texture or timbre, for examples), and to develop a musical expression that is related to the style of the studied music but that takes unique turns away from the model. Every musical work is a potential gateway to something new (but, in the WMP way, not too new as to disassociate itself from the influencing work). Models for launching creative work may include a choral song of the South Africa Xhosa people, a *maqam* for Iranian *ney* (flute), a Swedish *rohrspol* (dance form) for violin, a kaen-and-singer duet (*mawlum*) from Northeast Thailand, or a social dance song of the Navajo. The newly created music is a certain declaration that the earlier experiences with a selected recording have paved the way for the newly evolved musical composite. In the creative process, the rhythm, melody, texture, and timbre of a newly learned musical work can grow "legs" through occasions for students to make the music their very own, built upon their previous experience with it.

Children, youth, and other learners are also at liberty to invent anew, even while they take on more (or less) of the music they have learned. In standard World Music Pedagogy fashion, learners new to a musical culture, style, or form may go at creative expression in any number of ways: Extending a musical work with additional verses, transitions, bridges, or codas; fusing one melody (or rhythm, harmonic plan, or stylistic nuance) with another; improvising on the musical features of the musical work, trying this and then that in working out an idea that still "tastes" a little like the work but with new expressions; and composing within the framework of the learned music, holding to some components while determining new angles on it, new routes to take. Teachers and community musicians can suggest devices and techniques from the simple to the more complex, demonstrating and then shaping students in their use of techniques such as ostinato, drone, sequence, imitation, fugal form, word painting, augmentation, and diminution. In Creating World Music, learners are a little like the music teachers and community musicians with whom they work, merging the learned with the spontaneous, crafting an expression that is yet rooted in the music that came before.

Episodes for Expressive Change

The seven episodes to follow give attention to sequential steps for the support of creative avenues into the realm of composition and improvisation, each of them inspired by a selected work of the world's musical cultures. The three Learning Pathways (Episodes 5.1, 5.2, and 5.3) take the now familiar selections of a Chicano romantic ballad, a Malay-inspired percussion work, and an East African choral song to another level of expressive experience. Further selections, including Brazilian samba, Chinese instrumental traditions, Quebecois-style fiddling, and a popular song that is already newly created as a Carnatic Indian-influenced popular fusion piece, offer insights into Creating World Music. Each episode suggests ways in which traditions can change in the hands of students who, after they have listened and performed the music, are ready to play with the possibilities for new expressions. There is an assumption across the episodes that the teacher's guidance is essential and that the presence of a community musician can effectively support the generation of new ideas that are in keeping within the essence of the musical style as it was shaped by musicians from the origin culture.

New Twists to a Familiar Song (Form)

Many musical practices in Latin America are grounded in the possibilities for creative expression, much of it arising from a spontaneous setting forth of musical variation and development, as in the case of dance forms such as *salsa, merengue*, and *cumbia*. As well, some vocal forms of Latin American folk and popular music lend themselves well to creative possibilities, including the *romance*; the *ranchera*; the *decima* or *copla*; the generic *son*; the *aguinaldo* (carol); and a grand variety of children's songs, work songs, and lyrical love songs. Episode 5.1 features a folk-styled song of love, Quetzal's "Todo lo que Tendo" that lends itself well to both lyrical and musical invention. As a band of innovative L.A.-based musicians, Quetzal enjoys a reputation for breaking through

---

Episode 5.1: Romance in East L.A.
"Todo lo que Tengo"
(Learning Pathway #1)

Specific Use: Elementary Music Education, Secondary School Innovations

Materials:

- "Todo lo que Tendo", Quetzal, (from *Imaginaries*), Smithsonian Folkways Recordings
- Guitar (hand drum, other percussion), keyboards, various available instruments (flute, clarinet, violin, other)

Procedure:

1. Establish a mood for "Creating World Music" by listening together to this familiar song that has already drawn students into the midst of it through various experiences in Attentive, Engaged, and Enactive Listening.

2. Brainstorm some topics to sing about in a newly created song still in the style of "Todo lo que Tendo", inviting students to share with the question "What's on your mind?" Write answers that may include single words (peace, justice, friendship) or full phrases ("Peace is a journey of the

heart", "Reach out for justice, for the right to be free", "The finest prize a friend can give is a listening ear and a warm embrace").

3. Together or in small groups, develop verses on a chosen topic (rhymed or unrhymed). Provide a metric scheme and a quantity of verses (2–3–4), and clarify whether a chorus section should be developed for insertion between the verses that might underscore the theme of the poem.

4. Challenge students to write all or part of their poem in Spanish, in a mix of Spanish and English, or in another of the world's languages.

5. Share the verses through a rhythmic recitation that may appear as a group-performed "choral speech".

6. Repeat #5. (Note that with repetition, the rhythmic flow will improve. Listen for a melodic inflection that may emerge, too, and encourage prospects for converting the verse from chant to song.)

7. Add instruments to the rhythmic recitation of the newly created verse. Suggest that harmonic accompaniment be provided on guitar, keyboard, or a combination of instruments and that counter-melodies, embellishments, and transitions between verses may add to the musical interest. Add non-pitched percussion instruments to accentuate particular textual or musical ideas. Hint: Consider retaining the same chord progression as in "Todo lo que Tendo" since it is already familiar, or work with a modified (even a simplified) chord progression.

8. Repeat #7 since familiarity with the verse and its sounding above the harmonic accompaniment will give way to a melody (especially with a little modeling of the teacher and community musician).

9. Perform the composed songs, and discuss ways to enhance or further develop musical ideas to pique the interest of listeners.

10. Can the song be danced? Experiment with freestyle, footwork and step patterns, and formations.

11. Listen to the original recording and compare the multiple ways in which the new musical creation is similar or distinctive. Ask a Mexican-heritage community musician to respond to the musical integrity of the work: Does it retain the flavor of the source recording?

the boundaries of Chicano music and fashioning music that mixes Mexican elements with popular and rock forms, rhythm and blues, and jazz and punk to communicate the ideals of social change in a complex world.

Because students have learned the song well enough to not only join with the recording but to perform it in a public space, they know well its melody, the harmonies, and instrumental nuances. They have developed a feel of the phrases, the separation of verse from chorus, and the harmonic changes of the chords that undergird the melody. They understand the meaning of the words, too, as it suggests that falling in love with another person requires a commitment and yet does not mean that one's own identity must be sacrificed, erased, and abandoned. While the creative activity could lean toward greater changes in the music or in the lyrics, the procedures in this episode suggest that the song form of verse and chorus can function as framework for a small-group song-writing experience that allows students to express themselves musically on a topic that is meaningful to them. Students can stay very close to the harmony, and even the melody, of the original song or select new musical features that fit the form of a song they know well.

Re-Expressing Malay Thunder

For insight into the creative genius of Malay musician Riduan Zalani, and a way in which musical tradition may undergo expressive change, Episode 5.2 offers compelling evidence. (See Chapter 4 for a brief description of his perspective on performance

---

Episode 5.2: "Kecuh! Riuh! Gemuruh!" (Learning Pathway #2)

Specific Use: Secondary School Innovations, Instrumental Ensembles

Materials:

- Track 4, from the album, *Kata Kita Kota* by NADI Singapura

Procedure:

1. "What is *kompang*?" Encourage students to Google for photos, descriptions, and video examples of the Malay drum and the percussion ensemble and its various interlocking patterns.

2. Because the music has already been listened to, learned, and performed (via Attentive Listening, Engaged Listening, and Enactive Listening), the fundamental rhythm underlying *kompang*, called *Inang*, is already known. Pat, clap, snap, slap, or stamp the *Inang* rhythm. To emphasis the accents, try saying "Clap—pat pat pat clap clap" while giving greater emphasis to the claps.

3. In partners, practice continuously playing the down-beat (*Lalu*, signified by "L") rhythm or the up-beat (*Selang*, signified by "S") rhythm, as an interlocking pattern.

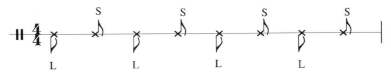

4. Practice the *Tinka* rhythm:

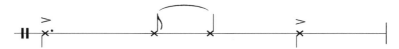

5. In groups of four, play the *Lalu* and *Selang* paired rhythms and the *Tinka* and *Inang* rhythms, one person to each rhythm.

6. In one large group, put together the interlocking rhythms first via body percussion and then on selected percussion instruments. Use three distinctive timbral sounds of skins, woods, and metals.

7. Ask students to create a brand-new rhythm that can also interlock with the *Lalu* and *Selang*, *Tinka* and *Inang* rhythms.

8. Divide the large group into three groups to create a rhythmic percussion piece based on all the now familiar rhythmic patterns (*Lalu* and *Selang*, *Tinka*, and *Inang*). Suggest possibilities, such as beginning with just the *Lalu* and *Selang* before layering the *Tinka*; dropping out the *Tinka* after two bars; adding the *Inang*; sounding all rhythms at once; fading the *Tinka* and *Inang*; and ending with *Lalu* and *Selang* in a burst of dynamics. Note that the rhythmic patterns can also be improvised upon or elaborated during the creation.

9. Listen to the original recording, and discuss ways in which the new piece compares with it. Does it retain a certain "Malayness"? Seek out the views of a Malay musician.

and teaching/learning.) As he performs Malay music, alone and with his contemporary group, NADI Singapura, Riduan invents new compositions that define tradition while also celebrating the capacity to seek out new musical innovations. He holds tradition close to his heart, and he and the group insist that traditional elements are important even as they create edgy Malay music that is accessible and suited to a more contemporary sound. As Riduan explains it, the music is new and yet "you need to hear the *Asli* (a traditional Malay dance form), you need to hear the *Dondang Sayang* (traditional poetic art form associated with the Malays and the Peranakans) . . . you still need to have the creeping of the drum, and there needs to be equal opportunity for the artists to shine".

"Kecuh! Riuh! Gemuruh!" refers to chaotic and thunderous sound. There are at least three deviations of this piece from traditional Malay *kompang* processional music: The combination of instruments that would not be typical in any traditional Malay ensemble, for this piece unusually features *gongs*, *jidur*, and *hadrah* (*jidur* is a Malay bass drum often played with mallets, while *hadrah* is a Malay hand-held tambourine); in traditional Malay ensembles, only one *jidur* is used, and then only as "enhancement" to the ensemble, so that the use of multiple *jidurs* and dedicating prominent rhythmic lines throughout the piece is an innovative step forward and away from Malay traditional practices; and composer Riduan Zalani has taken musical ideas from rhythms prominent throughout the Malay archipelago and "played" with them, extending, truncating, or repeating them in ways that are removed from Malay tradition. In the episode to follow, students have the opportunity to work creatively with Malay rhythms, using available instruments, combining the rhythms in any which way they choose, and building atop Riduan's already creative development of the Malay source traditions.

A "New" Sub-Saharan Collective Song

In some cultures more than others, creativity is encouraged, and a great joy arises as a new song evolves through efforts of a collective of musicians or when an individual musician leads or facilitates the entirety of singers, players, and dancers to develop something together that is new and meaningful. In the case of Wagogo musical practices in a Tanzanian village, there are identifiable melodies, harmonies, and instrumental designs that emerge in songs so that new songs may, in fact, be new lyrics that sound "familiar" and are at least partially based in songs that have come before. (Of course, much in the way of creative composition and improvisation—everywhere—is realistically anchored in familiar musical features, for the melodies, rhythms, textures, and forms that musicians know are quite naturally influential of new expressions.) Among the Wagogo, creative composition is fostered by an annual festival, *Tamasha la Muziki wa Cigogo*, that calls for the *ngoma* (song and dance) performance of new compositions by village groups on particular themes such as "arts for development", "community music", and "*ngoma* revisited". The newly created compositions that feature vocal and instrumental music, choreographed movement, and sometimes stories that are theatrically expressed are based in music that has come before.

"Nange" (or "Yange") is identifiable by Wagogo villagers as an initiation song, and thus it is viewed as fixed, permanent, and important to cultural identity. Children know the song, and adults readily join in when someone starts it up. In Episode 5.3,

---

Episode 5.3: Sub-Saharan Collective Song "Nange" ["Yange"] (Learning Pathway #3)

Specific Use: Early Childhood, Elementary Music Education, Choral Ensembles

Materials:

- Track 18, "Nange" [or "Yange"], from the album, *Tanzania—Tanzanie: Chants*

Procedure:

1. As a reminder of the song that has been learned via Attentive Listening, Engaged Listening, and Enactive Listening, share again the recording of "Nange" [or "Yange"] and invite students to join in.

2. Sing the song together without the recording, and show the feel of the song's rhythm in the body. This may include the transfer of weight from one foot to the other and from one side of the body to the other. The arms can swing forward together on pulse "1" and then back on pulse "2", and students can join hands as they move together once a solid feeling of pulse is established. See examples of Wagogo movement and dance, especially from the annually produced Wagogo Music Festival by the Chamwino Arts Center www.chamwinoarts.org.

3. Using the four measures of the learned song as the "return" section or chorus ("Sahani Yangu Hedukila, Yange Yange hedukila"), which is sung twice, invite ideas for developing a new four-measure phrase, also sung twice, between the "return" or chorus sections.

4. Working together in one large group, choose parameters within which to fashion a contrasting section. For example, the group may wish to continue the same meter, the same rhythmic flow, and the same melody but develop new words in English (or Swahili). Encourage students to sing about themes that have appeared in Wagogo songs of this ilk, such as the importance of family, of generosity and kindness toward others, and of growing up into a role of responsible community member. The challenge is in fitting new words to the melody and rhythm of the song, and so try these words as an example: "Com-mun-i-ty here with fam-i-ly, Fam-i-ly, friends, com-mun-i-ty".

5. If the melody begins to sound "old" or over-used, play with the possibilities of re-ordering the pentatonic pitches to create a new phrase of 8 or 16 beats, in four measures, that contrasts as well as complements the familiar melody.

6. Once the new contrasting phrase is collectively shaped, practice singing it in between the "return", or chorus, sections.

7. Extend the creativity by inviting further inventions of contrasting phrases that can be sung in between the "return" or chorus sections.

8. If the creation of the new phrase has taken students to a "standstill" vis-à-vis movement, reinstate the dance so that they can experience the importance of *ngoma*-inspired singing with dancing to the (somewhat) new song they have fashioned. If the dance movement has been performed in place, suggest that students spread across the performance space—in lines, double lines and circles, and freely, even as they maintain the same movements of the body.

9. Invite a community musician, whether Wagogo, Tanzanian, East African, or sub-Saharan African, to evaluate and further guide the effort to express the new creation as it addresses the essence of the source recording.

this known and notable song becomes a gateway to possibilities for creative expression by learners of every age. Without losing sight of the features of the music (and dance), the procedure outlines possibilities for adding a new section (and trying a new dance formation) that is inserted between the segments that are now entirely familiar to students who have moved their way through the WMP dimensions.

Circling 'Round the Samba Band

As a community ensemble, the samba band makes for comfortable gatherings of like-minded individuals who enjoy the friendly sociomusical experience, just as do shape-note sings, West African-inspired drum circles, gathers of "old-time" guitarists and fiddlers, and New Orleans second line percussion groups. There is a whole host of benefits from making music together in these ensembles, from alleviating stress and improving moods to fostering a sense of belonging, and samba bands have a way of enveloping music and dance in a party-like celebration of life itself. The samba scene is an international phenomenon, and communities across the world, from Australia to the United Kingdom and from Austria to the United States, have taken on this vibrant Brazilian music style and its fusion forms of *samba batucada*, *samba-reggae* and samba-rock (Higgins, 2007). Members of community samba bands enthusiastically tell of the gratification they feel from their participation that is "athletic" through the physically rigorous drumming and dancing that ensues. Samba bands cater to different age groups and skill sets, from amateur to professional levels, and can be used for celebrations and festivals as well as in various social and therapeutic settings in senior homes, work with marginalized youth, and special needs populations.

While Brazil claims the genre, the roots of samba are traceable to African traditions developed in Angola and the Congo and routed to Brazil through the slave trade that sent waves of captive populations across the Atlantic Ocean to the Americas. In the northeastern state of Bahia and in Rio de Janeiro, Brazilian samba style developed and became associated with the celebration of the pre-Lenten festival parades known as *Carnival*. As Episode 5.4 underscores, the samba features multiple layers of

Figure 5.1   In full voice, university singers rehearsing the songs of a community gospel choir

Episode 5.4: "Samba Batucada"

Specific Use: Elementary Music Education, Secondary School Innovations

Materials:

- Samba Brazilian Batucuda Band

Procedure:

1. Through plenty of listening that proceeds from Attentive to Engaged to Enactive, students have learned Samba Batucada parts by ear for *surdo*, *reco-reco*, *tamborim*, and *agogo*. (Note that the *surdo* part may be played on a bass drum, and the *guiro* can substitute for the *reco-reco*.)

2. Layer in the instruments, beginning with the *surdo* but then mixing up the order of entry of instruments, over many opportunities to play.

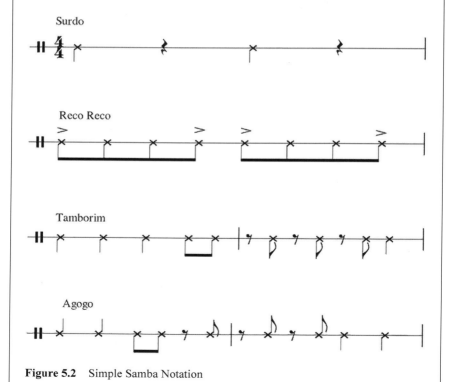

Figure 5.2 Simple Samba Notation

3. Try out the form below, and later change the order of sections:
   Call-and-Response Introduction
   Whole-Group Samba
   Call-and-Response
   Whole-Group Samba (layering in the instruments)
   Whole-Group Samba (with varying levels of dynamics, ending loud)
4. Listen to the model again to discern or be motivated to create more samba variations.
5. Choose a new form, add some new instruments, or try out movement with a swing to it.
6. Take the samba on the road: Down the hall, into the courtyard, to parking lots, on sidewalks, across neighborhoods.

duple-metered rhythms, often to a sung chorus, and may be played by percussion instruments alone, alongside various types of guitars, or even with a full set of wind and brass instruments. Samba bands of the sort during Carnival parades, and in the internationally popular samba bands, typically include the *tamborim* or *pandeiro* (a small hand drum played with a mallet); *reco-reco* (a ridged gourd played with a scraper); snare drums; *agogo* (metal) bells; a large drum called a *surdo*; a *ganza* (shaker); and the sound of the leader's whistle to cue players to start, stop, or move to a new section. As in the case of so many musical expressions of the African diaspora, samba bands bring players—and even listeners—to their feet to dance the dynamic rhythms.

Pursuing Inventions on Chinese Themes

The trio of musicians known as SA (三) are recognized for the bold and daring breaks they take into new musical territory, innovating even as they continue to acknowledge the musical roots of the instruments they play and the experiences they have known and continue to accumulate. They are players of instruments each with its own cultural history in Asia or in the West, even as they are musicians in the world at large with every reason (and right) to determine the repertoire they re-create and invent. Episode 5.5 documents the way forward for the collective creation of "The Pursuit" by SA (三) members Cheryl (Chinese percussion), Natalie (*guzheng*, the 13-string Chinese zither), and Andy (*dizi* ([Chinese flute], *didgeridoo*, and other flute-instruments). In their creative process, they return to fundamentals of rhythm and melody, experimenting with different possibilities. In early explorations, Cheryl would play in a regular 4-beat pattern on the *dagu* (large Chinese bass drum), Natalie would play in 5s on the *guzheng*, and Andy would play subdivisions of 1 on the *dizi* or other flute-instruments. With an interest in the spectrum of timbral possibilities on their instruments, they played also with the concept of "noise": Andy chose to play overtones on his flute, Natalie bowed on the untuned part of her *guzheng* while also playing random articulations on the tuned *guzheng* strings, and Cheryl played "spam" on cymbals ("spam" is defined as throwing out any and every idea that comes to mind in an instance, much like spam mail). As the SA (三) trio listened to Arabic music, they became increasingly enamored of the nature of Arabic melodies. They studied the tonalities of the Arabic *maqamat*, or modes, and were drawn to creatively adapting their instruments to these modes in order to approximate an Arabic sound.

The beauty and intrigue of musical creativity is already clear to learners who have had earlier experiences with a newly composed work, "The Pursuit", that features the innovative expressions of Cheryl, Natalie, and Andy. Students will have had earlier WMP experiences with this work but Episode 5.5 presses further, offering them a sequence of experiences that can draw them into experimenting with the possibilities of timbre and rhythm. Students can then pursue their own musical creativity through this innovative work and decide their way forward to further innovations of their own.

Episode 5.5: "The Pursuit", SA (三)

Specific Use: Secondary Music Innovations, Instrumental Ensembles

Materials:

- "The Pursuit" (2015)—SA

Procedure:

1. With their earlier experiences in Attentive Listening, Engaged Listening, and Enactive Listening already in tow, guide students to listening again with these challenges: "Identify one interesting or unusual musical element that catches the ear, and describe your choice" and "Identify the instruments and their featured timbres (and note how these timbres are created)".

2. To provide occasions for playing with rhythmic patterns, provide students with number cards of "2" (representing two eighth notes), "3" (representing an eighth-note triplet), and "4" (representing four sixteenth notes), allowing them to form different patterns with the cards, to explore different rhythmic ways on body percussion to articulate the patterns formed, to use various note values and accents, and to create a rhythmic piece based upon these number cards.

3. Explore a variety of ways to play instruments. Using non-pitched percussion instruments, ask students to explore conventional and non-conventional ways of producing sound. Use instruments to play the rhythmic piece created in step 2.

4. Follow the beginning phrases of a transcription of SA's music (Notation 5.2). Choose a phrase or two, and play with the possibilities of expressing these phrases as written and in new and unique ways.

5. Expand the palette of possible ways to make music by inviting a composer from the community to help guide students through exploration and experimentation with instruments and with an array of materials and objects with sound-making potential.

Figure 5.3   Notation for "The Pursuit"

Courtesy of SA, transcribed by Andy Chia

Fiddling With a Cajun "Jig"

As a lively and lilting dance and music form, the jig is identifiable by its "tri-po-let" feeling, a quick-moving three pulses, ad infinitum. There are jigs in 6/8, slip jigs in 9/8, and double jigs in 12/8, and they are present in music of the European Baroque period, as well in the music of Irish, Scottish, and French dances, and throughout much of the music of the Metis people of Canada whose cultural roots are traced to North American indigenous people and French immigrants. In Eastern Canada, where many of the French colonists landed in the 17th and 18th centuries, an Acadian culture developed as a distinctively separate colony of New France. When the Acadians were deported by the British following their defeat of the French in 1763, many of them migrated to the region of Louisiana. They brought their French dialect, music, and dance to New Orleans and inland from there to small settlements on the bayous. They fused their French-Canadian cultural traditions with those of the Spanish colonists then living in Louisiana, the West Africans who were coming in from the Caribbean, and Anglo-Americans who were present and then purchased the territory in 1803. Louisiana's Cajun culture evolved from the Acadians, and the jig, as played by fiddles and accordions, became prominent in the Cajun country dance halls. The dance music of Cajun culture continues today, as do (amplified) fiddles and accordions that play along with drums, electric bass, and guitars, but the music is often in duple 1-2 (or 1-2-3-4) meter rather than triple meeting, including the form known as the Cajun (6/8) jig.

Episode 5.6 provides an experience in Louisiana's Cajun dance music and in the form that is known as the duple-metered Cajun jig. The well-known Cajun band, BeauSoleil, offers a rendering that stimulates listeners to join in singing and playing the melody and dancing the rhythm and to adding a lilting melodic phrase of their own that settles nicely within this duple-metered "jig". While any instrument, and even singing voices, can contribute new variations, the presence of a fiddle or two can capture the lively lilt of this dance tune.

Episode 5.6: "Le Jig Francais"

Specific Use: Early Childhood, Elementary Music Education, Instrumental Ensembles

Materials:

- BeauSoleil, from 15 Louisiana Cajun Classics

Procedure:

1. In addition to earlier occasions for listening, participating in, and performing this Cajun jig, a return to these experiences will stimulate the ear for creative ventures ahead.

2. With available percussion instruments (for example, drums, hand drums, or sticks on the floor), ask students to play the melodic rhythm of both verse and chorus, sections A and B, twice through. (Note: If a fiddle is available, play the A and B sections while the students play their percussion instruments.)

3. With available pitched instruments (including the singing voice), ask students to play the melody of both verse and chorus twice through. Separate out the instruments by timbre (for example, first featuring the singing voice, then flutes [or recorders], then keyboards [or xylophones], then stringed instruments, then other winds and brass instruments). (Note: If violins (fiddles) are available, feature them.)

4. In call-and-response fashion, deliver slight variations to the two-measure phrases of just the verse (section A), to be immediately imitated by all players (and singers). Repeat the same variations back and forth until they are learned.

5. Invite students to create new variations of section A, again with immediate imitation by all. Consider parameters or "rules" for variations: Same meter, same rhythm, same starting pitch, same range of pitches.

6. Collectively select three variations as "keepers", calling them A-1, A-2, and A-3. Practice them. (Challenge students to notate them to assist in memorizing the different versions.)

7. Perform the new work of variations on the verse-theme, interspersing them with the chorus section (B). Begin with the original verse melody (A), and follow the form: A-original, B, A-1, B, A-2, B, A-3, B. (Note: If violins (fiddles) are available, feature them in playing the B section as it occurs.)

8. Invite students to listen further the music of Cajun fiddlers, and fiddlers of Irish, Scottish, and Metis (and even French) traditions, to understand the value of variation in these styles. With luck, there may be a fiddler in the community who would offer a live sampling of these musical expressions (and who might play a rendition of "Le Jig Francais").

Reshaping a Popular Song

Due to its widespread familiarity, a popular song like "Shape of You" may be more quickly learned by students than music that is more removed from familiar experiences. Such a popular song can be examined and experienced through Attentive Listening, Engaged Listening, and Enactive Listening. It can be performed close to the way it sounds, as it can also be the launch to a new musical expression. It can motivate song-writing activity, firing up the creative impulse in young learners. Episode 5.7 illustrates songwriting as a creative activity, working on basic skill development and leading to the invention of a new sound. Following a quick review of "Shape of You", the episode introduces a virtual composition that arose as three musicians, in three different locations, worked with Indian solfege syllables and electronic potentials to fashion a distinctive South Indian Carnatic flavoring of "Shape of You". These musicians worked together virtually from their home studios in Los

Episode 5.7: "Shape of You"

Specific Use: Secondary School Innovations; Choral Ensembles; Instrumental Ensembles

Materials:

- "Shape of You" (Ed Sheeran)

Procedure:

1. A review of the learned song is always welcome, and even after all the earlier experiences in listening, participating, and performing it, "Shape of You" can be enjoyed again in these ways. For a new twist to the song, suggest that students add a vocal drone or other harmony to the section that begins "Girl, you know I want your love" to make for a textural change from a monophonic or solo performance of the verses.

2. Search for Aditya Rao's Carnatic (South Indian) mix of Ed Sheeran's "Shape of You" at https://indianraga.com/music-download, and listen for similarities and distinctions in this rendition.

3. Ask: "What syllables do you hear?" (Note that the syllables are referred to as *swaras* in Hindustani North Indian music; they are the solfege syllables that express particular pitches within the octave.) Display the *swaras* in ascending order: Sa, Ri (or Re), Ga, Ma, Pa, Dha, Ni, with Sa as the octave above.

4. Sing the *swaras* up and then down the scale, pitching them from e to e' so that they sound in a Phrygian mode. Sing the swara syllables slowly at first then twice as fast while tapping a steady pulse.

5. Experiment with singing in call-and-response form, having different singers lead out on short improvised phrases of 8 beats that are imitated by the group. Examples of short phrases follow: In solfege, Sa-Ri-Ga-Sa-Ga-Ma-Pa-(letter names e-f-g-e-g-a-b-); in solfege, Sa-Pa-Ma-Ga-Sa-Ni-Sa- (letter names e-b-a-g-e-d-e-); in solfege, Sa-Ga-Pa-Dha-Ni-Sa(high)-Pa- (letter names e-g-b-c-d-e'-b-). Listen again to the Carnatic mix for how the *swaras* are used to replace the original lyrics and to derive inspiration for another way of developing the song through the use of *swaras*.

7. Ask students to divide into small groups to work out short musical expressions of just 32 beats (4 phrases consisting of 2 bars of 8 beats each) that are vocally based in *swaras*, utilizing e-e' pitch patterns. Suggest that they consider adding a drone or harmony vocally and/or on instruments such as guitars, keyboards, xylophones, and any other available pitched instruments and that they create also a pulse or rhythmic pattern for keeping their ensemble "in the groove".

8. Share the new small-group works, performing them for one another, listening for the *swaras* in their vaguely familiar Phrygian-mode "Shape of You" pitch set.

9. Perform the piece as a rondo-form creation that features the entire group on the section that begins "Girl, you know I want your love", acting as A, with small groups entering one at a time (between the multiple renditions of the A section) to perform their new Phrygian-mode creations.

10. Shifting to the potential of students to work in an online music collaboration, suggest that students explore the means of creating a cover track through collaborative musical work of an online band. Have them explore links to creating a new rendition of "Shape of You" (or other popular song): www.bandhub.com, www.kompoz.com/music/collaborate/recommended, and www.bandmix.com.

11. Plan a sharing of cover tracks as a demonstration of these online music collaborations.

12. Listen and discuss the new renditions as related to the original song via these questions: What components are new? What remained the same? Are different instruments being used from the original? How is the articulation of the melody different from the original? Are there differences in tempo, dynamics, or style?

Angeles (Aditya Rao), Minneapolis (Vinod Krishnan), and Dubai (Mahesh Raghvan) to create a new "shape" and sonic envelope for the familiar song. Beginning with a Google Hangout call, they then produced the new song on music production apps on iPad Pro (Fernando, 2017). (The trio's work, referred to as Aditya Rao, had three million hits within three days of its first launch.) The episode continues into experiences that acquaint students with the Indian solfege syllables and that invite playful meandering on these syllables within parameters of mode, rhythm, and phrase, encouraging students to lean into their own vocal and instrumental expressions on acoustic instruments.

There's more to the encounter, too, for learners who wish to explore virtual work in the online community. Creating a new rendition of a popular song, a "cover" song, such as the mix of Indian Carnatic facets and features, is the cutting edge of musical invention by musicians who are keen to connect their lived realities of technological and social media platforms with familiar musical training and traditions. The online music community provides opportunities for collaborative creation and performances. Thus, the final step of the episode is a gateway to recommendations for student expression through virtual songwriting that features online musical creation among friends.

Online Musical Communities

Following on the journey of Episode 5.7 into online learning and musical creation, it is worth noting the obvious: Young learners are now regularly watching, listening, and picking up musical skills from YouTube videos and other internet sources. They easily learn the basics of playing guitar, ukulele, taiko (drum), bagpipe, mandolin, steel drum, erhu, accordion, and a whole range of instruments from around the world simply by Googling these keywords. With skill development, these students can then insert these instruments into their new musical inventions. Beyond a passive learning experience through pre-made online videos, students can further customize their learning through one-on-one web-based lessons with master teachers from different parts of the world. A quick search on the internet finds web-based lessons with masters of *shakuhachi*, *djembe*, *tabla*, *'ud*, and blues guitar, with clear sequential instructions and (of course) payment modes. These new online modes of learning are particularly beneficial for those who do not have particular music specialists in their locale and need further guidance in advancing their musical studies. The online community of musicians can thus be a rich teaching and learning resource for amateur and professional musicians, and the new sonic possibilities on the internet add flavor to the songwriting, compositions, improvisations, and arrangements students choose to create.

U Win Maung, Burmese Harp Player

In Myanmar, the "Land of the Golden Pagodas", there are as many musical expressions as there are ethnic cultural groups. In cities like Yangon, Mandalay, and Bagan, there are multiple musical communities of performers and avid audiences for Burmese classical music, as well as folk traditions of many groups of people who have lived within

U Win Maung, Master Burmese Harp Player

the borders of the modern nation-state of Myanmar, and also popular music from as early as the 1930s to the present. There are musically creative masters such as U Win Maung, artist of the Burmese harp known as the *saung kauk*. From an early age, U Win Maung enjoyed the surrounds of the traditional folk and drum in his family village in the delta region of the Irrawaddy River. He learned his music by ear and through careful imitation of musicians with whom he studied. After his time in the army, in 1962 he began to learn the Burmese harp, studying with early masters of the instrument. He became known through the ensemble they called "Sit Thi Suang Than" (music of the soldiers), and they performed on Myanmar radio and TV, producing recordings for play throughout Myanmar. U Win Maung understands the balancing of the Burmese harp tradition with the creative musical impulse and has forged his own artistic way of improvisatory expression on the *saung kauk* by continuing musical references to masters whose music he has heard live and on recordings. He is a renowned teacher of young performers, privately at home and at the Gitameit Music Institute, and judges the annual performing arts competition called "Sokayeti Pyaing Pwe". He credits his own performing ability to other harpists whose music he has listened to, yet he himself has created a community of young players who gather at his home and in other places where he teaches. A national treasure, U Win Maung is keen to raise up young musicians in Myanmar to the expressive ways of playing *saung kauk*, so that they will honor and preserve tradition while also extending it through their own creative expressions.

Q: Should children and youth experience the music of their local community cultures?
A: Yes, they should experience and study their local music community. Many young people in Myanmar do not like the traditional music of their culture. If they are given opportunities to experience the music, and to study the music in their schooling, they will grow to understand and appreciate it—and even to value it. Over time and experience, they may become musicians themselves. Further, young people everywhere should be educated in the musical cultures of the world. When they experience music from beyond their community, they will develop insights on that distant music as well as their own local music through the comparisons that they will make.

Q: Does the study of diverse musical cultures enhance musicianship?
A: Yes. Students who study their local music, and the music of other cultural communities, will have further choices when they begin to creatively express themselves. They can adapt the musical features into the music they compose and improvise.

Q: Who learns saung kauk *(Burmese or Myanmar harp) from you?*
A: My students range in age from 5 to 70 years of age. They come from various social classes. Many students are girls and women, but there are strong male musicians, too, with whom I work. The harp is a musical companion for a lifetime, and elderly people who study harp will help themselves from becoming lonely. I teach children at their family home and also at a professional music school nearby.

Q: How do you help your students to play in a stylistically accurate manner?
A: I am sensitive to the situation of each of my students, and I adapt my teaching depending upon their needs. It is important that students practice with me there, during

instruction, and I do not allow students to practice at home until they show me that they can play in front of me; once they can play a passage, I encourage them to practice at home but not until then. I watch their fingers as they pluck the strings, and I monitor their correct elaboration of pitches and appropriate ornamentation. Of course, as my students play the *saung kauk*, I am playing the *si* (bell) and *wa* (clapper) to keep them in good Burmese timing and metric accuracy.

Q: Do you use notation in your teaching?
A: Notation is not the way to learn Burmese *saung kauk* or any other Burmese music. Music is learned by listening, and that is the long-standing oral tradition. I play the *saung kauk* as a means of demonstrating to students what to play and how to play. Students can record me and then go home and listen again and again until the music becomes very familiar.

Q: How do you develop the musical creativity of your students on the saung kauk?
A: I ask students to listen repeatedly to the music so that they can be familiar with its musical features. Then, I encourage them to adapt the music, picking up phrases they know bit by bit, playing with them, adapting them, finding their own style. By listening, they will develop "let kwet", an improvisatory patter of their hands.

Q: Is it challenging to teach improvisation on the saung kauk?
A: Yes. I do not ask beginning students to improvise. If they do not have the proper instrumental techniques and fingerings, they will be unable to play in a technically and stylistically correct manner. Only after sufficient study, and that varies from one student to the next, are they ready to create their own improvisations.

Than Zaw Aung, Burmese Musician and Dancer

The music of Myanmar is many splendored, involving the various performing arts in a single program: Music, dance, brief dramatic scenes, even comedic touches. Once in a rare moment, there comes along a single artist who can engage at a very high level in multiple artistic expressions. Master musician Than Zaw Aung sings, dances, and plays a grand variety of instruments. A gold medal player of Burmese-style mandolin since the age of six years, he performs on *pattalar* (xylophone), *hsaing waing* (drum circle), *done min* (zither), and Burmese slide guitar. He studied dramatic skills and duet-dancing, and performed in a troupe for many years as a singer and player of the *maung saing* (*gong* circle). Than Zaw Aung began to study Burmese classical dance at the age of 12 years and has danced as he has also performed musically on stage in various highly regarded venues in Myanmar and on recordings and films. As is the case with artists of traditional Burmese forms, he has learned the instruments, the singing, and the dance forms over many years of concentrated sessions of observing and imitating the teacher, each of which is followed by continuous practice of positions, figures, and segments. He values artistic creativity and understands that it can be nurtured once the fundamental skills are solidly in place. Only then, atop the study of the traditional repertoire, are interpretation and improvisation possible. His performance experience and carefully constructed pedagogical technique, too, inspire and hone the skills of his students at the State School of Fine Arts in Yangon. There, he has nurtured a community of

Than Zaw Aung, Master Burmese Musician and Dancer

young artists who offer hope for the sustainability of Burmese classical expressions from now into the future.

Q: What are your thoughts about educating young students in music that comes from local communities as well as music of the world's cultures?
A: I think that all children should study the music of their local cultures so that they can have a greater understanding of the place in which they live, the people who have made their village or neighborhood what it is over the generations. I also think that musical study can help all children and youth to become better persons—by singing, playing instruments, and dancing. They should also listen and learn music from other places in the world, especially because their studies will provide them with ideas for how they might become more musically creative on their local instruments—whether it be the piano, the guitar, or the *pattalar* (xylophone).

Q: Who are the students with whom you have worked, teaching them music and dance?
A: My private studio students are mostly between the ages of 12 and 20 years, but occasionally I teach children as young as 5 years old. They are Burmese and Chinese; in fact, about 20 percent of my students are Chinese. Many of my private studio students are girls. The students of the State School of Fine Arts include many young men, in an all-male dance class, and many are very fine students who are practicing their art form every day.

Q: Can you describe some of the techniques you use in teaching music and dance to students?
A: The most important quality in teaching is patience: Waiting, watching, prompting, allowing enough time for students to develop a skill. I am with the students in both private studio lessons and class sessions, monitoring their progress; ensuring that they are getting the details of the movement of their fingers, hands, wrists, and arms on an instrument; and helping them figure out the feeling of their arms, legs, and torsos in the dance movements. Skills come slowly, and teachers must encourage the small developments even as they are thinking of the long-term development they hope for their students.

Q: Do you teach music by ear or by eye (notation)?
A: I use cipher notation, learning the musical pitches by the pitch numbers, but have great respect for the oral tradition. Often, I may mix ear training with cipher notation, as that is an efficient way to feature more repertoire within the limits of time. Interestingly, I have some older students, especially those with failing vision, who I teach entirely by ear because the notation is too difficult for them to read.

Q: Do you play for the students in person or use recordings in your music and dance sessions?
A: I like to feature live music in my lessons and classes, so I play the instruments that I teach. In a dance class, I model the movement, and we work through positions and the various arm movements and footwork. Once they have a general sense of how their body is positioned and will move, then I go to the *pattalar* to play the melody that accompanies a dance piece. Little by little, we put the phrases and sections of dance together with the music.

Q: Do you feature any sort of creative work for students—composition or improvisation?
A: Beginning students do not reach the level of improvising on their instruments because it's important that they first have the fundamental skills and musical knowledge on the instrument before they can begin to invent the music (or dance). I do show them on my instrument how they might interpret a phrase and how they may eventually discover their own style of interpreting a melody. Students do not ask me to teach them how to compose, either; they want to learn the instrument, and the musical pieces that fit the instrument. While I am a composer and feature my compositions in performances, most of the creative work that students can develop requires years of experience to learn.

Music as Creative Artistic Expression

While some music is meant to be fixed and frozen so that it can be re-created as it was first conceived, the human impulse is to personalize it, to try out new possibilities that render it fresh and new for singers and players. As demonstrated through the episodes in Creating World Music, students can be encouraged to explore new sounds, to experiment with musical features on unfamiliar instruments, and to play instruments that differ from the recordings to which they have been listening. They can sing and play in a new musical mode, with a new pitch pattern, in a new meter, or with a new rhythmic groove, even as they maintain other aspects of the learned musical work. In this way, the new music is still linked to the initial version that students had listened to and performed, even as students take small steps away from the origin music (or even leap to a major outtake from the music they have learned). They can return to the music they have listened to, participated in, and performed as closely as possible to the recording that started them on their journey. They quite naturally can be encouraged to pay tribute to the musicians of the source recordings, those who initially performed the music, and lean into understanding why the music sounds the way it does. Their analytical listening and the carefully studied performance of the music can be accomplished, even as they are also invited to seek out their own "voice", musically speaking, and allow for the realities of the creative process to take hold as they make the music their very own.

References

Fernando, B. (2017). *Here's why Ed Sheeran's "Shape of you" got an Indian classical twist.* Retrieved June 6, 2017 from www.mid-day.com/articles/ed-shreeran-shape-of-you-carnatic-version-indian-classical-music-sia-ellie-goulding/18228150

Higgins, L. (2007). Acts of hospitality: The community in Community Music. *Music Education Research, 9*(2), 281–292.

Higgins, L., & Campbell, P.S. (2010). *Free to be musical: Group improvisation in music.* Lanham, MD: Rowman & Littlefield Education.

Ketbungkan, K. (2017). *It's innovate or die for Thailand's "demon" dance master.* Retrieved March 14, 2017 from www.khaosodenglish.com/life/arts/2017/03/12/innovate-die-thailands-demon-dance-master/

Listening Episodes

"Kecuh! Riuh! Gemuruh!", Riduan Zalani and NADI Singapura, https://itunes.apple.com/sg/album/kata-kita-kota/id924288831

"Le Jig Francais", BeauSoleil, www.folkways.si.edy/beausoleil/le-jig-francais/cajun-zydeco/music/track/smithsonian

"Nange" ["Yange"], Tanzanian Wagogo musicians, https://itunes.apple.com/us/album/tanzania-tanzanie-chants-wagogo/424221991

"Shape of You", Ed Sheeran, Carnatic-fusion, https://itunes.apple.com/us/album/deluxe/id1193701079 and at https://indianraga.com/music-download

"The Pursuit", SA (三), https://sathecollective.bandcamp.com/track/the-pursuit

"Todo lo que Tengo", Quetzal, www.folkways.si.edu/quetzal/imaginaries/latin/music/album/smithsonian

Samba Brazilian Batucada Band. https://itunes.apple.com/pe/album/pure-brazilian-batucada-percussion-madness-from-brazil/id843426072?l=en

6

Integrating World Music

The eighth grade students at Jefferson Middle School were immersed in a school-wide curricular thrust on "the quest for social justice". They were reading novels meant to supply them with courage to stand for equal rights for all people within their neighborhood. These included Sharon M. Draper's Stella by Starlight, about a community that bands together against racism and injustice following a girl's witnessing of a Ku Klux Klan activity; Winifred Conkling's novel Sylvia & Aki, set in the midst of a court case for the desegregation of California schools for Latino children; and Deborah Ellis' The Breadwinner Trilogy about a young Afghan girl living in the time of Taliban rule who disguises herself as a boy to be able to work to help her family. These stories fit the curricular theme as well as societal times, particularly as a wave of social and political activism was sweeping through the country. There was much discussion in language arts and social studies classes about what young people might do within their daily lives to ensure (multi- and inter-) cultural sensitivity, and how they might act out their beliefs in order to make a difference in their world. The Jefferson Middle School music staff—Mrs. Miller, band; Mr. Adams, choir; and Mr. Smalley, orchestra and general music—were fast at work on their own music-curricular designs and had not expected to be involved in the school project that they quite frankly felt was intended for the academic subjects and not "the specials" like music and art. They were taking seriously, as they always did, the preparation of their students in the approved repertoire for the year's upcoming scholastic festivals and programs.

It was their principal who drew the music staff into active involvement in the school's plunge into meaningful curricular encounters with issues of social justice and of matters of diversity, equity, and inclusion. "You're part of our teaching team", she told them, "and your contributions are important to the scheme of things. Let me know how you'll reflect our social justice goals into your program". The trio of teachers were initially taken aback with thoughts of how to mix in yet another curricular aim, what with their time at a premium and so many professional music standards already to meet, yet they were responsive to the principal's invitation. The choir guy was first *in suggesting that he could feature a few more of the West African, Latin American, and Asian choral works in his classes and for his programs. The instrumental teachers reviewed recently published works for school ensembles and found a few "world music works" that might satisfy the new curricular mandate. Mrs. Miller wondered aloud, "Does the mere inclusion of an arrangement of a Brazilian samba tune qualify as a contribution to the social justice aim?", to which Mr. Adams remarked that "it's a start down that road, isn't it?" while Mr. Smalley slowly shook his head and remarked that "they just don't get it, what all we music teachers already have on our plates".*

The breakthrough in the conversation came when Mr. Adams suggested that they agree to try out some world music pieces in their classes, with three caveats: "(1) We can have the kids sight-read the music—they would experience it but not necessarily perform it; (2) We can have them listen to some recordings that are eclectic, diverse, global . . . you know, multicultural; and (3) We can invite in some folks to share their music, show their instruments, tell their stories". Mr. Smalley perked up: "Oh, like an accordion player for a Polish song, a gospel musician from the downtown AME church, one of those zithers from China or Vietnam, or Rashid's uncle from Oman if we do an Arab song". "Bingo! That's what I'm thinking", Mr. Adams responded, to which Mrs. Miller added, "Or . . . we could do all three: scores, recordings, and guests. And maybe the first two would be more focused on music skills while the guests could open up the kids to some ideas about people, cultural values, and social justice". The music staff at Jefferson Middle School nodded their agreement that they would go forward with a reasonable plan to pitch in on the school's journey to social justice, diversity, equity, and inclusion.

Music: Integrated and Interdisciplinary

Music is a powerful means of expressing the verbally inexpressible, of reaching beyond words to the conveyance of deep sentiment, of reflecting upon ideas and ideals, of taking hold of a concept and expressing it. It has a way of wrapping itself around us in its sonic power and of seeping itself into our consciousness for so many of its socio-cultural meanings. Why shouldn't a team of teachers find ways of factoring in music as a means of driving home a meaningful theme? Why shouldn't music be integrated within school-wide missions and across topics and themes that are routinely valued by faculty and students? Why wouldn't music "fit" into classes that are not music classes, such as those in language arts, social studies, math, science, and the visual arts—to make a point, to reinforce a reality or a belief? Why wouldn't music teachers join with teachers of other subjects to collaborate on achieving educational and social aims? Why shouldn't community members, including community musicians, be tapped to join with school personnel to support and strengthen knowledge, skills, and valued beliefs? The power of music is there, awaiting opportunities to be interfaced with an array of topics and themes and to be understood not only for its sonic features but for its multiple topical meanings.

"Integration" is a noteworthy concept in the school curriculum, attendant to a student-centered way of learning that cuts across subject matter in order to achieve relevance and meaning for learners. The point of integrating curricular subjects in schools is to help make connections for students, to deepen their understanding by enveloping all relevant ideas, and to resonate with the human penchant to learn in a global, holistic manner. Integrated learning is not bounded by the unnatural barriers of learning one subject (such as music), then another subject (such as social studies), and still another subject (such as the visual arts), each of them separated and even isolated from the others. Curricular integration advances knowledge (and skills) and presses students to grow their understanding by looking both center and sideways to associated "areas" that help to shape the greater meaning of their growing insights on life, their futures, and the world.

A key focus in a historical trace of curriculum integration is the identification of real-world problems stemming from children's interests that require an amalgamation of various subject disciplines as process to explore the issues leading toward further examination and/or resolution (Beane, 1997). There are also three different desired levels of curriculum integration that community musicians and teachers can consider: Thematic (the selection of a theme and a curriculum, such as "social justice", that is organized around the theme where connections between disciplines are limited); Knowledge (the establishment of interactive and connective relationships between the knowledge and skills in two or more disciplines, such as music and history); and Learner-initiated (the uncovering of connections by learners on their own to apply their previous knowledge and to independently integrate new information, such as attention to people's valuing of freedom through a study of freedom songs) (Burton, 2001). Excursions into new knowledge, on themes with cross-disciplinary "connection-potential" and with learner-initiated questions as guide to discovery, are critical to all music education practice that is relevant and timely. The process of World Music Pedagogy, and its outcomes, is grounded in the real-world realities of music as it interacts with and informs cultural and historical understandings.

"Interdisciplinary" is a term utilized in higher education as well as in other educational contexts to describe the combining of academic disciplines for learning ideas more thoroughly. Specialists from two or more fields pool their ideas and guide their students in the discovery of a more expansive and sometimes new knowledge. In chemical engineering, for example, interdisciplinary studies in chemistry and engineering have forged not only new insights but a new field that informs the petrochemical and pharmaceutical industries. In music, programs in ethnomusicology require study in music, anthropology, and sociology, as well as in such realms as communications, history, religion, political science, sociology, and area studies (such as African Studies and Southeast Asian Studies). Like integrated learning, interdisciplinary study maintains that through connections across the disciplines, students develop deeper and broader understandings. In interdisciplinary approaches, the design of curriculum is essentially connected with achieving specific skills and contents from each discipline. Interdisciplinary approaches should only be adopted when there are meaningful and common areas of knowledge and when connections between disciplines are strong and apparent (Chrysostomou, 2004). A musical unit that connects the study of Tex-Mex *conjunto* music with contemporary issues facing Mexican migrants can benefit studies in both music and immigration policy, and a study of K-pop can enlighten students in music and economics as to the nature of the transnational flows and influences of the music industry in Korea, in Korean communities abroad (such as in Koreatown, Los Angeles), and across East Asia where Korean pop culture, called "hallyhu", has made great strides.

To know music is to be able to listen analytically to it, to sing it, play it, dance it, and create it afresh based upon the components that have been ferreted out for framing improvisations and compositions from the original or "source" work. The full scope of knowledge is also about understanding music as music, music as culture, and music in context (Campbell, 2018). The more one can know about the history of a song, its origins and development, and its cultural meaning, the greater the understanding of the song that is listened to, sung, and created anew. A comprehensive experience with the song guarantees an unabridged and unsimplified grasp of it.

In a school curriculum, the integration of music into the study of various subjects can enlighten students of the dimensions of music as well as of the selected subjects. Thus, the weave of a song into language arts can enhance the development of literacy, of reading, writing, and speech. The meshing of music into lessons in history, geography, even civics and economics classes can do more than amuse and go all the way in illuminating insights into current and historical events here and there in the world. The mix of music with the visual arts, as well as with dance and drama, can illustrate the ways that expressive practices are fluid in many cultures and communities. Integrated learning happens when teachers join together to determine that there are multiple ways in which learning develops and that themed units such as "social justice", "respect", "friendship", "water for life", and "community" can be developed and delivered by a team of teachers across subjects and disciplines.

Relevant to an integrated curriculum is the pedagogical response to ways in which students learn. It is commonly understood that learning is enhanced and deepened when more than a single modality is activated so that learning is more than just visual, just aural, or just "doing". Because learners naturally acquire knowledge in a multimodal manner, effective teachers are those who provide experiences that channel their students' learning through auditory, visual, and kinesthetic means. As students learn aurally through carefully channeled listening, their learning is reinforced and supported further through observations of musicians in their performance practice (as well as through standard notation and their own invention of iconic and symbolic systems). They learn kinesthetically, too, by joining actively in the pursuit of music as an embodied experience that involves them as singers, players, and dancers. Successful teachers recognize that a combination of these learning pathways into multimodal experiences may result in deeper learning by students so that they retain information for the long run.

As community musicians and teachers attempt to integrate music of the world's cultures into the folds of the curriculum, they can clarify to colleagues and administrators that a greater attention to music and the arts be given that is on par with the other subjects and disciplines. Curricular integration requires that meaningful lessons are drawn up that connect to the worlds in which students live and that build upon prior experiences that allow students to create new knowledge, experiences, and a deeper understanding of life (Appel, 2006; Fogarty & Stoehr, 2008). As math, language arts, history, and the sciences are important to the making of thoughtful students, so, too, does their education in the ways that the arts contribute to the development of logic and reason, understanding, and expression. By integrating music within curricular subjects, and inserting disciplinary perspectives within music studies, the naturally global and holistic learning by students can be ensured.

Integrating World Music via World Music Pedagogy

Integrating World Music takes as its challenge the bridging of music with other fields and disciplines and the designing of music experiences that serve to teach concepts and understandings that extend beyond music. Music teachers and community musicians share an interest in integration, of merging and meshing music with all the arts, of connecting and combining music with topics that stretch from history and the humanities to the social sciences and all the way to the sciences. The possibilities for Integrating World Music are boundless; as music opens to understandings of the world, so, too, do experiences have the potential to develop and enrich musical and cultural understandings. In collaboration with one another, music educators and community musicians can also intersect with disciplinary specialists in the arts (actors, dancers, playwrights, poets, painters), as well as with those in history, geography, civics, literature and languages, health sciences, environmental studies, and all the sciences. Projects may spontaneously arise from casual conversations and late-breaking contemporary events, even as they may be a result of long-term study of timeless issues that are universally experienced and felt. Themed lessons and curricular units can be shaped around issues of communication, cooperation, the environment, freedom, friendship, identity, and peace.

Because it developed out of an ethnomusicological consciousness of music as reflective of cultural meaning and infused with cultural values, World Music Pedagogy gears itself toward curricular integration as a means of conveying music's connections to time and place. By threading music into the study of other subjects and drawing other subjects into music study, the point is made of music as central rather than peripheral to knowing the world. One means of studying music across subjects in a WMP-integrated fashion is the Cultural Prism Model (Campbell, 2004), which features a set of questions that "help to shed splinters of light from the multiple sides of a crystal prism, turning the music into a veritable treasure-load of cultural information" (p. 218). These questions emanate from students who wonder and welcome insightful musical beginnings (Who created the music? Who first performed it?), musical continuities (Who performs it now? Does it always sound the same way, or is it a genre with variability and a flexible nature?), and musical meanings (What function does the music fulfill? Do particular groups of people, as defined by age, gender, ethnicity religion, socioeconomic status, nation, or region, identify with this music?) (Campbell, 2018). Integrating World Music opens music up into the intersection of subjects, disciplines, and fields and can happen earlier or later in the scope of experiences—at the point of first listening (Attentive Listening) or in between and around experiences in Engaged Listening, Enactive Listening, and Creating World Music.

Community Musicians as "Integrative Forces"

Community musicians regularly join with dancers, actors, and painters—and could potentially be joining also with geographers, mathematicians, and physicists—to pursue principles that may be more richly understood through parallel and intersecting experience and study. In the process of making music, they may seek to artistically express constructs that derive from distant and distinctive disciplines. Artist-musicians may choose a concept such as "rest", "symmetry", "repetition", "contrast", or "chaos" to explore with fellow musicians, visual artists, poets, playwrights, filmmakers, or experts from further afield. They may work outside schools, inviting students to join them in ventures that launch from one (or several) of the world's musical cultures. They may also bring their specializations (and a few specialist-colleagues) with them into schools, tailoring projects alongside music educators that will fit the needs and interests of students.

Community musicians and culture-bearers frequently serve as important information sources for understanding music as the sociocultural expression that it is. The who-what-when-where-why-how questions that surround musical cultures can often be answered by these musicians who know who they are, what music they perform, when and where they perform it, why the music functions as it does, and how it is performed—vocally, on instruments, or in a blended way that encompasses music, dance, drama, and even the visual arts. Granted, information on music's functions and meanings can be unearthed from local libraries or by discussions with ethnomusicologists on musical cultures in question. Still, there's much to be revealed in straight-ahead dialogues with living musicians right there in a classroom (or community location) who can perform, demonstrate, facilitate participatory musicking possibilities, and talk informally about the music they know. Such dialogues can enter into matters of how a musical practice has been taught and learned (or learned but not taught) and how it has been preserved, renewed, or transformed from its original source. Living musicians are, to many students, "the real thing", and they tell stories, offer colorful descriptions, and in a conversational manner bridge the gap from the classroom to the musical culture that learners need to know.

Some community musicians engage with communities in various settings for musical, social, religious, and cultural purposes. Musicians also work with artists from different art forms to explore and experiment in cross- and inter-disciplinary ways toward the creation of new knowledge and expressions. Engaging with people and subjects outside the realm of music helps musicians to grow as they are exposed

Figure 6.1   SA(仨) collaborating with visual artist Andy Yang in a secondary school assembly performance

Courtesy of the SA Collective

to a range of familiar and unfamiliar creative processes and ways of seeing the world, enriching their repertoire of possibilities. This is particularly significant for musicians who work with different communities, trying to understand their needs and how to effectively establish musical ideas and programs that would be mutually beneficial to all parties.

Interdisciplinary Studies of Music as Cultural Expression

World Music Pedagogy commences with the sound of the music so that recordings (and video recordings and live performances) can guide learners into the world of music and into particular cultures, genres, composers, and pieces. The episodes that exemplify ways of Integrating World Music launch from the assumption that learners have listened to the music, since cultural questions and answers in the practice of teaching world music derive from the music itself. These episodes can be delivered all or in part, early or later on in the WMP process. By now the Learning Pathways (Episodes 6.1, 6.2, and 6.3) are familiar to the reader, and it's fair to say that interdisciplinary ideas on Mexican identities, Malay culture, or East African values may be inserted earlier in the musical learning process than at the tail end of study. Similarly, with regard to Episodes 6.4, 6.5, 6.6, 6.7, and 6.8, knowledge of people, cultures, and the circumstances of the music of the Japanese, the Chinese, African Americans, Native Americans, and Puerto Ricans may be visited in interdisciplinary fashion at any time within the spread of experiences in listening, participating and performing, and creative expression. Insights can emerge at the pleasure of a student who asks a burning question that, when answered, may result in her further interest and involvement. An integrative "moment" can happen at the teacher's discretion to respond to a student's "need to know" something more about the music's function and meaning. Interdisciplinary studies of music as cultural expression can lead to the realization that a particular piece of music, at a given time, may teach a powerful life lesson—about the human condition; the histories and heritages of people of a place and time; local and global communities; and the social power of music to act upon the principles of diversity, equity, and inclusion.

A Love Song in Any Language

Music illustrates everyday and momentous events in life, including the complications of falling in love, finding a balance of independent identity within the union of two people, or maintaining the self even while becoming committed to the interests and needs of another. The strategies of Episode 6.1 guide students through topics that spread from language arts to social studies, from the particularities of the love song "Todo lo que Tengo" to the similarities of love songs across cultures. The lesson embedded within a love song may spring from the personal or observed experiences of the artist, but may also be intended as a message worth telling to all who will listen. In the case of this particular song, the lesson is a wise warning for all young people to hear, to think about, and to apply. Attention can be given also to the study of Mexican-heritage musicians in the L.A.-based fusion band, Quetzal, as it may assist them in understanding Mexican musical identities in the United States as well as in the place from which the musical style they perform (*son jarocho*) originates, on the east coast of Veracruz in Mexico. Spanish language is another channel of integrated study (this has already been partly demonstrated in Episodes 3.1 and 3.4), as is a study of the historic and contemporary flows of migration and immigration from Mexico to the United States. A further stretch of music could be had through the examination of various poetic forms as expressions of love, including the Shakespearean sonnet, the sung *ghazal* poetry of Persian origin, and the popular Japanese form known as *haiku*. Astonishing as it seems to be, a single song can open the doors to many rich interdisciplinary learning experiences.

Episode 6.1: Romance in East L.A. "Todo lo que Tengo" (Learning Pathway #1)

Specific Use: Elementary Music Education, Secondary School Innovations

Materials:

- "Todo lo que Tengo", Quetzal (from *Imaginaries*), Smithsonian Folkways Recordings
- Guitar-*pandeiro* (hand drum, or other percussion), hardwood floor (*tarima*, a raised wooden platform)

Procedure:

1. Discuss the meaning of the love song, and ponder the main message that love of another does not require giving up one's own identity.

2. Clarify that love songs are present in many cultures. Challenge students to find examples of love songs in the repertoire of singers in far-flung places such as Senegal; Spain and Samoa; and Japan, Germany, and Jordan.

3. Search for information on the band Quetzal, including their location (Los Angeles), their musical influences (*son jarocho, musica ranchera, salsa,* Chicano rock, rhythm, and blues), and the struggle for social justice and dignity they express through their music. See questaleastla.com.

4. Discover more about *son jarocho* as a regional musical style from the Mexican state of Veracruz. Listen for the fusion of features that are Spanish, indigenous, and African in the recordings of artists such as Mono Blanco, Son de Madera, and Siquisiri. Find a contextualized description, with interview and sound bytes: www.npr.org/2011/10/29/141723031/a-musical-style-that-unites-mexican-americans.

5. Return to the featured recording, and discuss how the stylistic elements of the song express love and romance. Converse about whether other love songs, from elsewhere in the world, utilize similar expressive components. Decide whether the message of love can be conveyed through the music, even when the language is not understood?

Community/Culture Connection

- Invite a *son jarocho* musician into the classroom, not only to perform and lead others in performing but to share the stories of *son jarocho* musicians: Why they perform, when and where they perform, and how they were drawn to the music. Ask about the making of a *fandango* event, and find out how to develop a local fandango at which *son jarocho* is a centerpiece.
- For any visiting musicians, request a performance of their favorite love song.

Traveling With Drums

There are opportunities in Episode 6.2 to draw students into the midst of Malay culture's penchant for percussion music and for understanding the commonalities and distinctions of drums across cultures—from Malaysia to Indonesia to other parts of Southeast Asia, all the way to the eastern, western, and southern reaches of Asia. Percussion instruments are pervasive in every culture; by guiding students in tracing the origins of particular instruments, the links that cut across historical time and vast geographical spaces are clarified. In using musical instruments (such as Malay drums) as beginning points of inquiry, community musicians and students alike can uncover, by delving into history, geography, and sociocultural matters, the routes drums have traveled from country to country and the ways they are transformed in new cultures in which they land.

Episode 6.2: "Kecuh! Riuh! Gemuruh!" (Learning Pathway #2)

Specific Use: Elementary Music Education, Secondary School Innovations

Materials:

- Kecuh (Ruckus) Riuh (Chaos) Gemuruh (Thunderous)
- Track 4, from the album *Kata Kita Kota* by NADI Singapura

Procedure:

1. Note that "percussion instruments are prized in many of the world's cultures, and those that are featured in Malay musical expressions are prized for their array of various timbres". Ask students to imagine and to try to describe or represent vocally or with body percussion various percussion timbres.

2. While earlier WMP experiences have opened the ears, continued listening (with directed questions) can aid the identification of drum types:

   "Can you identify how these drums are shaped differently just by listening to the sound?" (The larger the surface area of the drumskins, the lower is the pitch of the drum.)

"Are they made of metal, or wood?" (Frames are typically made of hardwood. The *hadrah* also has brass jingles attached.)

"What do you think the playing surfaces of the drums are made of?" (Usually made out of goatskin).

"How is each drum type played?" (Some with hands and others with a mallet of different density heads)

3. Name and describe, or find illustrations of, the percussion instruments that appear in Kecuh! Riuh! Gemuruh!—the *kompang, jidur, hadrah*, and *gong*. See sites such as www.srimahligai.com/articles/instruments.htm.

4. Plot a geographic map of where these instruments (or instruments similar to these) are found in Malaysia, Borneo, Singapore, and neighboring countries such as Indonesia, Thailand, the Philippines. Ask "Have some of these instruments originated from further afield? Do the instruments belong to people of similar cultural backgrounds across these countries?" Note that the similarities of these instruments across geographic boundaries are evidence of cross-border sharing and of the mixing of cultures across history.

5. Find substitute drums/instruments in the music classroom that might simulate the timbre of these drums. If they don't sound similar, raise the question: "How can you change the timbre of your substitute instrument by affixing different materials onto the surface or the side of your substitute instrument to make them sound alike?" Explore and experiment sticking modeling clay, putting hands on the skin when playing, and listening carefully to distinguish the similarities and differences in timbre.

6. Direct further probing into the acoustical properties of instruments with these questions: "What do you notice about the size of instruments in relation to the pitch? What do you notice about timbre of sound in relation to the material being used? Can pitch and volume be adjusted by particular materials attached to the instruments? How do these explorations link to the ideas of amplitude and frequency in your science lessons?"

Community/Culture Connection

*   Arrange for a visit from a percussionist to the classroom (ideally a specialist in percussion music from Malaysia, Indonesia, Singapore, or elsewhere in Southeast Asia). Ask about the origins of the musician's instruments, and discuss familiar "relatives" of these instruments as may be found in various contexts.

*   Consider some of the scientific principles that are evident through the study of an instrument's composite materials and acoustical properties.

Musical Life in an African Village

The brilliant choral music of the Wagogo people of Tanzania piques the curiosity of first-time listeners to want to know who the singers (and players and dancers) are, why they make this music, how they learn it, why it is distinctive from other East African cultures, and where and when are they performing it. Episode 6.3 shifts the musical experiences with sub-Saharan collective song into high gear with suggested routes into the discovery of the Wagogo people, their village life, and sub-Saharan African culture at large. A visit to everyday habits and customary practices of parts of rural Africa happens through music and the interface of stories, studies of maps, and available images of people and their village surrounds. Integrated studies of music, maps, and stories are a gateway into understanding different views of the everyday and of the world, even as knowing about one African village may deepen the musical experience through a recognition of the human connection.

Episode 6.3: Sub-Saharan Collective Song
"Nange" ["Yange"]
(Learning Pathway #3)

Specific Use: Elementary Music Education, Secondary School Innovations, Choral Ensembles

Materials:

- "Nange" [or "Yange"], from the album, *Tanzania—Tanzanie: Chants*

Procedure:

1. In identifying the source of the music, explore the people and places of the Wagogo culture. On a map of Africa, go to the eastern countries, south of Kenya, and locate Tanzania. Find the old capitol, Dar es Salaam, and the new capitol (since 1978), Dodoma. In a close-up map of Tanzania, look north and east of Dodoma to the land of the Wagogo people and of some of the traditional Wagogo villages (iklulu) such as Chamwino.

2. Explore the internet for images of Africa, east Africa, Tanzania, and the Wagogo, with special attention to everyday depictions of life in urban and rural areas. Note the wearing apparel, cuisine, places of residence, schools, hospitals, business districts, and modes of transportation. Compare city life to village life, utilizing a variety of images.

3. Find examples of Wagogo music and dance, and make note of the locations in which the performances occur (at the village hall, in open communal spaces, on the ground rather than onstage). Describe the instruments, the nature of the music and dance, the interactions between and among performers, and the attire of participants. See, for example, chamwinoarts.org as a site of the annual Wagogo Music Festival featuring multiple village groups who gather for a celebration of their music and cultural heritage.

4. For children, storybooks can be interesting "shares" of insights of lifestyles and cultures and of philosophical ideals that govern their daily interactions. Explore books such as *Why the Sun and the Moon Live in the Sky* (Elphinstone Dayrell and Blair Lent), *Wangari's Trees of Peace: A True Story from Africa* (Jeanette Winter), *Giraffes Can't Dance* (Giles Andreae

and Guy Parker Rees), and *The Water Princess* (Susan Verde, Georgie Badiel and Peter H. Reynolds). For secondary school students, *Things Fall Apart* (Chinua Achebe) is a classic work that illuminates the African village experience in all of its everyday rituals, routines, and challenges.

Community/Culture Connection

- Contact Chamwino Connect for possibilities of virtual (or in-person) exchanges with Wagogo villagers, including musicians, dancers, teachers, and students. https://chamwinoconnect.org/united-states-volunteer-board/.
- Invite in culture-bearers from Tanzania, Kenya, and other East African nations, and from the wider realm of sub-Saharan Africa, to tell stories of their lives in urban and rural locations. Some stories may relate to music, musicians, and musical instruments, and a few stories may even have songs woven in for occasional singing at the cue of the storyteller.

The Concept of Ma (間)

Picture books with attractive visuals and alluring narratives can capture the hearts of children and adults alike. These books can also come alive with a colorful storyteller of the sort that is sometimes seen in the children's corner of a bookstore or a library. One can learn many things from picture books, ranging from the aesthetics of the picture books themselves (such as the beautiful intertwining of prose with the subtleties of color in the visuals) to the simple ways with which difficult and challenging topics such as poverty and loss can be brought across in a seamless and emotive manner. Episode 6.4 serves to illustrate the power of a picture book in bringing out the philosophical concept of *Ma* in the Japanese culture through the everyday soundscapes of life, supported by and seasoned with interjections of Japanese traditional music. The experience illustrates the use of a thematic approach in integrating a sophisticated concept through the use of music (and soundscape) with visual art, narrative, and connections to architecture and poetry.

Episode 6.4: The Concept of Ma (間)
"Rokudan"

Specific Use: Early Childhood, Elementary Music Education

Materials:

- "Rokudan: 16th Century Kengyo Yatsubashi", Shinichi Yuize (0'00–1'00")
- "November Steps" Toru Takemitsu (Track 1, 1:30–2:30")
- The Sound of Silence (picture book by Goldsaito & Kuo, 2016)

Procedure:

1. Read the picture book aloud to students. Pause on the page with little Yoshio, who searches for the sound of Ma (silence) after hearing the beautiful sounds of the *koto* ("The most beautiful sound", the *koto* player said, "is the sound of Ma, of silence".)

2. Play "Rokudan", 0:00"–1:00", and ask "What is the *koto* player referring to when she mentions 'the sound of Ma'?" (Silence)

3. With attention to local geography, continue reading the picture book aloud; with each space that little Yoshio encounters, ask students if they have listened to the sounds of nature, of a busy commute to school, of dining at home, of a shower or bath, of just before sleeping, or just at awakening. Ask whether any of the sounds in these places are musical and whether they have heard the Ma in between the sounds.

4. Listen together to the sounds of papers rustling, pencils and pens clicking, woodblocks tapping, guitar strings strumming, rattles shaking. Ask students whether they hear the Ma in between the sounds.

5. In a visit to spaces in the school, stop to listen to the sounds in the school lobby, the gym, the cafeteria, and the playground. Ask students whether they hear the Ma between the sounds.

6. Play "November Steps" (1:30"–2:30"), directing students to listen to the solo instruments (*biwa* lute and *shakuhachi* flute). Ask students to identify the Ma as it occurs.

7. Task small groups of students to create four or five sounds related to a space (a city street, a farm, a kitchen, a construction site, a park) and to create sounds with instruments or via body percussion that deliberately make use of Ma as silent transitions, breathing points, or pauses between one sound and the next.

8. Suggest that students take time on their own to listen to the sounds of their environment at home and in the community and to find the Ma in between the sounds.

Community/Culture Connection

- Arrange for a visit to a Japanese garden, cultural center, or museum to underscore aspects related to Ma, including the principle of "maximal influence of minimal material". Examine Ma in the clean lines of a Japanese painting or Japanese architecture and discover it in the power-packed yet brief words of the Japanese *haiku*.

- Draw attention to another interesting Japanese aesthetic concept, *wabi-sabi*. This concept is tied closely to the acceptance and appreciation of transience and imperfection. Through different disciplines, *wabi-sabi* can be explored through the visual arts, music, architecture, philosophy, and the everyday sociocultural lives of the Japanese people.

Singing for Justice (and Against Slavery)

The circumstances of slavery are heartbreaking, and the guilt of slavery is a blemish on the history of modern nation states. The American episode of enslaved Africans had moved many to express their sorrow and defiance in songs of protest. Episode 6.5 draws attention to a young mother in the time of American enslavement of Africans whose baby will be taken from her at the purchaser's option, that is, at the marketplace at which slaves are sold. Grammy award-winner Rhiannon Giddens, a singer, violinist, and banjo player (and former member of the Carolina Chocolate Drops), is drawn to the country, blues, and old-time music. She collects traditional songs of African Americans and studies their historical meaning and has spearheaded an effort to understand the complexities of America's history of slavery, racism, and misogyny. She is inspired to write songs such as "The Purchaser's Option" that are reminiscent of work songs, slave songs, and spirituals and that speak to moments of African American history, including slavery, the quest for freedom, the inequalities, and the continued hardships. This song of an enslaved mother is a modern-day protest song, an expression of resistance even in the face of the inevitable. Like many protest songs, it functions to express the struggles of people in an historical moment even as it also offers occasion for reflecting upon the right to freedom of expression, thought, and culture.

Episode 6.5: Singing for Justice (and Against Slavery) "The Purchaser's Option"

Specific Use: Secondary School Innovations, Choral Ensembles, Instrumental Ensembles

Materials:

- "The Purchaser's Option", Rhiannon Giddens

Procedure:

1. As the song is listened to and learned, ask "What is the situation of the young woman who is singing the song?" (She is a slave for purchase, soon to be sold separately from her nine-month-old child.)

2. Share the content of the 19th century slave advertisement that was once printed in a newspaper: "For sale, a remarkable smart healthy Negro wench, about 22 years of age; used to both house work and farming". Initiate discussion as to how the songwriter drew from the ad to create the song's narrative.

3. Reflect upon the chorus that cries out in defiance: "You can take my body. You can take my bones. You can take my blood, but not my soul". Ask: "How does the melody and accompaniment give accent to the words and their meaning?" (Answers may vary, including the manner in which simplicity and repetition of music and text can communicate powerful feelings.)

4. Invite students to search out details of the enslavement of African Americans, following with questions such as "What was the period in which slavery was legal in the United States? Where did the slaves come from?" (From the colonial period, as early as the 16th century, slavery was made legal in 1776 and was technically abolished in 1865. Most slaves in the United States during this period arrived from regions in West Africa, from locations of modern-day countries such as Ghana and Nigeria.)

5. Ask students to examine the situation of modern slavery in which people have been "trafficked", including the sexual exploitation of women who have no control over their bodies (or their children). How is the forced labor of human trafficking similar to slavery? Encourage students to survey the internet for insights.

6. Research the variety of songs that function to protest inequities and injustices, and probe the many ways in which socially conscious musicians express themselves. Visit https://shadowproof.com for examples of music by contemporary dissenters.

7. Explore the genre of slave songs, work songs, songs of the Underground Railroad, and Negro spirituals that were used by African slaves to motivate and energize them and give them hope for a better life beyond slavery. Find recordings of "Steal Away (to Jesus)", "Wade in the Water", "Go Down, Moses", "Follow the Drinkin' Gourd", and "Swing Low, Sweet Chariot".

Community/Culture Connection

• Invite a performer of historic and contemporary African American song forms, be it spirituals, gospel, or blues, to share these songs and their meanings.

• Invite community musicians to perform and discuss how they use music to call out racism, classism, capitalism, and issues of gender and sexuality.

Unraveling the Mysteries of Chinese Opera

The Chinese Opera is a theatrical art form that has a long history in China extending back to at least the 12th century. The integration of rich narratives, music, song and dance, martial arts, and elaborate costumes and make-up substantiates the significance of Chinese opera, and Yue Opera in particular, as a unit of study by students alongside comparisons with musical theater and Western opera. Recommended means of study and experience are offered in Episode 6.6, running the gamut of in-class and out-of-class discovery of Chinese history, geography, and literature, along with listening and viewing examples of the famous "Butterfly Lovers" melody. The episode is drawn from a project that was intended as an interactive arts experience for seniors in a multiservice facility in which secondary school students were guided by the teacher and community musicians into a study of Yue Opera. This then led to work with senior citizens of Chinese descent in a multiservice center in their own re-discovery of an opera that was likely well known to them in their youth. While this episode refers to a specific set of successful events, in a specific community, the transfer to other communities is obvious in which a musical work or tradition is learned by students and then inroads are made with residents of a senior center who can appreciate and find the interactions with young people on the music they know to be a thoroughly gratifying experience.

Episode 6.6: Unraveling the Mysteries of Chinese Opera "The Butterfly Lovers"

Specific Use: Secondary School Innovations (students working with seniors of Chinese descent)

Materials:

- Track 1 ("The Butterfly Lovers"—Chinese Folk Song)
- Track 1 ("Butterfly Lovers Violin Concerto")

Procedure:

1. Assign students in small groups to find out basic information about the history, geography, and literature surrounding Chinese opera from internet sources. The following guidelines can help teachers to facilitate discussion surrounding the topic:

    i. Assist students in a discovery of The People's Republic of China (PRC) as the world's most populous country and has a huge landmass with bordering countries that stretches from India to Russia to Mongolia. Ask students to locate where Shengzhou, Zhejiang province is on the map of China, the home of Shaoxing opera, also known as Yue Opera (geography).

    ii. Lead students in knowing the tragic love story of the Butterfly Lovers, one of the four great folktales of China. Assign them to finding out more about the history of these folktales and how they might be connected to narrative accounts in China's history (history and literature).

    iii. Note that the legend has been adapted to Chinese opera, known as Liang Zhu (梁祝) in Yue Opera. Guide students to an understanding of Chinese opera as a dramatic art form that involves spoken dialogue, song and dance, and music in which elaborate physical gestures and costuming are important components as well. Clarify that there is not just one opera style but multiple styles that range from the Peking Opera in the north of China to the Cantonese Opera in southern China (The Arts).

2. Ask students to share and compare video clips of Liang Zhu and to note the different art forms coming together to create the Yue Opera. Ask: "If one were to compare the Chinese opera with a Broadway (New York) musical, what are some similarities and differences?" (The teacher can discuss with students in terms of the varied art forms used [from visual to theatrical

forms] to instrumentation and vocal styles, including discussions about historical, social, and cultural links)

3. Subsequently, Liang Zhu has been adapted into film and television and most notably in music into the "Butterfly Lovers' Violin Concerto", composed by He Zhanhao and Chen Gang in 1958. Listen to the two tracks (folk song and violin version), and compare how each is aurally presented.

Community/Culture Connection

•   Organize an event in which community musicians, music teachers, and students can produce musical activities for seniors who might be familiar with "The Butterfly Lovers" (especially seniors of Chinese descent, typically 60 years or older, who will likely know this repertoire). Community musicians, music teachers and students can re-acquaint seniors with the repertoire and its historical context, through conversations about what they may recall about "The Butterfly Lovers."

•   Provide a performance of the repertoire (by students as trained by community musicians/teachers, featuring an arrangement of the famous Liang Zhu melody on any instrumentation that is available.)

•   Follow a performance on video with a sing-along session for seniors (or even "karaoke"), encouraging individuals or some groups to enter a dramatization of "The Butterfly Lovers" as the community musicians, teacher, and students serve as accompanists. They can also be encouraged to enact the scenes from "The Butterfly Lovers" through dance and movement, joining with community musicians, teachers, and students.

"Hillbilly" *Jibaro* Music of Puerto Rico

Puerto Rican music is alive and well in Puerto Rico, in the United States, and elsewhere in the Caribbean and in Europe. The music is a blend of influences from Spain and West Africa, and there are hints of the indigenous people, the Taino, in the vocabulary of both speech and song and in the hollowed-out gourd, the *guiro*, that is rhythmically scraped. Episode 6.7 features the country music of the small farmers of the mountainous inland communities, including the song types known as *seis* and *aguinaldo*, the latter of which is still performed during the Christmas season as a reminder of when neighbors sang, danced, and shared food as they moved from house to house. The *jibaro* tradition looks historically to an earlier time when most of inland Puerto Rico was inhabited by poor farmers who eked out a living for their families on their small plots of land and whose manual work was balanced with their expressive output as poets, composers, and storytellers. They learned to play guitars and smaller guitar-like lutes known as *cuatro* and ensured that the rhythm was always present in their lives—in the percussion instruments they played, in their dancing, and in their singing voices. Holidays were meant for celebrations in music and dance, and fiestas were important for the hard-working farmers. While *jibaro* culture is more a glance at the past than a current way of life, the music lives on among Puerto Ricans everywhere.

Episode 6.7: "Hillbilly" *Jibaro* Music of Puerto Rico
"Sies de Andino"

Specific Use: Early Childhood, Elementary Music Education, Secondary School Innovations, Instrumental Ensembles, Choral Ensembles

Materials:

- "Sies de Andino" and "Exodo Boricua" from *Boricua Roots/Raices Bor-cuas: Sings Puerto Rican Songs* (by Sandra Roldan)
- "El Alma de Puerto Rico" by Ecos de Borinquen

Procedure:

1. In study of the *jibaro* music of Puerto Rico, the attention shifts from the better-known tropical sounds of *salsa* and other popular music forms so pervasive in San Juan and in Puerto Rico's coastal communities to the folk songs of the interior mountain region of the island. On a map, locate Puerto Rico; on a close-up map of the island-nation, find towns where the *jibaro* live, such as Cidra, Milonga, Andino, Comerio, and Vega Alta.

2. Explore the culture of *jibaro*, who were historically poor *campesinos*, (farmers) living inland and working the soil, herding cows, and holding much natural wisdom. Note that while they were isolated from urban life (and have been compared to American hillbillies), they were self-sufficient, had developed their own cultural expressions, and greatly treasured their song and dance.

3. Explore "Puerto Rican hillbilly music", or *jibaro*, by listening to Sandra Roldan's songs and to the interview with Aaron Levinson, producer of *jibaro* recordings at www.npr.org/sections/world-cafe/2014/02/27/283116784/latin-roots-jibaro-music-is-puerto-rican-country-music (Wait for the performance by Quinque Domenech of "Cumbanchero" that is spliced into the interview). The essence of *jibaro* music is heard in the sounds of the guitar, *cuatro* (small guitar of five pairs of double strings), and percussion instruments such as the *guiro* (gourd rasp, or "scraper") and the bongo. Discuss *jibaro* music as it compares to Puerto Rican *salsa* and urban popular music.

4. Using Sandra Rolduan's "Exodo Boricua", observe that the song tells of Puerto Ricans who have moved to the United States for economic reasons. Assign students the task of understanding the migration of Puerto Ricans to New York City and other American locations and the relationship of "Newyoricans" (Puerto Rican heritage residences of New York) with New York and San Juan (and elsewhere in Puerto Rico).

5. View together the video recordings of Ecos de Broinquen, with attention to instruments and their techniques, the styles of the singing voices, the contexts of the music—as the gatherings in the countryside and in the recording studio—and the involvement of not only musicians but the community at large.

Community/Culture Connection

- Through in-person visit or by Skype, discover through conversations the identity of Puerto Ricans as American citizens whether they were born on the island or on the US mainland. Engage them in conversations about family and neighborhood get togethers as to the role that music and dance play in their celebrations (and do not be surprised to learn how music [and food] are standard ingredients).

- Request a culture-bearing community musician to perform a *jibaro* song like Victor Jara's "Al Ver Sus Campos" or to offer a lesson in dancing to *salsa*, bomba, or a recording of reggaetón.

Handshakes, Moccasins, and Dancing in the Round

Indigenous people of North America, even within a particular region, may be distinguished from group to another by language, cultural traditions, and customary practices. While they may borrow and be influenced by their neighbors and by the ideas that appear on TV, films, and the internet, they nonetheless assemble trademark expressions of culture. Adjusting the lens to particular tribal groups that reside within the same region, however, there is diversity by way of the songs they sing and the instruments they play. Episode 6.8 shares some of the repertoire of Native American groups living in the southwestern United States, in "the land of enchantment" known as New Mexico, including the Navajo, the Mescalero Apache, and Pueblo groups in Taos. They continue the old music, including the ceremonial songs, the ageless game songs, and the social dance songs, even as they play with the creative possibilities for performing it differently—adding guitars, tambourines, and an occasional synthesizer. They sing out every sentiment, from disappointment, loneliness, and fear to the joys of friendship, homecoming, and human kindness.

Episode 6.8: Handshakes, Moccasins, and Dancing in the Round "The Handshake"

Specific Use: Early Childhood, Elementary Music Education, Secondary School Innovations, Choral Ensembles, Instrumental Ensembles

Materials:

- "The Handshake", by A. Paul Otega, "Moccasin Game Song", by A. Paul Ortega and Sharon Burch, and "Taos Pueblo Round Dance Song", by Ruben Romero, Ernest Martinez, and Juan O. Lujan, from *Music of New Mexico: Native American Traditions*

Procedure:

1.   As this trio of songful melodies are learned, there are descriptions of origin and function that give meaning and value to them. For each of the selections, encourage students to ask questions that will offer further perspective on the songs and singers.

2.   Compare the opening (and closing) melodic phrase of "The Handshake" to recordings of the "Zuni Sunrise Song", from which the song is adapted, noting that songs are shared across cultural groups (in this case, from the Zuni to the Mescalero Apache). See https://itunes.apple.com/us/album/native-american-flutes-11-relaxing-indian-songs-performed/997264365 for examples of sunrise songs.

3.   Describe "The Handshake" as pointing out the poverty of Native Americans who have relocated from rural areas and reservations to large cities, as well as the song's expression of the Native American value of human kindness. Ask students to explain the possible relationship between the two meanings.

4.   Challenge students to respond to questions about the moccasin: "What is a moccasin?" (A shoe of deerskin or soft leather chiefly meant for outdoor use.) "Who wears moccasins?" (Many indigenous people of North America wore moccasins.) "Why are moccasins worn?" (To protect the foot while also allowing the wearer to feel the ground.)

5.   Play the moccasin game by lining up a row of moccasins (or other shoes) and hiding a treasure (or a pebble) in just one of them, allowing the opponent(s) opportunities to guess the location of the treasure. Clarify that the moccasin game songs derive from a creation myth that tells of day and night creatures who would come out to play the game to determine whether day or night should prevail; because the game did not end before sunrise, the result was undetermined so that both day and night were continued.

6.   As students learn to sing the "Taos Pueblo Round Dance Song", ask "Why do indigenous people perform dances in the round?" (The round dance is a healing ceremony that became a social dance for indigenous people, and the joining of hands in a circle creates unity even as the beat of the drum for the dance has been compared to the community's heartbeat.)

7.   Ask students to explain the presence of the guitar in "The Handshake" and "Moccasin Game Song" while noting its absence in "Taos Pueblo Round Dance Song". Encourage them to consider that cultures have older and newer layers of interest and influence and that the round dance song derives from an early time when singing was all that was necessary for inspiring the dancing, while the use of the guitar in the other two songs may indicate the migration of the Spanish and the Western cowboy to New Mexico, both of whom favored the guitar. That said, challenge students to listen for the addition of instruments that contemporize the dance (the tambourine and the synthesizer).

Community/Culture Connection

- Talk with indigenous people, whether in person or over the internet. Ask questions about their uses of music and of the older and newer songs in their repertoire. Find out whether there is a tendency of the group to preserve or innovate (or both) and reasons for the decision.

- Under the guidance of a culture-bearer, explore the relationship of indigenous people to nature. Invite the science teacher to join in conversations of understandings of the natural elements (earth, wind, water, sky).

Music for Active Citizenship

Beyond episodes that are inserted here and there across the curriculum, teachers can guide students in taking on roles that they can play as active artist-citizens in school and community settings. Music, dance, drama, and the visual arts can provide a safe space to express, dialogue, and even confront issues that impact a community, and they can also turn feelings into actualities that make life better for all concerned. Living together in a globalized, fluid, and technologized world often means encountering increasingly unfamiliar and diverse settings and human "flows". An understanding of others in ways that surpass mere tolerance is necessary yet challenging in these tumultuous and changing times. Empathy and a genuine commitment to cultural sensitivity and inclusion is a noble educational goal that can be accomplished through active artistic citizenship. Cultural diversity can be embraced for "its dynamic nature and the challenges of identity associated with cultural change" (UNESCO World Report, 2009, pp. 3–4) rather than as just an asset to be preserved. All the arts serve as platforms to highlight and bring to the fore these historical, sociocultural, and political shifts, "making special" (Dissanayake, 1999) the human activities that are embedded within the community, as all the arts can be used to critically reflect upon valued ideals and ideas.

The emotional power that music invokes in gathering, invoking, and motivating people into action has long been evident. Music is notable for raising an awareness in students of political, social, environmental, and cultural causes and concerns. Large-scale charity concerts have been organized to support people affected by natural disasters and health epidemics, even as political songwriting has been aimed at furthering positions and music videos have been produced to promote peace and harmony. In school, music teachers and community musicians are known to be open-eared about issues that are important locally, nationally, and globally, and to lend their voices as they engage in active citizenry through artistic means.

One exemplary program of music for active citizenship comes out of *The Playing for Change Foundation* (https://playingforchange.org/about/). The foundation provides free classes in dance, musical instruments, world languages and musical theory, all with the intent of fostering resilience and joy, especially for marginalized and at-risk children and youth. In Argentina, Bangladesh, Brazil, Ghana, Mali, Nepal, Rwanda, South Africa, Morocco, Mexico, and Thailand, these programs are guided by principles of economic empowerment (using local materials and labor when building and employing locals as teachers and administrative staff for each program), the importance of local leadership (affirming the capacity of local village and community leaders), the use of music to transform lives and communities (emphasizing for example, tolerance and shared understanding), and the connection of communities through technology (encouraging learners to tell their own stories in order to know peers who live in different regions and circumstances). Write-ups and short videos of the various programs can be found at https://playingforchange.org/programs/ and are noteworthy for inspiring experiences grounded in principles of diversity, equity, and inclusion.

"Seeing" World Music

The multimedia experience is commonplace in today's hyper-global and technologized society, so that communities of musicians and musical communities are variously portrayed by the media to the public. Students now experience and value music as sound *and* image, with these images ranging from the familiar and unfamiliar, from standard and stereotypical to the uncommon and even the bizarre, serving commercial, historical, socio cultural, and political functions. Musical-visual pairings include musicians in their traditional wear playing traditional instruments, and festivities and celebrations of music, dance, and theater forms. At times, these pairings attempt to represent culture in a single instance, which can lead to stereotypical mapping: Indian sitarists, Mexican-heritage *mariachi* trumpet players, African American blues guitarists, Spanish guitarists, Chinese *erhu* players, Iranian *tar* players, and Brazilian *sambanistas*. On the other hand, when an image appears of a Chinese person with a *sitar*, for instance, the immediate reaction may be surprise and awe, with praise for the musician who plays music outside her culture (no matter how well she may really play). No critical examination of the musician's background and training may come forward, nor an attempt to explain the musician's perspective, which then may lead the observer to simply offer that this player is exemplifying "harmonious multiculturalism". Neither stereotypes nor unexplained images do justice in the messages they carry, but with discussion and study by students with teachers, the inaccuracies and confusion could be clarified and alleviated. Community musicians can be invited in to tell their stories and share their impressions of the use and misuse of images and clarify their own sense of who they are before and beyond the visual images.

Visual images are powerful communication tools and become even more so as sound is added. Musical-visual pairings should be studied as "political texts for the purpose of developing critical citizenship in the cause of social reconstruction" (Duncum, 2005, p. 154). A study of the world's musical cultures can benefit from multimedia experiences to enable students to enter into critical and reflective dialogue on musical, historical, national, sociocultural, or political issues. They can become grounded in the questions they may wish to raise as to how musicians represent their first culture as shaped by race, class, and gender and how they may choose to step outside this representation, and their "first culture", to perform music in ways that are personally shaped by their particular interests and training

Learning about artists and their choices of the musical style(s) they express can entice students of every age, especially through their live interactions with community musicians. Splitting a class into multiple smaller groups of four or five students, these study groups can be charged with going together to a local concert for observation and pre-arranged post-concert interviews. Performers of a wide range of musical styles, whose programs may be scheduled in concert halls, clubs, community centers, parks, and places of worship, make good choices for the assignment, including Brazilian *capoeira*, Korean *samulnori*, Estonian choir, Native American *powwow*, Cantonese opera, Afro-Cuban drumming, Filipino *rondalla*, and so many more. Observations can be made of the demographics of the concert audience, the physical appearance of the performers (clothing, hairstyles, shoes) as well as audience members, the performance space itself, the concert publicity (posters, social media announcements, banners), and audience reactions that can be observed during the concert itself as well as through conversations at intermissions and following the performance. Of course, program contents can be listed by title, and descriptions of the music can be researched and offered. Post-concert interviews by the study groups can explore questions of representation: Does the music represent the performers with regard to race, class, gender, and power? What are some of the anomalies that students notice about the performance with regard to musical-visual representation? How do the observations and interviews inform the study group of the demographics and sociocultural norms of performers and audiences in the local community? Results of the small groups can be shared and compared with findings by other groups.

As a furthering of the musical-visual pairing in socio-media space, students can attempt to search for a music video of a world fusion band on the internet. Examples include "Deep Impact" or "Akatsukino Ito" by Wagakki Band (Japanese Fusion Rock Band), "Xiger Xiger" or "Baifang" by Hanggai (Mongolian Folk Rock Band) and "Little White Boat" or "Gratitude" by the TENG Ensemble (Singapore Fusion Ensemble). Students in their groups can attempt a visual and musical analysis of the selected music video. For visual analysis, features for study can include the physical environment in which the video was shot, the physical appearances of the musicians, the instruments used, the narrative to the video, the close-ups and pan shots, the pace of the video against the music, other characters/objects appearing in the video, etc. For musical analysis, students can listen for musical elements of different genres that might have been fused by the musical groups and try to see if there might also be visual cues to indicate these fusion elements. Students, along with their teachers, can also have critical dialogues that surround the intentions of musicians through their music videos along the lines of national, sociocultural, or political commentaries or innuendos.

Music and Culture in the Hands of Community Musicians

Community musicians make lives worth living as they don their dynamic roles as players, singers, dancers, and actors in their quest to shape the musical sounds they can express for all who will listen. They play pianos and *pipas*, steel pans and *sitars*, flutes and fifes, *kotos*, koras, and *concertinas*, *djembes* and *jew's harps*, *tablas* and tambourines, and so much more. They leverage changes through the songs they sing, advocating civic decency, human respect, and social justice. Community musicians can be interdisciplinary, too, selecting for performance the types of music that can draw the imaginations of listeners to far-flung places across the globe and to historic, recent, and current times. They are often integrators, piecing ideas together in musical ways that have punch and power. Some community musicians are activist-artists, speaking truth through the music they make. Many teach music in the community, and enjoy opportunities to bring their ideas to the schools—if only teachers would invite them in.

Joe Seamons, Banjoist and American Folk Musician

From the backwoods of northwest Oregon, American roots musician Joe Seamons learned the old-time clawhammer-style banjo, acoustic guitar, and harmonica. He plays and sings all sorts of "American music", including folk, gospel, early jazz, blues, and "old-time" fiddle tunes. He recalls the community that would gather at his family home, with his parents and their friends pitching in the sounds of their guitars, autoharps, hammered dulcimers, and banjos. They would play their locally composed songs, too, and learn the history of their region's logging and fishing cultures. Joe grew up hearing them, and the music of his parents' record collection, all of which brought him to seek out modern interpreters of enduring American music traditions. He credits some of his professional life with the intensive instruction he's had with master finger-pickers (guitar) John Miller, Guy Davis, and Andy Cohen and banjoists Hobe Kytr and Jerron Paxton. Joe learned Piedmont-style harmonica from Phil Wiggins, a nationally known harmonica player, and he freely admits learning music from listening to record collections as widespread as Joni Mitchell, Bob Dylan, OutKast, Nas, Boys II Men, and Lauren Hill. He claims that the music of black America, from ragtime through jazz, blues, and rap, was among the most influential to him. He is "Joe" of "Ben and Joe", two community musicians who perform, teach, and celebrate the integration of the musical experience in the study of people, place, and historic time.

Joe Seamons, American Folk Musician

Q: Can you offer some thoughts regarding experiences by young people in the music of locally living cultures?
A: Children should absolutely experience and study their local cultural heritage—whether it be music, food, basketweaving, or any form of folk art. Knowing, manifesting, and transmitting that cultural heritage is a tremendously grounding force—it creates an unshakeable part of one's identity and gives one more confidence and curiosity to step outside of your comfort zone and experience a wide range of other cultures.

Q: Do you think that children/youth should experience and study music of people and places throughout the world?
A: Yes. Intelligent thinking, the process of generating insights and growing knowledge, is based on the ability to form analogies. "This reminds me of that, but is different because . . . " is an essential line of thinking for any well-rounded human being to undertake. When you recognize that your own identity is just one lens with which to view the world, your perspectives on the world become flexible and adaptable. My experience in traveling the world and exploring local cultures has taught me that learning all you can about other cultures is simply the flip side of the coin—the first side being your own culture. My study of the music of black Americans has opened doors and widened horizons for me throughout my adult life, despite the fact that I did not know African American culture in my developing years. In studying the musical heritage of people, at first we experience wonder, bewilderment, and a gentle sort of shock. Then, we either turn away from the experience due to the difficulty of processing it, or we seek out those who can help us to understand the people behind the music. If we choose to engage with the music and the people, this leads to new relationships, unanticipated connections, and personal growth.

Q: Who do you teach?
A: As a working community musician, I've worked with many dozens of students in schools, and I've performed for thousands more. The children with whom I've managed to establish strong working relationships are generally ages 10–13. I work with colleagues like Ben Hunter in after-school settings and teach workshops and school-day residencies. We offer educational concert programs nationwide through our non-profit's program, *The Rhapsody Project*.

Q: How do you help students to come close to re-creating the music of a given culture in a stylistically accurate way?
A: Ultimately, the greatest American roots musicians are at their best when they sound like themselves. So, we do well to expose students to a wide variety of recordings (of American roots music as well as other musical styles in the world) and to show them the techniques that will ultimately allow them to come closest to the sounds they're hearing and imagining inside their heads. We probably cannot attain complete stylistic accuracy among our students as they perform the music, but we can develop their keen awareness of stylistic conventions. We can also consider that students need to develop their own personal musical styles, and they should feel free to borrow stylistic traits from traditions that resonate with them—on the condition that they are willing to acknowledge those stylistic debts when possible.

Q: Do you use notation in teaching music?
A: I deliberately avoid notation with our students so that they are compelled to "learn by ear". I am trying to revive aural traditions that free young musicians from feeling that they need a piece of paper in front of them to learn a song. I will, occasionally, write out a chord chart and instruct the students in how to spell a given set of chords. I regularly play recordings of the music I want them to know.

Ben Hunter, Violinist-Fiddler and American Folk Musician

A player of many instruments and styles, Ben Hunter holds a university degree (BA) in Violin Performance, having studied violin from an early age. He grew up listening and doing music while a child in Zimbabwe at an after-school program of *marimba, mbira*, and Shona-style song and dance and later in Phoenix, Arizona, where he came to know the hip-hop, R&B, and popular music of his generation as well as the music of his mother's generation: Motown, blues, jazz, soul, funk, folk, rock n roll, classical, and opera. Through the travels in his youth, he also listened to a lot of Mexican, South American, and African music. He played trumpet, saxophone, and drums while

Ben Hunter, American Folk Musician

in school, and today he enjoys singing and playing violin, mandolin, guitar, piano, and percussion instruments and exploring specific genres such as Manouche Jazz, Choro, and Quebecois. Some of his own compositions employ these instruments and genres, too, from blues to soul, and he counts some of his major influences the music of Sam Cooke, Marvin Gaye, The Supremes, The Temptations, Michael Jackson, Billy Joel, Paul Simon, Wynton Marsalis, Joshua Bell, OutKast, and Habib Kouite. He is "Ben" of "Ben and Joe", two community musicians who perform and teach American Roots music and who delve into the histories of the music they make.

Q: Can you offer some thoughts regarding experiences by young people in the music of locally living cultures?
A: Music, period, is indispensable in the lives of young people. I think that learning music from local cultures is just a more effective way to let music into the lives of young people in a way that will make them keep music throughout their entire lives. This is particularly hard, though, because American society, as much as we brag about diversity, is actually about homogenization. While there are pockets in the United States where musical traditions live strong, there are lots of places where trying to fit in to a mainstream culture is more important. The obvious benefits of knowing living cultures are: A sense of self and identity; learning one's heritage and culture (hopefully, paired with food and lore); and finding strength in knowing one's roots and expanding on them with each generation, allowing each new generation to contribute to the inherently changing, evolving nature of culture.

Q: Do you think that children should experience and study music of people and places from throughout the world?
A: Absolutely! One of the greatest things about our shrinking world is the exchange of knowledge in the pursuit of our human history on this earth. The more we are able to explore the music, and the art, food, and traditions of different cultures around the world, the better we can understand our common humanity—and trace common and distinctive components of our lineage. Music and art hold the stories of our past in ways that often are excluded from the history books. Musicians documented what they experienced, and the observations and ideals of a time are passed down over the generations. I also just think that children are adept at connecting dots in more profound ways than adults can. They are further away from the prejudice and the kinds of judgments that society fosters in us as we grow older, more cynical, more "experienced".

Q: Who do you teach?
A: I teach predominantly in the city of Seattle and have worked as a community musician in the South End for about ten years with colleagues like Joe Seamons. Many of my students are middle school children, all backgrounds and races, although I also work with adult students. I also founded an organization called Community Arts Create, which offers a variety of arts opportunities and events; one of our programs is called The Rhapsody Project, which takes our program of folk and blues music into grade schools, middle schools, high schools, and universities all over the country.

Q: How do you help students to come close to re-creating the music of a given culture in a stylistically accurate way?
A: I find "stylistically accurate" a hard term to cope with when teaching American folk music. I can show students the music, play it for them, tell them the history, and

give them the techniques of those recordings or styles. As mentioned before, though, especially in a place like America, those styles and techniques are naturally going to evolve. There are those real sticklers, calling themselves "traditionalists" and trying to maintain one perfect sound that is frozen in time. But "tradition" is a contradiction in terms because traditions change with each generation. The best thing I can do in my teaching is to make, play, and sing the music as we can while also ensuring that my students understand where the music came from to give respect to the people and the conditions that produced that music. With the world's musical expressions, there are stylings to observe and real attempts to get the dialect and the nuances of the music—as best as we can to respect the music and the musicians. But really, I try and use music as a way to teach how to engage in life and with people. It takes a lot of listening, a lot of self-work, and it always works best when we collaborate with the musicians who know this music.

Q: When you teach and/or facilitate music learning, do you use notation? What sort of notation?
A: Not often but sometimes. It depends on the music that I teach. Jazz, choro, manouche jazz, classical—these genres almost require notation because there are a lot of notes to know, and a visual often helps students absorb it. But this style of music is generally for more adept players who likely read music already. But when I teach American folk music of any sort, I do so through listening. I play "live", and I play recordings so that students can hear just how weird and awesome music can be. Kids want to be able to play it the way they hear it, and they often appreciate the music more when they can hear an old recording. I often tell a backstory about the song, the composer, the performer, or the time period, and we listen and make sense of the recording in that way.

Weaving Music Into Schools and Communities

When integrated with understandings of people, places, historic times, and contemporary issues, music is made all the more colorful. It sometimes becomes more humanly meaningful when the backstories behind the music and musicians are offered, when functions and uses can be relayed, when music then and there can be understood as expressive of people's dreams and yearnings as well as their everyday circumstances and settings. Music teachers, and teachers of all subjects, can effectively guide students' understandings of life's lessons, and of important skills, too, when they weave music into language arts, social studies, and community concerns and by looping various subjects into music. Likewise, community musicians who visit schools and co-create (with students) school and community performances are all the more interesting when they can tell the stories behind the music. Because music is so much more than a sonic experience, the integration of insights that arise from attention to interdisciplinary meanings is a vital part of teaching world music.

References

Appel, M. (2006). Arts integration across the curriculum. *Leadership, 36*(2), 14–19.

Beane, J. A. (1997). *Curriculum integration: Designing the core of democratic education.* New York: Teachers College Press.

Burton, L. (2001). Interdisciplinary curriculum: Retrospect and prospect. *Music Educators Journal, 87,* 17–21.

Campbell, P. S. (2004). *Teaching music globally.* New York: Oxford University Press.

Campbell, P. S. (2018). *Music, education, and diversity: Bridging cultures and communities.* New York: Teachers College Press.

Chrysostomou, S. (2004). Interdisciplinary approaches in the new curriculum in Greece: A focus on music education. *Arts Education Policy Review, 105*(5), 23–30.

Dissanayake, E. (1999). "Making special": An undescribed human universal and the core of a behavior of art. In B. Cooke & F. Turner (Eds.), *Biopoetics: Evolutionary explorations in the arts* (pp. 27–46). Lexington: International Conference on the Unity of the Sciences.

Duncum, P. (2005). Visual culture art education: Why, what and how. In R. Hickman (Ed.), *Critical studies in art and design education* (pp. 151–162). Bristol: Intellect.

Fogarty, R., & Stoehr, J. (2008). *Integrating curricula with multiple intelligences: Teams, themes, and threads* (2nd ed.). Thousand Oaks, CA: Corwin Press.

Goldsaito, K. & Kuo, J. (2016). *The sound of silence.* New York, NY: Little, Brown & Company.

UNESCO World Report. (2009). *Investing in cultural diversity and intercultural dialogue.* Paris: UNESCO.

Listening Episodes

"El Alma de Puerto Rico", Ecos de Borinquen, www.folkways.si.edu/ecos-de-borinquen/el-alma-de-puerto-rico-jibaro-tradition/latin-world/album/smithsonian

"Exodo Boricua", Sandra Roldan, *Boricua Roots/Raices Borcuas: Sings Puerto Rican Songs,* www.folkways.si.edu/sandra-roldan/boricua-roots/raices-boricuas-sings-puerto-rican-songs/caribbean-latin-world/music/album/smithsonian

"Kecuh! Riuh! Gemuruh!", Riduan Zalani and NADI Singapura, https://itunes.apple.com/sg/album/kata-kita-kota/id924288831

"Moccasin Game Song", A. Paul Ortega and Sharon Burch, *Music of New Mexico: Native American Traditions,* www.folkways.si.edu/ruben-romero-ernest-martinez-and-juan-o-lujan/taos-pueblo-round-dance-song/american-indian/music/track/smithsonian

"Nange" ["Yange"], Tanzanian Wagogo musicians, https://itunes.apple.com/us/album/tanzania-tanzanie-chants-wagogo/424221991

"November Steps", Toru Takemitsu, https://itunes.apple.com/ip/album/toru-takemitsu-november-steps-viola-concerto-corona/id05699045

"Rokudan: 16th Century Kengyo Yatsubashi", Shinichi Yuize, *The Concept of Ma* (間), www.folkways.si.edu/shinichi-yuize/rokudan-16th-century-kengyo-yatuhashi/world/music/track/smithsonian

"Sies de Andino", Sandra Roldan, *Boricua Roots/Raices Borcuas: Sings Puerto Rican Songs,* www.folkways.si.edu/sandra-roldan/boricua-roots/raices-boricuas-sings-puerto-rican-songs/caribbean-latin-world/music/album/smithsonian

"Taos Pueblo Round Dance Song", by Ruben Romero, Ernest Martinez, and Juan O. Lujan, *Music of New Mexico: Native American Traditions,* www.folkways.si.edu/

ruben-romero-ernest-martinez-and-juan-o-lujan/taos-pueblo-round-dance-song/
american-indian/music/track/smithsonian

"The Butterfly Lovers", Chinese Folk Song, https://itunes.apple.com/us/album/fairy-
ballad-chinese-folk-songs-butterfly-lovers/id153856000

"The Butterfly Lovers Violin Concerto", https://itunes.apple.com/sg/album/butterfly-
lovers-violin-concerto-tchaikovsky-violin/id295341526

"The Handshake", A. Paul Otega, *Music of New Mexico: Native American Traditions*,
www.folkways.si.edu/ruben-romero-ernest-martinez-and-juan-o-lujan/taos-pueblo-
round-dance-song/american-indian/music/track/smithsonian

"The Purchaser's Option", Rhiannon Giddens, *Singing for Justice (and Against Slavery)*,
https://itunes.apple.com/us/album/freedom-highway/1179556528

"Todo lo que Tengo", Quetzal, www.folkways.si.edu/quetzal/imaginaries/latin/music/
album/smithsonian

7

Surmountable Challenges and Worthy Outcomes

A visiting artist from the community (who shall go unnamed) arrived late for an assembly at the K–8 grammar school and did not deliver "the goods" as promised. The entire student population, the teachers, and a fair sprinkling of parents were already gathered when the artist strolled into the gym with his collection of instruments (and a hot, steaming latte in hand). While the late arrival could have been a part of the show, the artist was fixed on pulling instruments out of cases, setting them out on makeshift stands of chairs and atop the cases themselves. He tap-tap-tapped and tested the microphone and then proceeded to tune the instruments to one another. Ms. Wilcox, the music educator, was quite literally beside herself, attempting to assist him in hustling along his preparations, explaining to the principal (three times) that the show would soon begin, and asking students to "talk quietly among themselves". At 25-minutes past the scheduled time for the assembly, the visiting artist began to play, sing, and talk with his assembled listeners. His performance was riveting, and his repartee with the audience colorful and animated. He had immediately captivated them and held them in rapt attention even as he also invited their participation rhythmically and in singing a repeating phrase at the close of every verse. All were in flow, and the gym was filled with happy patting, clapping, and singing. It was unfortunate, then, that just 20 minutes into the program, Ms. Wilcox (at the insistence of the principal who always adheres to the realities of school schedules), stepped to the microphone to thank the artist and dismiss the students back to their classrooms. The letdown was unmistakable, with a collective roar of "aws" and moans filling the room. In the 45 minutes of the program's allotted time, the roller-coaster ride of emotions was widely felt by the captive audience—from frustration to elation to exasperation and disappointment.

Mr. Ferris was keen to enrich the musical lives of his secondary school students, to offer them diverse experiences in music of the world's cultures. For the sake of his students who were enrolled in his two wind bands, the chamber orchestra, a mixed choir, and a course in "musical explorations", he decided that he would take seriously the school's diversity mandate by expanding the repertoire to which his students would *listen and learn to perform. As per the dimensions of World Music Pedagogy, he would also ensure that they played with some creative ways of launching new musical expressions that could be based on the selected recordings and that he would guide his students in trying to make sense of the cultural meaning of the music through interdisciplinary cultural and historical understandings of the songs and styles they were learning. He was delighted with the idea of having a fully multiculturalized curriculum and hoped to bring in culture-bearing musicians he knew in the community who would share their homemade music on the Japanese* koto, *the* atumpan *(talking drum) of the Ashanti of Ghana, the Brazilian* berimbau *(monochord), the harps of Mexico and Myanmar, the Irish* bodhran *(hand drum), the Comanche wood flute, the* hardingerfele *(fiddle) of Norway, and the* sitar *and* sarod *of India. Alas! Mr. Ferris learned that the budget had been spent earlier than usual. Once he'd paid for repair of two violas and the string bass, choral stands to replace the rickety ones he'd retired last year, new reeds for the wind instruments, and the rental of scores for the spring musical, he was left with just enough funds for a single culture-bearer. Hands down, the artist Mr. Ferris had selected certainly knew his instrument (the bodhran) and could sing verse upon verse of Irish songs and ballads (in English and Gaelic), and student response was enthusiastic. However, his aim of offering up-front-and-personal experiences with a many-splendored diversity of music and musicians was not achieved.*

The plan did not go down well for the preschoolers, nor for the residents of the senior center, despite the very best intentions of the preschool teacher (Kim), the center's recreation director (Phyllis), and the African drummer (Gwen). The aims and outcomes they'd shared were far flung: To provide a program of West African songs and rhythms, to advance an intergenerational experience in arts and culture, and to provide a sociomusical experience for the elders and the young children. Kim and her two aides arrived at the center with the children in tow, each child connected to the other by means of colorful ties that were wrapped round the waists of the clustered little preschoolers. Phyllis had directed her staff to assist the elders in taking seats in the cafeteria-and-cards room and to arrange for the non-ambulatory to find good viewing positions in their wheelchairs. There were plenty of smiles to go around as the little ones filed into the room and followed their teacher's directions to sit cross-legged on the floor in two rows just in front of the seated seniors. All were in anticipation of the performer, who was dressed in a dazzling full-length dress with flowing sleeves, a matching turban, and a fringed shawl. Gwen opened with a complicated rhythm on the djembe *drum that led into a full-voiced song in an "African language", the meaning of which was lost to the listeners. Several more rhythms and songs followed the first, without break and in the same order:* Djembe *rhythm and African-language song. The preschoolers soon began to wiggle to the rhythms, while the seniors clapped and nodded, their smiles fading as the performance proceeded without greeting nor performer-to-audience exchange nor translation. The sound system was effective in fully magnifying the drum's tones and overtones and the singer's voice, but it was probably unnecessary given the small space. Before the third song was finished, the children were bursting with wiggles and giggles, while several of the seniors were holding their hands over their ears to muffle the sounds.*

A middle school student group, led by their music teacher, Mr. Jackson, had worked collectively over the winter months in the studio of a trio of Japanese musicians (play-ers of koto *[zither],* shamisen *[lute], and* shakuhachi *[flute]) to come up with a joint performance in late April at a local community club. The Saturday of the performance was perfectly set in the sun-dappled courtyard where the cherry blossoms were in full bloom. The 22 students were poised to sing and to play on their wind, brass, and percussion instruments, and the Japanese musicians were sprinkled in between the middle schoolers. The melodies sailed, the rhythms ebbed and flowed, and there were moments of individual and coalescing group expressions. Midway through the performance, Mr. Jackson's school principal suddenly turned to him and confided, "I thought the students were supposed to immerse themselves in Japanese music? But this is not Japanese music, not at all. What have they been learning in the last few months?" Mr. Jackson was suddenly tense and confused because he heard the music as clearly musical, expressive, and with attention to important Japanese principles: There were transparent, unhurried, and uncluttered melodies, some virtuosic passages, and occasional silences. This was no "Sakura" arrangement for wind band but rather a more profound experience meant for expressing a Japanese mode or character. The middle school students were thoroughly "present" and engaged, and the audience was quietly fascinated. As the performance ended, and, following enthusiastic applause, the students gathered around the Japanese artists to thank them for the opportunity to perform the collaborative pieces they had composed. Clearly, the students understood, through their own experience, the Japanese essence as it can be musically expressed. Mr. Jackson stood by, observing the post-concert banter, while the principal quipped, "Whatever. I liked the music, anyway".*

Successful School-Community Intersections

In the spirit of World Music Pedagogy, with the aims of diversity, equity, and inclusion in mind, there is increased interest by teachers in connecting schools to communities of living musicians. School-community intersections are happening during school time and on school sites—in classrooms, auditoriums, gyms, cafeterias, and even in the outdoors. They are happening in community contexts ranging from libraries and museums to church basements and music shops. They are happening after school, sometimes before school, and over the course of special summer enrichment programs outside the scholastic year. Young learners are primed and ready to absorb music anywhere and across many cultures. They are drawn to the musical energy of active musicians for what they sing, play, and have to say about the music and are enamored by stories of the people and the places from which the music comes. Successful school-community intersections are often transformative for students (and their teachers) when it comes to learning music, understanding culture, and growing their grasp on human life.

Success is never automatic. In the cases described above, there were flaws from the start, or that surfaced along the way, that resulted in a lessening of the learning outcomes. Despite the best of intentions by teachers, without thoughtful planning, the best-imagined projects were spinning sideways and losing their way. Ms. Wilcox of the first vignette had missed an opportunity to prepare the community music for the gig. She could have clarified to the visiting musician at the time of her invitation to him just what it would mean to offer a program within a tightly wound school schedule. One adage should have been known to her late-arriving artist: "To arrive early is on time, to arrive on time is late, and to arrive late is unacceptable" (and possibly with deduction of payment!). She might have used the artist's set-up time as a teaching moment, that is, a time when she could contextualize the music, tell a relevant story of life in the origin culture of the music, pick up one of the instruments brought by the artist and begin to tell about it (or even to play it), or sing a song with participatory elements that could involve all members of the waiting audience. Then there was Mr. Ferris, on track in wanting to multiculturalize his curriculum and who might have realized his plan but for the budget that had dissipated. He invited one artist, correctly maintaining that artists should be paid for the performance, yet there might have been ways to proceed with a roster of multiple artists: Proposing to the principal the benefits of multiple artist residencies to receive a temporary boost in the budget; requesting the support of the PTA for achieving the noble goal of diversifying musical study; reaching out to teachers, staff, and parents to arrange for them to sing a treasured heritage song, a show-and-tell of a story of a musical instrument, a family keepsake, or household item of multicultural interest; and even seeking the possibility of arranging for a "ticketed world music event" in which the proceeds could be earmarked for the support of performing artists. Kim, Phyllis, and Gwen were up for hosting an intergenerational event that would prove musically, culturally, and socially beneficial. They did not appear to have carefully planned for the event, however, which could have benefited from advance discussion among themselves and with Gwen about the content and tone of the program. They might have planned out how the program could meet the needs of preschoolers and seniors, who would take responsibility to adjust the sound system "to taste", and whether the program could be participatory—for example, through a dialogue by Gwen with her audience or by way of an invitation by Gwen's invitation to all to "perform" specific rhythms in claps, pats, and stamps. Mr. Jackson's uncomfortable moment with his school principal could have been easily avoided if he had articulated the objectives of the school-community collaboration in advance of the performance or in a public announcement at the performance. The project with the local musicians was meant for understanding "the point" of Japanese music through performance, conversation, demonstration, and a group composition experience that would underscore the characteristic elements of Japanese traditional music. Mr. Jackson could have programed the Japanese trio to begin the program with a performance on their own that would demonstrate Japanese features, followed by their brief explanations and a Q&A with the audience that could help to clarify contemporary practices and the fusion of traditional facets and features.

It becomes clear, in reviewing well-intentioned but ineffectual projects like those described, that the success of school-community intersections requires even-handed collaboration between key players. When teachers plan assemblies, residencies, workshops, and field trips, it's vital that they convey their expectations even as they listen and heed the comments of those with whom they're engaging. Community musicians and culture-bearers, along with persons within community agencies, organizations, and cultural centers, need to know the rules and regulations of an event in which they are to be involved. Detailed communication in advance of the event is key, and consultation in person, by phone, email or other electronic means can ensure success. The teacher needs to take the reins, know something of the community and the local musicians with whom she is working, gauge the appropriateness of the content of an event to the students, establish start and stop times for the event, help to tailor the educational value of the event through pre- and post-event experience and study, and facilitate the course of the event. All programs may present challenges but most are "surmountable".

School Music in Transition

Music education programs are leaning into multicultural-intercultural-global aims, although this is a fairly recent development. The European influence had been strong in the shaping of music as a curricular subject in schools. In the United States and Canada, there was from the start of school music programs an intent to preserve the art music of European masters. European-flavored songs found their way into American school music programs, and songs by Mozart, Beethoven, and Brahms were standard fair in school choirs by the close of the 19th century. Orchestral music was something to strive for in schools, and instrument makers were supplying the demands made by secondary schools to gear up their students with strings, winds, and brass instruments. The wave of European art music was felt in schools across the globe, and the mark of strong Western-based music education programs was often the extent to which students could perform the music of the Germans (and the Austrians, British, French, and Italians) the way it was meant to sound. Folk music was often forbidden in schools, as was jazz, popular music, the expressions of indigenous peoples, and all that was not art music was viewed as "primitive", simplified and unsuitable, and even deleterious to the development of musically expressive students.

Change came slowly to the school music curriculum, but transportation and technology brought a wider cultural consciousness that began to shave away at the content and delivery of music to children and youth. By the mid-20th century, television and other media began to bring the world into the family home, and air travel became the means for traveling the world. Little-known places could now be reached, and visual and aural images of far-distant cultures were available at the flick of a switch. The establishment of the United Nations, and UNESCO, and the International Music Council (IMC) shared in the fundamental belief in world peace, both at large and through music. In the United States, the Civil Rights Movement of the 1950s and 1960s stirred up the need for schools and societies to address inequities and injustices. Curricular reform gradually reflected these societal movements, and North American music programs were experimenting with the possibilities for music of the world's cultures, including folk music, jazz, popular music, and art music beyond Europe. Multicultural mandates in schools further drove the change in content as well as pedagogical approaches to a vast array of music and student interests, needs, and learning style.

Technology became thoroughly enveloped within educational endeavors, developing over a century of revolutionary change, and school music programs have been impacted by instructional radio, television lessons, computer-assisted instruction, digital technology, and the internet. Learning became increasingly autonomous, recently through flipped learning models in which students are consuming content at their own pace and through communication online with teachers and peers. The convergence of technology with cultural awareness goals is timely, and culturally responsive educators are finding the "edtech explosion" of the last two decades particularly useful for exploring issues such as hunger, poverty, education, racism, sexism, bias, and stereotypes through online games, interactive images, and exercises of every sort. For school music, music apps are available to introduce listeners and learners to a world of music, musical instruments, and related artistic expressions in dance and drama—from Japanese *kotos* and *taiko* drumming to Indian *tabla* and *sitar*. Internet-connected whiteboards are available for displaying images of musicians and the cultural contexts of their lives in cities and villages across the globe. Digital audio workshops are often included in a computer's basic software package, providing the capability for users to record, edit, mix, and master audio files. GarageBand is just one example of a pre-installed platform that allows students to compose all the music they can imagine and as it is influenced by various local and global styles. The interfaces of technology in the arts, and by music professionals, are widely evident, and the potential for using technology for knowing music as a world phenomenon is unmistakable and well within reach.

Historic hallmarks of music education are continuing in North America and in many schools across the world, even as change is evident everywhere. Bands, choirs, and orchestras are established school music cultures with hard-earned reputations for developing musically educated students who perform vocally and on instruments, read standard staff notation, and understand Western historical and contemporary musical forms particularly pertinent to art music's structures and nuances. Elementary school music programs, particularly those that are labeled "general music" (or classroom music), are steeped with experiences in learning to sing in tune and in time, to play pitched and non-pitched percussion instruments, and to read notation that will then qualify them for membership in the music ensembles that become available to them in the intermediate grades and on into secondary school. Music teachers have made inroads in establishing musical opportunities such as jazz bands, keyboard and guitar study, composition and song-writing classes, and popular music performance. Since the last decades of the 20th century, an awareness of cultural diversity has influenced the music that is experienced and studied across the curriculum, at all levels. Notational literacy reigns supreme in Western-styled music education practices, and music continues to be defined for its sonic essence without much attention to its relationship to movement and dance, nor to cultural meanings, contexts, and functions of the music. Yet, school music is in transition, as it always was, and the influences of society, local and global cultures, and the music of local and global communities will continue to inspire and influence music education practice.

Critical Diversity-Directed Educational Movements

As populations have diversified, educational movements have arisen to reform the school curriculum in ways that pay tribute to the learning styles of all students and to educate and empower them to realize their potential as thoughtful citizens. James Banks (2018) envisioned Multicultural Education as a curricular framework that would ensure that students of every race, ethnicity, gender, and ability could achieve academic success in schools. The framework is based on five features, all of which guide teachers in shaping equitable learning conditions for students while also removing them from the long-standing obstacles of racism and prejudice that have stood in the way to block learning. The five realms of Multicultural Education delineate how a belief in equity and justice can be put into practice by teachers through ever-deeper levels of commitment to multiculturalizing the curriculum: Content integration, the knowledge construction process, prejudice reduction, an equity pedagogy, and an empowering school culture and social structure. Along with these dimensions are four levels of curricular reform, labeled as "contributions, additive, transformation, and social action".

These are immediately evident in the work of teachers who have genuine commitment and considerable experience in guiding the multicultural sensitivity and understanding of their students.

The influences of Multicultural Education are visible in music education programs, projects, and publications over at least three decades, particularly in influencing a repertoire that is more inclusive of the world's cultures. Classic works like *Multicultural Perspectives in Music Education* (Anderson & Campbell, 1989, 1996, 2011), the publications of World Music Press, music-culture curricular units designed for Smithsonian Folkways, and instructional units prepared for the Association for Cultural Equity are coloring the repertoire featured in school music practice. Meanwhile, growing attention to the local communities in which students live is driving teachers to consider crafting curriculum and instruction in music at all levels of involvement, all the way to social action and the interactions of schools with communities in collaborative projects. After all, the meaning of Multicultural Education to music education is more than diversifying the repertoire, and World Music Pedagogy asserts that deep listening is critical to performance, creative new musical expressions, and an understanding of culture. Teaching-learning techniques that underscore the origin culture of the music in study illuminate reasons for the music to sounding as it does, just as attention by teachers to the culture of students is critical to effective pedagogical plans that motivate learning.

A recognition of students as individuals, shaped by their families and communities but also as unique unto themselves, helped to form a pedagogical philosophy known as Culturally Responsive Teaching (Gay, 2010). As a student-centered approach to teaching, Culturally Responsive Teaching holds teachers responsible to adapting to the demands of multicultural student populations and to ensuring that the unique cultural strengths of students are nurtured to promote their academic achievement and general sense of well-being. For the majority of teachers who come from middle class European American backgrounds, they are challenged to overcome their own cultural biases and to open their eyes, ears, and minds to other perspectives. Culturally Responsive Teaching is three-pronged, suggesting the necessity for teachers to explore their own cultures, to learn about other cultures, and to learn about their students' cultures. It maintains that cultural identities of students and teachers are important, which resonates well with the attention by World Music Pedagogy processes to knowing the cultures of music that are listened to and learned within school music programs. Music fits well with the larger goal of making knowledge relevant to students, and it may ease them into the study of their own and other cultures and of society at large and human life. As Lind and McKoy (2016) have suggested, Culturally Responsive Teaching in music can be manifested in course offerings such as songwriting, popular music, and the manner in which a diversity of music cultures can be interspersed within more standard classes such as music theory, piano, and bands, choirs, and orchestras.

With the emergence of social justice in schools, aspects of Multicultural Education and Culturally Responsive Teaching dovetail with World Music Pedagogy to create an activist approach to music education practice that is aimed at the achievement, in music and through music, of an educational democracy and a cultural democracy. In a socially just curriculum, all cultures count, and all members of society are entitled to educational opportunities regardless of class, gender, race, ethnicity, social status, disability, sexual orientation, religion, political affiliation, or other group membership status. Disparities in arts funding are real, such that resources for the study of music, the performing arts, and the visual arts are less available for students of color. Power inequities occur at the classroom level as part of teacher-student relationships and may require the earnest efforts of teachers to move aside from the authority role and relinquish some of the decision-making to students; this may more naturally occur in

Figure 7.1   Zimarimbas! Sounding Zimbabwean Music, as facilitated by Jocelyn Moon (on hosho, front left) and Zack Moon (on marimba, front right)

composition and improvisation experiences than in performance ensembles. The democratization of the classroom is aided by teachers who diversify the musical content of the curriculum in the name of social justice. As World Music Pedagogy insists, not only should the canon of musical expressions be expanded to include music of many cultures, but projects can be developed as well to align music with the targeting of specific injustices and as a way forward to understanding and resolving these injustices. Curricular implications of social justice ideals in music education practice have led to the singing of protest songs at the site of a union gathering or drumming in solidarity in a parade for gender or racial equity. A musical democracy is attained when all the world's music, including quite local community expressions, are open and available for experience and study in schools, both for the beauty and logic of their sound as well as for the powerful messages that are communicated.

Community Values and National Standards

There are national and state-wide standards for students and their teachers to attain within the realm of a school curriculum, even as there are also community interests and values to honor. The long-standing school priorities of literacy and numeracy have been joined in recent decades by broader views of "the basics" for all students, including a comprehensive view of education in mathematics, science, and technology, as well as classic and contemporary aims of language arts, the social sciences, and the arts. Government policies and professional organizations determine much of the content and rigor of skills and knowledge across the subjects, per age and grade level, and the approved content shows itself not only in class lessons and assignments but also in assessment practices, accountability systems, and teacher education practices.

With widespread agreement as to the necessity of a nation, state, and locality to share educational goals, there is also the need to recognize contextual forces that influence what is taught and in what manner it is best learned. Schools and their curricular standards interact with and are influenced by the needs and interests of the local community. Within every school, there are external forces that shape and influence the details of "the basics" and the specific ways in which learning is designed. Even with reference to regions within a single nation, there are ways of doing things in the American South that differ from the American Northwest, as sure as there are different values to uphold in South China than in the far western region of Xinjiang. Context is critical, and community values are to be respected so that schools are relevant to children coming from their family and community environments.

In music, there are certain shared aims and standards that are prized by music educators and teaching musicians in schools everywhere, and local communities are there to draw from while flavoring the content and teaching-learning process. Making music reigns supreme as critical to music education practice, both vocally and on instruments, and this encompasses the recreation of canonized and contemporary musical works as well as the process of composing and improvising new and original music. Listening is viewed by educators as core to the musical enterprise, as is the connection of the listening ear to the physicality of music in movement and dance. School music educators across the world are well aware that some musical practices are typically learned through notation, while orality (and aurality) is the way forward to learning various other musical styles. Music educators strive to support the capacity of their students to create, perform, and respond to music, and they frequently agree as to musical works (often Western art music "chestnuts" by Bach, Beethoven, and Brahms) that every learner should know.

Still, with these common educational aims in mind, communities vary with regard to what values they place on which musical styles. The responsibilities of music teachers carry all the way to identifying these community values, including preferred instruments, musical styles, songs, and dance tunes that are embraced by students, their families, neighbors, and others living locally. The challenge then for teachers is to work the local music (and the local musicians) into the curriculum as ways to attain widely held standards of music and multiculturalism. Thus, school music experiences can encompass Western art music alongside the remembered songs of a Ukrainian grandmother, the merengue rhythms of a Dominican uncle, and the flute melodies of a Khmer musician-turned-restaurant owner. Students in school music classes can exercise their ears by learning a Navajo social dance song. They can grow their notational literacy skills through efforts to read transcriptions of Kenyan choral music, Appalachian-style Bluegrass tunes, and Cantonese opera arias, choruses, and instrumental accompaniments. They can converse with visiting community musicians who play Burmese harp (*saung kauk*), Malian *balafon* (wood xylophones), Hungarian *cimbalom* (hammered dulcimer), and Ethiopian *krar* (lyre). Music can be learned, and national standards can be met even as community connections are made.

Music and Community, Altogether

Music exists in every community, and every community is musical. Communities are hard-core, real-life people living side by side, street by street, apartment after apartment, sharing the same services at grocery stores and gas stations. They are also communities defined by similar identities, as in the case of a Carnatic South Indian community, a Syrian (American) community, or a Mexican (American) community. Opening to further meanings of community, people cluster for other values, too, such as a community of soccer players, book club members, yoga practitioners, video gamers, birdwatchers, or churchgoers. Communities can be virtual, as in the case of Beyoncé fans or online bloggers on a selected topic. They can be both musical and virtual, as in the case of an online choir whose 100 members contribute their voices to a musical performance or online arrangers, composers, and producers of music.

Some communities embrace their local music and are proud of achievements by locally living individuals and groups. In the case of a Bolivian village or a Japanese neighborhood with a tradition of frequent festive musical celebrations, a significant segment of the community may be musically active. There are regular community gatherings of musicians, and there are circles of singers and guitarists and players of marimbas, steel pans, and ukuleles—all of whom are open and welcoming of others to join in. Within neighborhoods, there may be multiple musical communities, too, as music shared on one city block may differ from the music down the next street, or on the playground, in the park, or wafting from restaurants and cafes. It seems that no community is without its trademark musical expression(s).

The emergence of Community Music is a phenomenon that recognizes musical communities, and the interest there is by people to bond together as a musical group. Community Music builds upon the premises of music as socialization, for social bonding, friendship, and well-being. Remarkably, Community Music, as a government-supported and grant-funded venture to unite and empower people, has developed in some places a means of allowing individual voices to be heard and a collective resonance to be felt. Higgins (2012) described a key focus of Community Music as knowing how the music of a community is relevant to participants in terms of its connections to their identities, traditions, and aspirations and how it is particularly meaningful because of the social interactions that occur in the process of making music together. Community Music is a wide-ranging set of involvements, and it is inclusive of a diverse range of people, not just the activities of professional musicians or the recreation of standard works of notated school music repertoire.

Communal music-making is the hallmark of Community Music, which involves exposure, participation, and performance with the help of a music facilitator(s). Often, community music-making is seen in settings outside formal institutions. More recently, however, community musicians are working closely with music teachers in schools and across other formal music education settings (Higgins & Willingham, 2017). The ethos that Community Music brings to schools has already begun to change how music-making transpires, in that community musicians are utilizing their partnerships with music teachers to advocate for "active participation, sensitivity to context, equality of opportunity, and a commitment to diversity" (Higgins, 2012, p. 174).

In the Thick of Community Musicians

In the midst of any music, in any community, are the community musicians. They perform, they teach and inspire learners, and they facilitate musical expressions. Some community musicians are culture-bearers, carrying the music of their cultural heritage onward into the lives of those who will listen, learn, and join in a participatory or performative manner to sing, play, and dance, and to create and re-create. Community musicians and culture-bearers (and culture-bearing community musicians) are important to World Music Pedagogy, to the aims of fostering a respect for diverse musical and cultural expressions, and to the realization of school-community intersections. It is surprising, and also regrettable, then, that community musicians are not as much a presence in the school music curriculum as they might be—not in group lessons nor the classroom and rehearsal sessions. The idea of school-community projects and programs is undeniably useful in developing cultural sensitivity, yet music educators sometimes find it challenging to figure ways of reaching out beyond the school (and jam-packed school schedules). Fortunately, there are productive ways for music teachers and their students to come into the thick of knowing community musicians, and there are exemplary school music programs in which students have gained both musically and culturally from their encounters.

One of the teacher's direct duties is to grow the musical network of their students, tuning them in to the local music scene and introducing them to musicians in the community. A small-scale fieldwork exercise recently undertaken by one music educator and his students illustrates an orientation by students themselves to the music of their community. On gathering students into small working groups, the music teacher tasked them with working together to identify musicians in their community who enjoy performing standard repertoire or performing new repertoire that they themselves create for the specialized musical genre or instrument. Students were drawn into the search through internet sources for information on musicians in their community. They discovered the instruments the musicians play (or vocal styles they sing), the repertoire in which they specialize, and the stories of how they came to be working musicians. Students searched the internet for the musicians or musical groups they had identified and determined their ages, their sociocultural composite, even their socio-political views. If there was musical repertoire of the musician(s) available online, students were directed to listen to selected pieces and to attempt to analyze the music in terms of their musical influences, sonic elements, and cultural meanings. They were led into a discussion as to similarities and differences of the musicians they researched, which developed into comparisons with other music they have studied, whether in the community, in the national mix of musical practices, or across geographic regions and international boundaries.

For all students, if the opportunity arises, there can be occasions for them to interview a community musician or musical group, on their own time, at the convenience of the community musician in the studio or field, or on the school campus. Students may go so far as arranging for their own presence in the rehearsal space, tracking the creative processes of a designated musician once, twice, or over multiple visits. The resourceful music teacher may also make arrangements for students to learn selected repertoire of the musician or group and negotiate with the musician the possibility for informal performances of students in tandem with the musician. By coming into the thick of musicians in the community in these ways, the bridge between what is often seen as a gap between school music and music in the community can be filled so that both students and musicians in the community can benefit.

The Nexus of Ethnomusicology and (Music) Education

Any consideration of diversity as it relates to music as a local and global phenomenon, and to the education and training of students to know music broadly and deeply as a pan-human phenomenon, is ultimately linked to ethnomusicology. This hybrid field, a discipline that might be best described as a "humanistic social science", arose from the work of musicologists whose interests are traditionally the sonic structures of music and anthropologists who examine the human experience within societies and cultures. As the study of music as a reflection of culture, ethnomusicology is focused on understanding human musical life—how people use music, perform it, compose it, and think about it (Nettl, 2015). Ethnomusicology seeks to understand the nature of music as it is expressed, learned, listened to, and valued by the full spectrum of humanity. Young and old, urban and rural, "Western" and "non-Western", people are defined by the music they make, the musical communities in which they live, the sonic features of the music, and the behaviors and beliefs of musicians and listeners that are of interest to scholars of ethnomusicology.

Research in ethnomusicology embraces the study of individual music cultures (such as the Irish flute of Clare County, Ireland), comparative study of multiple cultures (such as "pitch", "tuning", or "improvisation" in India, Iran, and Turkey), music within its cultural context (such as rhumba music in Havana, Cuba) or music in diaspora (Mexican American music in East L.A., or Houston, Chicago, New York or Miami). Early research in the field was more or less musicological, replete with musical descriptions, sonic-structural analyses, and transcriptions in Western staff notation. It was also anthropological, with attention given to the people as they behave musically, attending to how music is used (such as in ritual, for social occasions, in political messages, in churches and schools). Ethnomusicology today is typically the study of living cultures, whether long-running or in new formations. These cultures are geographic, conceptual, and virtual, and include issues of music with gender, race, and class. Ethnomusicology seeks out the function, meanings, and values of music to people and the role of music in communities and cultures.

For music educators and teaching musicians, ethnomusicology sends a clear message that music is more than the sound itself. Music is what people do with it and what it does for people. Music is emotional expression for people everywhere in the world, a means of cultural identity, and a way of building relationships with those who enter into the music together. The stories behind the music are important for clarifying music's uses, and it is the work of ethnomusicologists that help to paint the picture of music in the lives of those who value it. By going to the musicians, getting the backstories, the histories and herstories, even the "mythistories" that people share, ethnomusicologists provide a fuller sense of music as sound, behavior, and values. Now, there is a growing acceptance that ethnomusicology's emphasis on music-culture studies offer prospects for teaching and learning music, about musicians, and about the social and cultural context of a musical work (Rice, 2014).

Decades of work by music educators in the movement to diversify musical content in the curriculum have prompted connections and collaborations of educators with ethnomusicologists in searching out songs, instrumental music, and dances that may personify and exemplify a musical culture. Frequently, teachers have been intent on connecting with scholars who might help them with recommending music that would reach-and-teach students in elementary and secondary school music settings. In a reductive sense, ethnomusicologists sometimes have been seen by teachers primarily as sources of "the goods": Music as "material" only, without attention to transmission processes and learning behaviors, or music's contexts, functions, or meanings. Today, there is evolving understanding of the outcomes of collaborations between educators, ethnomusicologists, community musicians, and culture-bearers in providing learners with music that stands for itself and music learning experiences that comprise oral/aural experiences or experiences in reading other notation systems. Musical selections are less often seen as representing all the people in a cultural group but as opportunities for learners to slip inside artistic and social expressions that are musically beautiful and meaningful to a few, or even to an individual, within a culture (rather than to the entirety of a culture).

From an ethnomusicological perspective comes the attention in World Music Pedagogy to honoring orality/aurality in the teaching-learning process, finding meaning through interdisciplinary probing of why the music sounds the way it does in a culture and recognizing the importance of music as a living expression that may sound differently (and distinctively) in the voices and instruments of people who are closer and further from the cultural center of the music (Schippers, 2010). Music educators and community musicians do well to listen carefully with their students to origin-source recordings of the music and to pay tribute to the musicians whose music it is. At the same time, they logically recognize that with every performing musician, and in every performance rendition, the music is uniquely expressed in ways that are genuine and true to the musician even while the link to the origin music is clearly in evidence. Further, given the vast array of the world's musical styles that highlight spontaneous creative expression, the WMP process is again within the scope of the ethnomusicological perspective in encouraging listeners to figure out the music in order to assimilate it into their systems. In educationally valid terms, musical experience and study flow easily into the creative act as learners progress through a full sweep of the music to the point of making the music their own in inventive new ways.

Ethnomusicologists are uniquely drawn to the struggles of the oppressed, the challenges of minority groups, and the lives of those who have been ill-treated, subjugated, even tyrannized. Teachers, too, tune to the need by their young students to be understood, respected, and supported—across the board—and many are aware of the neighborhoods their students call home and what color, creed, or class may characterize them. For teachers, an ethnomusicological lens on their work can strengthen their own conviction of the critical importance of music in building human relationships. Ethnomusicology is a music-centered and people-centered field that is imbued with an impassioned spirit of activism, and teachers with a lens on ethnomusicology gain further understandings of how best to support the struggles of the marginalized.

Confronting Constructs in the Application of World Music Pedagogy

The cross-fertilization of music education with ethnomusicology has produced a culturally sensitive approach to teaching music as a human phenomenon, in which locally and globally available music is open territory to choose to experience, study, learn, and teach. World Music Pedagogy has evolved from the conscientious attention by teachers to want to *teach music with a capital "M"—"Music"*, as it is variously expressed across the world (Campbell, 2004). Being in touch with ethnomusicologists, co-teaching courses with them, collaborating with them on scholarly projects, several generations of pioneering music teachers were increasingly intent on drawing cultural diversity into their lessons. They read the monographs of ethnomusicologists, listened to their field recordings, and eventually honed pedagogical techniques that could facilitate musical experiences as closely as possible to the manner in which it was experienced in the bush, the barrio, the courtyards, clubs and cafes, the family homes, and the city streets. Through a careful study of the music, the musicians, and the contexts in which the music was made, today's music teachers are now crafting encounters, "episodes", and events in which many of the world's musical practices can be discovered by children and youth. Because they understand child and adolescent development, they are able to figure ways in which the music can fit the learning preferences of students in various experience levels. Through the efforts of music educators and teaching musicians, World Music Pedagogy is focused on adapting ethnomusicological understandings to the ways of music teaching, learning, and development; ensuring that diversity, equity, and inclusion is meaningfully applied to school music experiences, and responding to the unique cultural strengths of individual students (as well as of local communities) so that music can be experienced and understood for its multiple facets, assets, and outcomes.

In schools and communities, and in the collaborations between schools and communities, an array of ethnomusicological concepts, constructs, and terms have come into play. All are relevant to World Music Pedagogy and to the school-community intersections that can transpire, and each of them have had due consideration in forging the design of this volume. They are briefly noted here as a closing catalog of ideals, a checklist of sorts, for reflecting upon teaching-learning practice as it is impacted by considerations of musical cultures living locally as well as across the globe.

Positionality

A recognition by a teacher of her (his) own identity, and of personally cherished beliefs, is important since it likely influences her (his) selection of musical content and peda-gogical strategies. Did she herself have piano lessons from the age of seven years? Did he himself play bass in a rock band? Did she come from a long line of American-born (or South African-, or Samoan-, or Chinese-, or Turkish-, or Mexican-born) parents, grandparents, great-grandparents? Did he have after-school tutoring rather than an after-school job from the age of 14 years? How does the teacher's experience compare to those of the students she teaches? A reckoning with teacher-student affinities and "disconnects", of similarities and dissimilarities, is consequential in designing cur-ricular content and method. In the United States, for example, a teacher raised in a middle class White family is unlikely to immediately grasp the needs and interests of students coming from greater or lesser affluence or from non-White families; it takes concentrated effort to listen and learn from the students themselves. World Music Pedagogy, and every other pedagogical approach to teaching-learning music, begins with the assumption that teachers need to know their students and to retrofit curriculum and instruction for the understandings and skills they need to acquire. The question, "Who can teach what to whom?" is answerable, in that all teachers can embrace the responsibilities they have in ensuring the learning of all their students, and that all music teachers, regardless of their experience and training, can be tuning all their students to the world's musically diverse cultures, and that all teachers can bridge the gap between school and community through visits both ways—community musicians to school and school music students to the musical communities.

Authenticity

Perhaps no concept has been more greatly discussed within the field of music education than that of authenticity. Teachers worry about their own misinterpretation of music from a tradition or practice that they did not study and that was never a part of their own experience at home, in their neighborhoods, in school or university study. They want students to perform it with utmost authenticity, as it sounds in the origin-culture—or not at all; this stance is driven by the respect they hold for the music and the musi-cians from these cultures. But music is not frozen in time (unless it is viewed as an object and a product); it is a living tradition, a creative expression, and an opportunity to offer a new expression by the individual musician or musical collective. For those who prefer to match the model (which is surely a more restrictive view of authentic-ity), we have described strategies that include intensive listening to the recorded or live model and working with a community musician who can coach students in situ to attain a rendering that is close to the origin-source. Matching the model is a musically challenging exercise of great merit, one that is useful in tuning the ears as closely as possible to the musical style (Campbell, 2018). At the same time, it's worth remember-ing that educational experiences in the world's musical cultures encompass not only listening as a pathway to performance but also increases opportunities for musical creativity and for knowing the cultural context of the music through interdisciplinary and integrative encounters. World Music Pedagogy asserts that listening is the way forward for going deeply into the music, whether or not it is performed, and however it is to be experienced.

Context (and Recontextualization)

The presence of music in schools is typically out of context, whether the music is Mexican *banda* (played in the streets), Burmese *nat pwe* (performed on a village green), Spanish *flamenco* (danced on a wood-platform), Inuit *katajjaq* throat songs (sung in a family home), or South African *kwaito* (chanted in clubs). Studying music in schools may be viewed as a decontextualized experience, but it can also be viewed in a more positive light as recontextualized, that is, moved from its source to a new space in the classroom or performance venue. World Music Pedagogy points to ways of knowing original contexts of the music through interdisciplinary studies, and video recordings, photos, and stories provide images and straight-ahead stories of music's place in the lives of the musicians who make it. Of course, field trips into the community open the possibilities for experiencing music in original contexts or as the music has been re-imagined by musicians seeking to partly preserve it while also providing a distinctive new flavor.

Identity

The association by people with musical styles is of interest to ethnomusicologists and educators, as is music's role in defining individuals and groups. Identity is behaviorally observable in speech, dress, hairstyle, and a host of choices that include the music in which one is engaged individually or collectively. The choice by students to listen to or participate in particular musical styles may mirror ethnicity, nationality, gender, race, economic class, and generation (or age). That there are multiple layers of identity is no surprise, either, so that K-pop (Korean popular music) is typically associated with Korean (and Korean American) male adolescents and millennials, while fans of *p'ung mul* ensembles of drums and *gongs* cross gender and generations in the rise of that music as a joyous celebration of Korean-ness. Listeners drawn to the L.A.-based Chicano group, Quetzal, hear their band's music as a mix of Mexican folk music, punk rock, and African American rhythm and blues and an expression of themselves; the band members individually and together comprise a community of multiple cultural realities such that they (and the music of their band) are not so straightforward or uncomplicated as to be referred to only as "Mexican American". Personal identities exist alongside group identities, and the scholarship of ethnomusicology includes accounts of everyday people who use music regularly to affect their mood and accompany their activity (DeNora, 2000). Even as students seek their own musical and cultural identities, World Music Pedagogy is a means of opening up ears and minds to the palette of possibilities that they may wish to call their own.

Musical Hybridity and Transculturation

The greater the contact between cultures, the more likely are the fusions between and among them. Musical hybridity is a constant reality in a time of globalization in which a worldwide flow of ideas can be experienced, "borrowed", and fully accepted as culture norm. The process of transculturation figures into musical transformations, too, and into the evolution of new musical norms. Composers of Western art music have hybridized their works for centuries, as in Italian composer Domenico Scarlatti's employment of Spanish and Portuguese idioms in his keyboard piece and the inclusion by Antonin Dvorak of African American spirituals and Native American melodies in his "New World Symphony". The sonic and social aesthetic of hip-hop is a worldwide phenomenon, and Jamaican *reggaetón* and Tanzania *bongo flava* are exemplar of the interplay of global and local forces that have forged internal and external in the making of these genres. Flavorings of close-and-far musical expressions feature in many artistic expressions, including dance, drama, and the literary arts, and today's music is more likely than not to be borrowed, adapted, and embraced. "True", "pure", and fully "original" music is not only hard to find but may be beside the point since all music is available for curricular inclusion, and the selection of music depends upon the blend of student interest and needs, teacher expertise, the school's local surrounds, and the presence of community musicians who will perform their music, however hybridized it may be.

Cultural Appropriation

When cultural elements of minority groups are selected and adopted by members of a dominant group, there is then a violation of the collective property rights. Cultural appropriation stems from colonialism, oppression, and an unequal balance of power between dominant and minority groups and involves the taking of various cultural practices, expressions, and symbols from minorities, especially indigenous groups, without their permission. The use of music, for example, a song of the Spokane nation, of the San Ildefonso Pueblo group of New Mexico, of the Luo people of Kenya, or the Sukuma of Tanzania, may be viewed in the same light as the donning of a Native American war bonnet or a Senegalese kaftan as a costume. Without permission or understanding of its traditional meaning of a song, the reduction of cultural practices to the "exotic" and playful amusement of outsiders is viewed as disrespectful to cultural insiders. Hybridity and transculturation, as noted above, can happen as part of the natural process of cultural flow, but cultural appropriation is more immediate and without thoughtful consideration of valued objects and ideas—and certainly without dialogue and discussion with those whose culture is appropriated. The musical selections within this volume are fully permitted and approved by culture-bearing musicians and are meant for teachers who wish to convey the musical integrity of the cultural origin group.

Representation

A whirlwind journey across the musical globe can realistically appear essentialist if, in limited time, just one song or musical selection is sampled from each of dozens of cultures. Teachers struggle with providing just "the right piece" that will represent the complex cultural matrix of a nation or ethnic culture. Which musical work best represents Japan, Germany, or Jamaica? Is there a piece that stands for all of Mexico, and should it be drawn from *mariachi, son jarocho, son huasteco, musica norteno,* or another of many regional genres? Which of dozens of instruments best portrays Chinese traditional music or Iranian (Persian) classical music? The reality is that no musical work, genre, or instrument can stand for an entire culture; rather, each musical selection stands for itself. Music within an ethnic culture varies, depending upon the age, gender, socioeconomic class, religious affiliation, and geographic region of the sub-groups within the culture. It is illogical to expect to highlight a single musical selection that is representative of all people, for all time, within a culture. In the application of World Music Pedagogy to a curriculum, multiple illustrations of a music culture are a worthy goal, even if it means that over the course of several years, a teacher and her students may return to the place on the planet where there are multiple new musical pieces and experiences to be had. In the meanwhile, a song or an instrumental work can be treated as its own entity, a single expression of logic and beauty and a connection to the particular musicians whose music it is, to be enjoyed for what it is rather than to be presented as *the* music of a given cultural group.

Transmission

The study of music's transmission, and of orality and literacy, in so many cultural circumstances informs World Music Pedagogy, for it is through an understanding of how musical works and practices are conveyed by musicians, and how they are received by listeners and acquired by learners, that music teaching and learning can be shaped to best support and facilitate the process. Because so much of the world's art, folk, and popular music happens through oral-aural transmission procedures, World Music Pedagogy has taken to heart the somewhat overlooked and under-valued importance of listening—again, and again, and again. The visual transmission of music is acknowledged, of course, as this encompasses not only music notation but also the observations of musicians in the music-making process for all the nuanced movements and gestures they require. With attention to many circumstances of music's transmission, in many cultural settings, notation is understated in the process of World Music Pedagogy, not only because of its complete absence from many cultures but also because notation systems invariably do not provide full information of music's rhythm, pitch, technique, or other sonic nuances. The ear is the instrument of utmost important, thus is WMP so committed to listening as means of ever-deeper understanding and skill development.

Social Justice

Evident in an application of the principles of World Music Pedagogy into practice is an activist commitment to social responsibility and social justice, partly in the intent to select music that is broadly representative of the world's diverse cultures as well as in the strategies meant to envelop every learner in listening, participating, performing, creating, and understanding the many-splendored meanings of music in culture. These aims bear all the attention that teachers and community musicians can muster and fit well with the ideals of ethnomusicology to honor the human genius of varied musical cultures and to accept the wide array of alternative musical uses, meanings, and channels of transmission. In the journey forward through music by teachers to foster in students both cultural understanding and human empathy (along with standard music curricular goals), the creation of equity and respect for all individuals is unquestionably a constant factor in the teaching-learning design. Social justice requires a consciousness by teachers to be alert to inequities and imbalances, to practice inclusivity in curricular content, and to resist and avert all manner of systematic racism and sexism, unequal power relationships, and biases that might rear themselves in curricular development and instructional practice. Socially responsible teaching practices are inclusive rather than exclusive, and social justice requires that, in addition to educational equity, all the world's musical cultures are within the realm of possibility for student experience and study.

Worthy Outcomes of School-Community Intersections

This book is a call for attention and action on a musical ecosystem that involves music educators, community musicians, and culture-bearers in service to students, their families, and the communities that surround schools. It is directed toward the development of musical knowledge, skills, values, and cultural understanding through music. It is grounded in matters of diversity, equity, and inclusion with regard to student interest and need, and it pays tribute to an education that is democratically configured. Within the framework of a cultural democracy comes considerations for a musical democracy, thus curricular development can embrace the music (and musicians) of locally living and globally available communities. A call for action entails a joining together of schools, community organizations, and even universities in partnerships that can be developed for the good of all in the musical ecosystem.

More than ever, the world we live in requires the development of a genuine cultural sensitivity for one another. Such empathy typically does not come naturally but is a result of an education that promotes cultural knowledge and provides for the development of respect for distinctive ways of thinking, doing, and being. Music is a powerful bridge between cultures and communities and a way into the heart of a people who may at first appear "strange" or "different", a perception that too easily can catapult to suspicion and fear, the very elements present in times and places when things (can) fall apart. Such circumstances can be avoided when teachers delve into the intricacies of a musical culture, genre, or particular work and facilitate the experiences that lead to their students' musical and cultural understanding. It is through experiences that fully activate their listening ears, as well as a resonating of their minds and the bodies, that music's many-splendored experience can lead to empathetic awareness and compassion. It is when schools and communities intersect, and when teachers, community musicians, and culture-bearers work together, that students are enlightened and their lives are enriched. Then, even the most distant music can captivate and compel the learner so that the riveting musical experience inspires a cultural curiosity and a cultural respect and honoring. Then, conviviality results so that multicultural interactions and processes become a part of everyday social life. Then, students can develop a dialogic empathy that fixes their focus on people beyond themselves, listening to and feeling for others, experiencing the power of cultural inclusion through artistic dialogue.

Avanti! In troubled times like these, it takes the commitment of thoughtful teachers to go forward in countering violence, in seeking remedies to student angst and unease, and in steering students from bias and bigotry to tolerance, acceptance, and genuine respect. With an embrace of music as a pan-human phenomenon in all of its rich cultural variety, thus qualifying it as worthy of inclusion in meaningful learning encounters, the capacity of teachers and community musicians is invincible for holding on to cherished traditions even as they respond to the inevitable transformations that abound in society and its schools.

References

Anderson, W. M., & Campbell, P. S. (1989). *Multicultural perspectives in music education.* Lanham, MD: Rowman & Littlefield.

Anderson, W. M., & Campbell, P. S. (1996). *Multicultural perspectives in music education* (2nd ed.). Lanham, MD: Rowman & Littlefield.

Anderson, W. M., & Campbell, P. S. (2011). *Multicultural perspectives in music education* (3rd ed.). Lanham, MD: Rowman & Littlefield.

Banks, J. A. (2018). *An introduction to multicultural education* (6th ed.). New York: Pearson.

Campbell, P. S. (2004). *Teaching music globally.* New York: Oxford University Press.

Campbell, P. S. (2018). *Music, education, and diversity: Bridging cultures and communities.* New York: Teachers College Press.

DeNora, T. (2000). *Music in everyday life.* Cambridge: Cambridge University Press.

Gay, G. (2010). *Culturally responsive teaching: Theory, research, and practice.* New York: Teachers College Press.

Higgins, L. (2012). *Community music in theory and in practice.* New York: Oxford University Press.

Higgins, L., & Willingham, L. (2017). *Engaging in community music.* New York: Routledge.

Lind, V. R., & McKoy, C. L. (2016). *Culturally responsive teaching in music education: From understanding to application.* New York: Routledge.

Nettl, B. (2015). *The study of ethnomusicology: Thirty-three issues.* Urbana, IL: University of Illinois Press.

Rice, T. (2014). *Ethnomusicology: A very short introduction.* New York: Oxford University Press.

Schippers, H. (2010). *Facing the music: Shaping music education from a global perspective.* New York: Oxford University Press.

Appendix 1
Learning Pathways

Three of the musical examples in this volume have returned in Chapters 2, 3, 5, and 6 as "Learning Pathways" episodes based upon the five dimensions of World Music Pedagogy. These progressive WMP episodes can be parceled out over many school and community sessions, repeated in part, varied and extended, so that learners can orient themselves to the nuances of new musical expressions. Although it's entirely plausible, these episodes are not intended explicitly as lessons to be taught one right after the other. The intent of each Learning Pathway is to map how teaching and learning of one piece of music might proceed over the course of time when using the dimensions of World Music Pedagogy, where listening, participatory musicking, performance, creating, and integrating experiences open students to the many splendors of a musical culture.

Learning Pathway #1

Romance in East L.A.

Episode 2.1: Romance in East L.A.
"Todo lo que Tengo"
(Learning Pathway #1: Attentive Listening)

Specific Use: Elementary School Music, Secondary Music Innovations, Instrumental Ensembles

Materials:

- "Todo lo que Tengo", from the album *Imaginaries,* by Quetzal

Procedure:

1. "What instruments do you hear and in what order?"
2. Play track to 1'53".
3. Discuss answers (guitar, *pandeiro*, violin, voice).
4. Play track up to 1'53" to check answers.
5. "Can you pretend play one of the instruments?"
6. Play track to 1'53".
7. Respond to the pretend-play gestures, noting for example that they were rhythmic, in-sync with the sound, and continuous.
8. "This is a love song. Raise your hand when you hear "todo lo que quiero" (all that I want) and "todo lo que tengo" (everything I have)".
9. Play track to 1'53".
10. "Given what you hear, where in the world might the musicians be living?" (Given the Spanish language and the instrumentation, Mexico)
11. Invite a musician of Mexican-heritage music to visit, to listen with the students, to exchange with students on the meaning of this music, to play or sing with the recording, or to offer a live rendition of the song.

Episode 3.1: Romance in East L.A.
"Todo lo que Tengo"
(Learning Pathway #1: Engaged Listening)

Specific Use: Elementary School Music, Secondary Music Innovations, Instrumental Ensembles

Materials:

- "Todo lo que Tengo", Quetzal (from *Imaginaries*), Smithsonian Folkways Recordings
- Guitar, *pandeiro* (hand drum, or other drum)

Procedure:

1. "Listen and show fingers for the chord numbers I, IV, V (G-C-D)".
2. Play track to 1'53".
3. Discuss duration of the chords (I/G-four beats, IV/C-two beats, V/D-two beats)
4. Play track to check answers.
5. "Tap the rhythm of the *pandeiro* (drum)".
6. Play track to 1'53".
7. Demonstrate and discuss the continuing eighth-note rhythms, two taps per beat.
8. "Hum along with the sung melody. Listen for sung words like "mundo", "tiempo", "quiero", "amor", "corazon" ".
9. Play track to 1'53".
10. Call for students to translate the words they hear: "mundo" (world), "tiempo" (time), "quiero" (I wish or I want), "amor" (love), and "corazon" (heart).
11. Play track to 1'53", while listening for the words, humming the melody, and tapping the rhythm of the *pandeiro*.
12. Arrange the visit of a Mexican-heritage musician who might perform the piece with and without the recording, demonstrate the *pandeiro* rhythm and the guitar's chord changes (in various strumming patterns), and inspire language learning through the use of occasional Spanish words.

Episode 3.4: Romance in East L.A.
"Todo lo que Tengo"
(Learning Pathway #1: Enactive Listening)

Specific Use: Elementary School Music, Secondary Music Innovations, Instrumental Ensembles

Materials:

- "Todo lo que Tengo", Quetzal (from *Imaginaries*), Smithsonian Folkways Recordings
- Guitar-*pandeiro* (hand drum, or other percussion)

Procedure:

1. "Sing the melody on "loo", occasionally adding some of the words: "mundo", "tanto", "tiempo", "quiero", "amor", "corazon", "vivir". The "text" may sound something like "loo-loo-loo-loo-loo mundo" ".

2. Assign a Spanish-speaking student to write out the words.

3. Play track to 1'53".

4. "Sing the melody with (and without) the recording". Note: Lyrics are provided for the first verse and chorus; additional lyrics are accessed through https://genius.com/Quetzal-todo-lo-que-tengo-all-that-i-have-by-quetzal-lyrics.

Verse 1:
Dicen, que el mundo, se acerca a su fin
Mi bien, da pena
Que tanto tiempo perdí
Ven, que te quiero
Te quiero decir
Que sin tu amor, no puedo vivir
Te quiero y no niego
Mi corazón es para ti
Te quiero y da miedo
Que pronto acabe de existir

Chorus:
Todo lo que quiero yo lo hare en la vida
La fe que me nace es por ti mi vida
Todo lo que quiero yo lo hare en la vida
Todo lo que tengo

5. Repeat #4, singing the melody with (and without) the recording.

6. "Take tambourines and hand-drums (if not *pandeiro* drums), and tap the rhythm of the *pandeiro* (drum)".

7. Play track to 1'53".

8. Repeat #6, #7.

9. "Take guitars and play the chord progressions with (and without) the recording".

```
4 X   G - - -   C - D -
2 X   Am - - -  G/em - - - C - - - G/em - - D - -
4 X   G - - -   C - D -
```

10. Play track to 1'53".

11. Repeat #9, #10.

12. "Sing and play guitar and *pandeiro* with (and without) the recording".

13. Play track to 1'53".

14. Repeat as necessary, building in practice time necessary to developing the skills for singing and playing the piece.

15. For advanced guitarists, challenge them to follow the hypnotic broken chord pattern of the small plucked lute known as the leona.

16. Challenge a violin student to learn the violin melody.

17. Clarify the meaning of the song's lyrics, which clarifies that to be in love with another person does not require losing your own identity. Share the translation of the chorus: "I love you, and I don't deny it: My heart is for you. I love you, and it scares me that life will soon no longer exist". Explain that this last phrase refers to living life alone, as it has been experienced, will change, as living life together demands new perspectives.

18. Host a community musician of Mexican heritage, particularly for demonstrating the various instrumental parts and techniques while also singing as well as interpreting the song's lyrics.

Episode 5.1: Romance in East L.A.
"Todo lo que Tengo"
(Learning Pathway #1)

Specific Use: Elementary Music Education, Secondary School Innovations

Materials:

- "Todo lo que Tendo", Quetzal, (from *Imaginaries*), Smithsonian Folkways Recordings
- Guitar (hand drum, other percussion), keyboards, various available instruments (flute, clarinet, violin, other)

Procedure:

1. Establish a mood for "Creating World Music" by listening together to this familiar song that has already drawn students into the midst of it through various experiences in Attentive, Engaged, and Enactive Listening.

2. Brainstorm some topics to sing about in a newly created song still in the style of "Todo lo que Tendo", inviting students to share with the question "What's on your mind?" Write answers that may include single words (peace, justice, friendship) or full phrases ("Peace is a journey of the heart", "Reach out for justice, for the right to be free", "The finest prize a friend can give is a listening ear and a warm embrace").

3. Together or in small groups, develop verses on a chosen topic (rhymed or unrhymed). Provide a metric scheme and a quantity of verses (2–3–4), and clarify whether a chorus section should be developed for insertion between the verses that might underscore the theme of the poem.

4. Challenge students to write all or part of their poem in Spanish, in a mix of Spanish and English, or in another of the world's languages.

5. Share the verses through a rhythmic recitation that may appear as a group-performed "choral speech".

6. Repeat #5. (Note that with repetition, the rhythmic flow will improve. Listen for a melodic inflection that may emerge, too, and encourage prospects for converting the verse from chant to song.)

7. Add instruments to the rhythmic recitation of the newly created verse. Suggest that harmonic accompaniment be provided on guitar, keyboard, or a combination of instruments and that counter-melodies, embellishments, and transitions between verses may add to the musical interest. Add non-pitched percussion instruments to accentuate particular textual or musical ideas. Hint: Consider retaining the same chord progression as in "Todo lo que Tendo" since it is already familiar, or work with a modified (even a simplified) chord progression.

8. Repeat #7 since familiarity with the verse, and its sounding above the harmonic accompaniment, will give way to a melody (especially with a little modeling of the teacher and community musician).

9. Perform the composed songs, and discuss ways to enhance or further develop musical ideas to pique the interest of listeners.

10. Can the song be danced? Experiment with free-style, footwork and step patterns, and formations.

11. Listen to the original recording and compare the multiple ways in which the new musical creation is similar or distinctive. Ask a Mexican-heritage community musician to respond to the musical integrity of the work: Does it retain the flavor of the source recording?

Episode 6.1: Romance in East L.A.
"Todo lo que Tengo"
(Learning Pathway #1)

Specific Use: Elementary Music Education, Secondary School Innovations

Materials:

- "Todo lo que Tengo", Quetzal (from *Imaginaries*), Smithsonian Folkways Recordings
- Guitar-*pandeiro* (hand drum, or other percussion), hardwood floor (*tarima*, a raised wooden platform)

Procedure:

1. Discuss the meaning of the love song, and ponder the main message that love of another does not require giving up one's own identity.

2. Clarify that love songs are present in many cultures. Challenge students to find examples of love songs in the repertoire of singers in far-flung places such as Senegal; Spain and Samoa; and Japan, Germany, and Jordan.

3. Search for information on the band, Quetzal, including their location (Los Angeles), their musical influences (*son jarocho*, musica ranchera, *salsa*, Chicano rock, rhythm, and blues), and the struggle for social justice and dignity they express through their music. See questaleastla.com.

4. Discover more about *son jarocho* as a regional musical style from the Mexican state of Veracruz. Listen for the fusion of features that are Spanish, indigenous, and African in the recordings of artists such as Mono Blanco, Son de Madera, and Siquisiri. Find a contextualized description with interview and sound bytes: www.npr.org/2011/10/29/141723031/a-musical-style-that-unites-mexican-americans .

5. Return to the featured recording, and discuss how the stylistic elements of the song express love and romance. Follow on whether other love songs, from elsewhere in the world, utilize similar expressive components. Decide whether the message of love can be conveyed through the music, even when the language is not understood?

Community/Culture Connection

- Invite a *son jarocho* musician into the classroom, not only to perform and lead others in performing, but to share the stories of *son jarocho* musicians: Why they perform, when and where they perform, and how they were drawn to the music. Ask about the making of a *fandango* event, and find out how to develop a local fandango at which *son jarocho* is a centerpiece.

- For any visiting musicians, request of them a performance of their favorite love song.

Learning Pathway #2

Kecuh! Riuh! Gemuruh!

Episode 2.2: "Kecuh! Riuh! Gemuruh!"
(Learning Pathway #2: Attentive Listening)

Specific Use: Elementary School Music, Secondary Music Innovations, Instrumental Ensembles

Materials:

- Track 4, from the album, *Kata Kita Kota* by NADI Singapura

Procedure:

1. "What instrument do you hear at the beginning and how do you think the instrument is being played?".

2. Play track up to 0'30".

3. Discuss answers. (*Gong*. Note that instead of a hanging *gong* that is played by striking with a mallet, this piece features a *gong* that is laid on the ground and played with two wooden rulers on the ground.)

4. "Can you find out more about the origins of this instrument (*gong*) and how it is normally being played?"

5. Discuss answers. Provide students with information about *gongs*—their composite material (bronze, metals), places of origin and use (especially in Southeast Asia), various sizes and shapes (flat or knobbed, thin or thick), types of beaters (wood, metal, wrapped with cloth, yarn or twine).

6. "Can you hear a constant pulsation throughout the track? Can you pretend play this pulsation on your lap or any other part of your body?"

7. Play track up to 0'30", modeling the pulse-keeping, observing the steady rhythm.

8. "How does the pulsation make you feel?"

9. Discuss answers. Consider responses of mood made by the music, and make note of those students who find it easy or difficult to keep up with the pulsation.

10. "Given what you hear, are you able to identify where in the world the music might have come from?"

11. Discuss answers, which may include continents (such as Africa, Asia) and countries (such as the Philippines, Japan), and draw out their reasons for these responses. (Note that Singapore, in Southeast Asia's "*gong* region", is the origin place of this music.)

12. Host a community musician who plays percussion in the local symphony orchestra or Chinese orchestra, and request a session on orchestral *gongs*; host a community musician or culture-bearer aligned with a local temple of Buddhist or Taoist practice, for which East Asian or Southeast Asian *gongs* may be available to show-and-tell *gongs*, their variety, their timbral qualities, and their cultural significance.

Episode 3.2: "Kecuh! Riuh! Gemuruh!" (Learning Pathway #2: Engaged Listening)

Specific Use: Elementary School Music, Secondary Music Innovations, Instrumental Ensembles

Materials:

• Track 4, from the album, *Kata Kita Kota* by NADI Singapura

Procedure:

1. "Listen and identify one distinct repeated rhythmic pattern in the track" (There are at least three distinct rhythm patterns that can be identified, all in distinct 8-beat patterns)

2. Play track from 1'00" to 2'00".

3. "Listen again and confirm what you hear. Try to notate this rhythm pattern in simple notation".

4. Play track from 1'00" to 2'00".

5. "Share and compare notation of the rhythm pattern with your classmates".

6. "Play this rhythm pattern with body percussion, choosing to use pats, claps, or slaps".

7. Play track from 1'00" to 2'00" and have students play their rhythmic patterns along with the track.

8. Encourage students to use the internet to source out the other four fundamental Malay rhythms (Masri, Joget, Zapin, and Asli) and check if any of the rhythms match their identified rhythm pattern.

9. Host a Malay musician with full knowledge of the rhythms and techniques for playing them on percussion instruments to provide a live performance and demonstration. Consider also inviting a percussionist to learn the work, demonstrate fundamental playing technique, and help to shape the participatory musicking of the students.

Episode 3.5: "Kecuh! Riuh! Gemuruh!"
(Learning Pathway #2: Enactive Listening)

Specific Use: Elementary School Music, Secondary Music Innovations, Instrumental Ensembles

Materials:

- Track 4, from the album, *Kata Kita Kota* by NADI Singapura

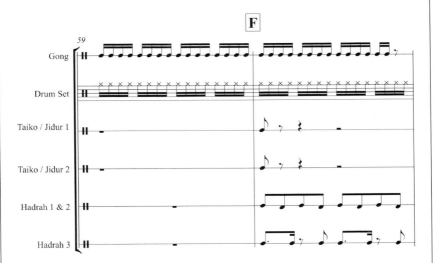

Figure 3.3   Notation reference for Kecuh! Riuh! Gemuruh!

Courtesy of NADI Singapura, transcribed by Riduan Zalani

Procedure:

1. "Listen and identify" the constant pulsating rhythm from the beginning of the track (this is the same rhythm identified from Episode 2.2), two *jidur* rhythmic patterns (found at 2'20"–2'23", teachers can refer to notation reference provided below [Bars 57–58]), and three-part *hadrah* rhythmic patterns (found at 2'25"–2'30", teachers can refer to notation reference provided below [Bar 60]. Note that Hadrah 1 and 2 play as an interlocking pair).

2. Play track from 2'00" to 2'45".

3. "In small groups, use body percussion to 'play' the identified rhythm and interlocking patterns".

4. Play track from 2'00' to 2'45".

5. "Transfer these rhythm patterns onto drums of different timbral qualities" (regardless of whether or not they are Malay in origin).

6. Play track 2'00" to 2'45".

7. Repeat #5, #6.

8. "Play the piece without the recording".

9. "Play with the recording, checking for accuracy".

10. Play track 2'00 to 2'45".

11. Recommend that students explore the internet for examples of silat movements that they may wish to add to each of the rhythm patterns they perform.

12. Arrange for a percussionist to visit the music class for purposes of facilitating performance techniques on available percussion instruments. While a specialist in Malay music is ideal, a community musician with performance expertise on various percussion instruments can be musically enlightening.

Episode 5.2: "Kecuh! Riuh! Gemuruh!" (Learning Pathway #2)

Specific Use: Secondary School Innovations, Instrumental Ensembles

Materials:

- Track 4, from the album *Kata Kita Kota* by NADI Singapura

Procedure:

1. "What is '*kompang*'?" Encourage students to google for photos, descriptions, video examples of the Malay drum, and the percussion ensemble and its various interlocking patterns.

2. Because the music has already been listened to, learned, and performed (via Attentive Listening, Engaged Listening, and Enactive Listening), the fundamental rhythm underlying *kompang*, called *Inang*, is already known. Pat, clap, snap, slap, or stamp the *Inang* rhythm. To emphasis the accents, try saying "Clap—pat pat pat clap clap" while giving greater emphasis to the claps.

3. In partners, practice continuously playing the down-beat (*Lalu*, signified by "L") rhythm or the up-beat (*Selang*, signified by "S") rhythm, as an interlocking pattern.

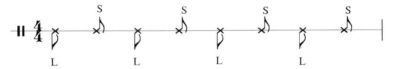

4. Practice the *Tinka* rhythm:

5. In groups of four, play the *Lalu* and *Selang* paired rhythms, and the *Tinka* and *Inang* rhythms, one person to each rhythm.

6. In one large group, put together the interlocking rhythms first via body percussion and then on selected percussion instruments. Use three distinctive timbral sounds of skins, woods, and metals.

7. Ask students to create a brand-new rhythm that can also interlock with the *Lalu* and *Selang*, *Tinka* and *Inang* rhythms.

8. Divide the large group into three groups to create a rhythmic percussion piece based on all the now familiar rhythmic patterns (*Lalu* and *Selang*, *Tinka*, and *Inang*). Suggest possibilities, such as beginning with just the *Lalu* and *Selang* before layering the *Tinka*, dropping out the *Tinka* after two bars, adding the *Inang*, sounding all rhythms at once, fading the *Tinka* and *Inang*, and ending with *Lalu* and *Selang* in a burst of dynamics. Note that the rhythmic patterns can also be improvised upon or elaborated during the creation.

9. Listen to the original recording, and discuss ways in which the new piece compares with it: Does it retain a certain "Malayness"? Seek out the views of a Malay musician.

Episode 6.2: "Kecuh! Riuh! Gemuruh!" (Learning Pathway #2)

Specific use: Elementary Music Education, Secondary School Innovations

Materials:

- Kecuh (Ruckus) Riuh (Chaos) Gemuruh (Thunderous)
- Track 4, from the album *Kata Kita Kota* by NADI Singapura

Procedure:

1. Note that "percussion instruments are prized in many of the world's cultures, and those that are featured in Malay musical expressions are prized for their array of various timbres". Ask students to imagine and to try to describe or represent vocally or with body percussion various percussion timbres.

2. While earlier WMP experiences have opened the ears, continued listening (with directed questions) can aid the identification of drum types:

   "Can you identify how these drums are shaped differently just by listening to the sound?" (The larger the surface area of the drumskins, the lower is the pitch of the drum.)

   "Are they made of metal, or wood?" (Frames are typically made of hardwood. The *hadrah* also has brass jingles attached.)

   "What do you think the playing surfaces of the drums are made of?" (Usually made out of goatskin).

   "How is each drum type played?" (Some with hands and others with a mallet of different density heads)

3. Name and describe, or find illustrations of, the percussion instruments that appear in Kecuh! Riuh! Gemuruh!—the *kompang*, *jidur*, *hadrah*, and *gong*. See sites such as www.srimahligai.com/articles/instruments.htm.

4. Plot a geographic map of where these instruments (or instruments similar to these) are found in Malaysia, Borneo, Singapore, and neighboring countries such as Indonesia, Thailand, the Philippines. Ask "Have some of these instruments originated from further afield? Do the instruments belong to people of similar cultural backgrounds across these countries?" Note that the similarities of these instruments across geographic boundaries are evidence of cross-border sharing and of the mixing of cultures across history.

5. Find substitute drums/instruments in the music classroom that might simulate the timbre of these drums. If they don't sound similar, how can you change the timbre of your substitute instrument by affixing different materials onto the surface or the side of your substitute instrument to make them sound alike? Explore and experiment sticking modeling clay, putting your hand on the skin when playing, etc. using your ears carefully to distinguish the similarities and differences in timbre. What do you notice about the size of instruments in relation to the pitch? What do you notice about timbre of sound in relation to the material being used? Can pitch and volume be adjusted by particular materials attached to the instruments? How do these explorations link to the ideas of amplitude and frequency in your science lessons?

Community/Culture Connection

*   Arrange for a visit from a percussionist to the classroom (ideally a specialist in percussion music from Malaysia, Indonesia, or elsewhere in Southeast Asia). Ask about the origins of the musician's instruments, and discuss familiar "relatives" of these instruments as may be found in various contexts.

*   Consider some of the scientific principles that are evident through the study of an instrument's composite materials and acoustical properties.

Learning Pathway #3

Sub-Saharan Collective Song

Episode 2.3: Sub-Saharan Collective Song
"Nange" ["Yange"]
(Learning Pathway #3: Attentive Listening)

Specific Use: Early Childhood, Elementary School Music, Choral Ensembles

Materials:

- Track 18, "Nange" [or "Yange"] from the album, *Tanzania—Tanzanie: Chants*

Procedure:

1. "What instruments do you hear and in what order?"
2. Play track to 0'29".
3. Discuss answers. (Voices, solo and group, children, some women; also claps)
4. Play track to 0'29" to check answers.
5. "Can you hear any of the sung words or syllables?"
6. Play track to 0'29".
7. Respond, fielding out "Yange", "Yange Yange" (sounding "yahn-gah nahn-GAY"), "Hedukila" (sounding "heh-DOO-kee-lah"), "Tanzania" (sounding "Tahn-zan-nee-YAH"). [Note: At times, "nange" may sound as "yange".]
8. "Can you follow the solo and group voices? Raise your right hand when you hear the solo voice, your left hand when you hear the group voices, and both hands when you hear the solo and group voices together. Feel welcome to rock gently to the pulse you hear".
9. Play track to 0'29".
10. Discuss the song's independent vocal parts, call-and-response features, the imitation of short lines in quick succession, and the threading of solo and group singing in between and around each other.
11. "Given what you hear, where in the world might the musicians be living?"
12. Discuss answers, which may include Africa (due to the full and open tone quality, the imitative voices, the claps).
13. Make time and space in the program for a visit from a community musician or culture-bearer who is Wagogo or from Tanzania, East Africa (Kenya, Uganda, Rwanda), or sub-Saharan Africa. Ask that they share their vocal music, particularly a selection that may feature several parts that together create harmony, and that the visitor tell a little of the presence of music in their "African childhood and youth".

Episode 3.3: Sub-Saharan Collective Song "Nange" ["Yange"] (Learning Pathway #3: Engaged Listening)

Specific Use: Early Childhood, Elementary School Music, Choral Ensembles

Materials:

- "Nange" [or "Yange"], from the album, Tanzania—Tanzanie: Chants
- Whiteboard

Procedure:

1. "Listen and track the contour of the melody: With the index finger, trace the descending, slightly ascending, and undulating melodic lines".
2. Play track to 0'29".
3. Discuss the melodic directions of the four short phrases: Phrases 1 and 2 descend, Phrase 3 ascends and then descends, and Phrase 4 descends (repeating the descending melody of Phase 2).
4. On whiteboard or other screen device, visually depict the four phrases as four independent lines that descend or ascend. Place them one under the other so that the four lines appear as rising, falling, and wavering lines.
5. Play track to 0'29" to check answers, tracing the lines in the air with the finger.
6. "Tap out the rhythm of the melodic lines while 'singing inside' ".
7. Play track to 0'29".
8. Demonstrate and discuss, noting that every syllable is a rhythmic unit requiring a separate tap. Suggest that given the speed of the melody, tapping the leg with alternate hands may work better than tapping with just one hand.
9. "Hum along to the melody while tracing the pitches or tapping the rhythm".
10. Play track to 0'29".
11. Clarify the meaning of the text: "Yange Yange" (it is shining), or "Sahani Yangu" (My plate), "Hedukila" (it is mine). [Note: "Yange Yange" may sound as "Nange Nange"].
12. "Sing 'Yange Yange' when it appears, humming all other components of the melody".
13. Play track to 0'29".
14. Bring in a community musician, especially from sub-Saharan Africa, if not East Africa specifically, or Tanzania or Wagogo culture. As the recording plays, it may be intriguing for students to observe that this musician may not only learn the song quickly by ear but may also be inclined to "dance" the music, or to move to its rhythm.

Episode 3.6: Sub-Saharan Collective Song
"Nange" ["Yange"]
(Learning Pathway #3: Enactive Listening)

Specific Use: Early Childhood, Elementary School Music, Choral Ensembles

Materials:

- "Nange", from the album, *Tanzania—Tanzanie: Chants*

Procedure:

1. "Sing aloud 'Nange, Nange' each time it occurs in the song". [Note: 'Yange Yange' may be substituted.]
2. Play track to 0'29".
3. "Repeat these words: 'Nange Nange', 'sahani yangu', and 'adukila'". Note: These words can be delivered rhythmically only, or as sung phrases.
4. "Sing aloud 'Nange Nange' and 'adukila' as these phrases appear in the song". Note: The second phrase is elongated, even played with, and can only be learned by listening carefully.
5. Play track to 0'29".
6. Divide the group into two parts, one group assigned to sing "Nange Nange" and the other to sing "adukila" with the recording. (In another run, ask the groups to switch parts).
7. Play track to 0'29".
8. "Sing the phrase 'sahana yangu' each time it occurs in the song".
9. Play track to 0'29".
10. "Sing the song—all parts—altogether, with the recording". [Note: Encourage students to feel the rhythm, nodding their heads, swaying, to the pulse.]
11. Play track to 0'29".
12. Play track again for opportunities to sing with and without the recording. Select a soloist, or a small group, to sing "Nange Nange" while the remainder of the group sings the "sahana yangu adukila".
13. Listen further to 0'45", clapping the pulse along with the singers, and learning by ear to sing the next section of "Nange" in two parts. (This step is well-suited to more experienced singers in upper elementary school and in secondary school choral ensembles.)
14. Arrange for a community musician with choral expertise, ideally with expertise in sub-Saharan African choral music, to lend a hand in shaping a coalescing choral sound, while also demonstrating basic movement that supports the musical feel of the piece.

Nange (Yange), melody line

1. Nan - ge Nan - ge (na - in-di-ye) sa-ha-ni Nan - ge a - du-ki - la
2. Ya - ngu Ya - ngu (na - in-di-ye) sa-ha-ni Ya - ngu he-du-ki - la

Nange (Yange), in two parts

Figure 3.4   Notation reference for Nange and Nange (2-part)

Episode 5.3: Sub-Saharan Collective Song
"Nange" ["Yange"]
(Learning Pathway #3)

Specific Use: Early Childhood, Elementary Music Education, Choral Ensembles

Materials:

*   Track 18, "Nange" [or "Yange"], from the album, *Tanzania—Tanzanie: Chants*

Procedure:

1. As a reminder of the song that has been learned via Attentive Listening, Engaged Listening, and Enactive Listening, share again the recording of "Nange" [or "Yange"] and invite students to join in.

2. Sing the song together without the recording, and show the feel of the song's rhythm in the body. This may include the transfer of weight from one foot to the other, and from one side of the body to the other. The arms can swing forward together on pulse "1" and then back on pulse "2", and students can join hands as they move together once a solid feeling of pulse is established.

3. Using the four measures of the learned song as the "return" section or chorus ("Sahani Yangu Hedukila, Yange Yange hedukila"), which is sung twice, invite ideas for developing a new four-measure phrase, also sung twice, between the "return" or chorus sections.

4. Working together in one large group, choose parameters within which to fashion a contrasting section. For example, the group may wish to continue the same meter, the same rhythmic flow, and the same melody but develop new words in English (or Swahili). Encourage students to sing about themes that have appeared in Wagogo songs of this ilk, such as the importance of family, of generosity and kindness towards others, and of growing up into a role of responsible community member. The challenge is in fitting new words to the melody and rhythm of the song, so try these words as an example: "Com-mun-i-ty here with fam-i-ly, Fam-i-ly, friends, com-mun-i-ty".

5. If the melody begins to sound "old" or over-used, play with the possibilities of re-ordering the pentatonic pitches to create a new phrase of 8 or 16 beats, in four measures, that contrasts as well as complements the familiar melody.

6. Once the new contrasting phrase is collectively shaped, practice singing it in between the "return", or chorus, sections.

7. Extend the creativity by inviting further inventions of contrasting phrases that can be sung in between the "return" or chorus sections.

8. If the creation of the new phrase has taken students to a "standstill" vis-à-vis movement, reinstate the dance so that they can experience the importance

of *ngoma*-inspired singing with dancing to the (somewhat) new song they have fashioned. If the dance movement has been performed—in place, suggest that students spread across the performance space—in lines, double lines and circles, and freely, even as they maintain the same movements of the body.

9. Invite a community musician, whether Wagogo, Tanzanian, East African, or sub-Saharan African, to evaluate and further guide the effort to express the new creation as it addresses the essence of the source recording.

Episode 6.3: Sub-Saharan Collective Song "Nange" ["Yange"] (Learning Pathway #3)

Specific Use: Elementary Music Education, Secondary School Innovations, Choral Ensembles

Materials:

*   "Nange" [or "Yange"], from the album, *Tanzania—Tanzanie: Chants*

Procedure:

1. In identifying the source of the music, explore the people and places of Wagogo culture. On a map of Africa, go to the eastern countries, south of Kenya, and locate Tanzania. Find the old capitol, Dar es Salaam, and the new capitol (since 1978), Dodoma. In a close-up map of Tanzania, look north and east of Dodoma to the land of the Wagogo people and of some of the traditional Wagogo villages (iklulu) such as Chamwino.

2. Explore the internet for images of Africa, east Africa, Tanzania, and the Wagogo, with special attention to everyday depictions of life in urban and rural areas. Note the wearing apparel, cuisine, places of residence, schools, hospitals, business districts, and modes of transportation. Compare city life to village life, utilizing a variety of images.

3. Find examples of Wagogo music and dance, and make note of the locations in which the performances occur (at the village hall, in open communal spaces, on the ground rather than onstage). Describe the instruments, the nature of the music and dance, the interactions between and among performers, and the attire of participants. See, for example, chamwinoarts.org as a site of the annual Wagogo Music Festival featuring multiple village groups who gather for a celebration of their music and cultural heritage.

4. For children as well as youth, storybooks can be interesting "shares" of insights of lifestyles and cultures, and of philosophical ideals that govern their daily interactions. Explore books such as *Why the Sun and the Moon*

Live in the Sky (Elphinstone Dayrell and Blair Lent), *Wangari's Trees of Peace: A True Story from Africa* (Jeanette Winter), *Giraffes Can't Dance* (Giles Andreae and Guy Parker Rees), and *The Water Princess* (Susan Verde, Georgie Badiel and Peter H. Reynolds). For secondary school students, *Things Fall Apart* (Chinua Achebe) is a classic work that illuminates the African experience in the village.

Community/Culture Connection

- Contact Chamwino Connect for possibilities of virtual (or in-person) exchanges with Wagogo villagers, including musicians, dancers, teachers, and students. https://chamwinoconnect.org/united-states-volunteer-board/.

- Invite in culture-bearers from Tanzania, Kenya, and other East African nations, and from the wider realm of sub-Saharan Africa, to tell stories of their lives in urban and rural locations. Some stories may relate to music, musicians, and musical instruments, and a few stories may even have songs woven in for occasional singing at the cue of the storyteller.

Appendix 2
References and Resources

These lists include references that have been cited through the volume, as well as some resources that the authors have found useful in teaching and learning (and facilitating the development of knowledge, skills, and values) of world music cultures. Also included are readings that inform further study of issues in ethnomusicology and music education, as well as recordings, video recordings, and internet resources of information that support the use of World Music Pedagogy in settings that feature school-community intersections.

References in Music, Education, Ethnomusicology, and Community Music

Allsup, R. E. (2016). *Remixing the classroom: Toward an open philosophy of music education.* Bloomington, IN: Indiana University Press.

Banks, J. A. (2009a). *Encyclopedia of diversity in education.* Thousand Oaks, CA: Sage Publications.

Banks, J. A. (2009b). *The Routledge international companion to multicultural education.* New York and London: Routledge.

Bartleet, B., & Higgins, L. (2018). *The Oxford handbook of community music.* New York: Oxford University Press.

Blacking, J. (1973). *How musical is man?* Seattle: University of Washington Press.

Bohlmann, P. V. (2002). *World music: A very short introduction.* New York: Oxford University Press.

Campbell, P. S. (2004). *Teaching music globally.* New York: Oxford University Press.

Campbell, P. S. (2018). *Music, education, and diversity: Bridging cultures and communities.* New York: Teachers College Press, Columbia.

Freire, P. (1970/2010). *Pedagogy of the oppressed*. New York: Continuum.

Higgins, L. (2012). *Community music: In theory and practice*. New York: Oxford University Press.

Higgins, L., & Willingham, L. (2017). *Engaging in community music*. New York: Routledge.

Howard, G. R. (2016). *We can't teach what we don't know: White teachers, multiracial schools* (3rd ed.). New York: Teachers College Press.

Keil, C., & Feld, S. (1994). *Music grooves*. Chicago: University of Chicago Press.

Kenny, A. (2016). *Communities of musical practice*. New York: Routledge.

Lind, V. R., & McCoy, C. (2016). *Culturally responsive teaching in music education: From understanding to application*. New York: Routledge.

Lum, C. H. (2013). *Contextualized practices in arts education: An international dialogue on Singapore*. Singapore: Springer.

Lum, C. H., & Chua, S. L. (2016). *Teaching living legends: Professional development and lessons for the 21st century music educator*. Singapore: Springer.

Miller, T. E., & Shahriari, A. (2017). *World music: A global journey*. New York: Routledge.

Nettl, B. (2015). *The study of ethnomusicology: Thirty-three discussions* (3rd ed.). Urbana, Chicago and Springfield, IL: University of Illinois Press.

Pavlicevic, M., & Ansdall, G. (Eds.). (2004). *Community music therapy*. London: Kingsley, Jessica Publishers.

Pettan, S., & Titon, J. T. (2015). *The Oxford handbook of applied ethnomusicology*. New York: Oxford University Press.

Rice, T. (2013). *Ethnomusicology: A very short introduction*. New York: Oxford University Press.

Schippers, H. (2010). *Facing the music: Shaping music education from a global perspective*. New York: Oxford University Press.

Small, C. (1998). *Musicking: The meanings of performing and listening*. Middletown, CT: Weslyan University Press.

Turino, T. (2008). *Music as social life: The politics of participation*. Chicago: University of Chicago Press.

Wade, B. (2009). *Thinking musically: Experiencing music, expressing culture*. New York: Oxford University Press.

Practical Resources in Music

Collections

Anderson, W. M., & Campbell, P. S. (2010). *Multicultural perspectives in music education* (3 vol.). Lanham, MD: Rowman & Littlefield Education.

Campbell, P. S. (2008). *Tunes and grooves for music education*. Upper Saddle River, NJ: Pearson.

Campbell, P. S., McCullough-Brabson, E., & Tucker, J. C. (1994). *Roots & branches: A legacy of multicultural music for children*. Danbury, CT: World Music Education.

Global Music Series: Experiencing Music, Expressing Culture (2004–). 28 volumes focused on world music cultures, book/CD/website of instructor's manuals for all ages and learning contexts. Retrieved from https://global.oup.com/academic/content/series/g/global-music-series-gms/?cc=us&lang=en&

Lomax, A., Elder, J. D., & Hawes, B. L. (Eds.). (1997). *Brown girl in the ring: An anthology of song games from the Eastern Caribbean.* New York: Pantheon Books.

Stock, J. (1996). *World sound matters: An anthology of music from around the world.* London: Schott.

Recordings

Gelombunk. Original compositions inspired by sounds of the Malay Archipelago. Retrieved from www.riduanzalani.com/js_albums/gelombunk/

Hukwe Ubi Zawose. *Vocal-choral songs of the legendary Wagogo musician of central Tanzania.* Retrieved from www.amazon.com/Tanzanie-chants-Wagogo-Kuria-Tanzania/dp/B004VQLHGA

Imaginaries. Grammy award-winning collection of an East L.A. soundscape by Quetzal, a Mexican-American band that mixes traditional son jaorcho with rock, *salsa*, and R&B; includes bilingual liner-notes. Retrieved from www.folkways.si.edu/quetzal/imaginaries/latin/music/album/smithsonian

DVDs and Films

Festival Chamwino Arts. Under "Media, Video", a sampling of festival music and dance from annual festivals. Retrieved from www.chamwinoarts.org/?page_id=273#prettyPhoto

Son Jarocho Master Musicians Cesar Castro, Artemio Posadas, and Louis Sarimientos. Performances of Mexican-American *son jarocho* musicians and dancers at the Library of Congress; begins at 9'00". Retrieved from www.youtube.com/watch?v=_aNlqdkdWMw

That *Beat of Faith.* Instructional DVD focusing on the Rebana Asli, including musical references, historical information and rhythm exercises. Retrieved from www.riduanzalani.com/product/that-beat-of-faith/

Websites

The Association for Cultural Equity. Retrieved from www.associationforculturalequity.com.

Kodaly Center American Folk Song Collection. Retrieved from http://kodaly.hnu.edu/collection.cfm

National Endowment for the Arts National Heritage Fellows. Retrieved from www.arts.gove/honors/heritage

Smithsonian Folkways Recordings. Retrieved from www.folkways.si.edu

Index

Printed and bound by PG in the USA